INFORMING THE FUTURE

Social Justice in the New Testament

INFORMING THE FUTURE

Social Justice in the New Testament

Joseph A. Grassi

PAULIST PRESS
New York/Mahwah, N.J.

Cover design by Valerie Petro

Book design by Theresa M. Sparacio

Library of Congress Cataloging-in-Publication Data

Grassi, Joseph A.
    Informing the future : social justice in the New Testament / Joseph A. Grassi.
        p.   cm.
    Includes bibliographical references.
    ISBN 0-8091-4092-6
    1. Social justice—Biblical teaching. 2. Bible. N.T.—Criticism, interpretation, etc. 3. Christianity and justice—History of doctrines—Early church, ca. 30–600. I. Title.
BS2545.J8 G73 2002
261.8—dc21

                                                        2002006291

Published by Paulist Press
997 Macarthur Boulevard
Mahwah, New Jersey 07430

www.paulistpress.com

Printed and bound in the United States of America

Contents

109776

Contents

PART III

Introduction

September 11, 2001, will always be remembered in world history for the tragic and unnecessary loss of so many innocent people. Most of the world's nations have united in a determined struggle to eliminate terrorism. This has inspired many people to search also for the roots of violence wherever they may be. A prominent root is the acute suffering of a major part of the Earth's people through unjust distribution of the resources of this planet.

Social Justice has been defined as the equal and just distribution of economic, social, and cultural resources to all people without discrimination of any kind. To what extent does the New Testament encourage or practice this human right? It would be easy to delete the word *equal* and define *just* in the sense of "generous" or "charitable." In that sense, justice would consist of a generous sharing on the part of those who are richly endowed with those who are less fortunate. Unfortunately, this view is built on the mythological view that this Earth has unlimited resources.

In contrast, the roots of the New Testament are based on prophetic justice with the following basic views of the land: 1) There are limited resources; 2) it is a designated sacred gift from God; 3) it was meant to be equally distributed. In this view, what one person has in abundance while others have considerably less is definitely evil.

In this book, we explore the dimensions of Social Justice as envisioned and practiced in the challenging yet hopeful views of the four Gospels, New Testament letters, and the early church. Then, we will compare this to the United Nations Millennium Declarations. Finally, we will present the challenge and hope that the New Testament brings to our world today.

PART I
OLD TESTAMENT ROOTS

Introduction

Reading the Scriptures

Jesus announced in his Sermon on the Mount that he had come to fulfill "The Law and the Prophets" (Matt 5:17; 7:12). This means that the roots for Social Justice in the New Testament must first be found in the Old Testament scriptures. In regard to the Hebrew Bible, a title often used instead of "Old Testament," there are some parameters and limitations:

1) The society in view had its origins in a patriarchal tribal structure that colors most of the texts that we will study. Social Justice will have its limitations within that structure.

2) Because our study is Social Justice in the New Testament, we will limit ourselves to texts that were either directly or indirectly referred to in those books. As for the specific references, we will usually wait until the New Testament section of our book. We are not attempting to survey[1] the whole Hebrew Bible because some parts were never, or rarely, read by the New Testament authors. They picked those texts that brought out the message of their particular books or letters.

3) Jesus and the New Testament writers had a special way of reading and understanding the Old Testament scriptures. They did not read them as mere ancient history. They were not primarily concerned about the original historical situation, the sources of each book, the literary composition and history. These are interesting and valuable questions for a modern scholar. However, Jesus and the Gospels followed the traditional Jewish outlook that

the Hebrew Bible, especially the Torah and Prophets, was the living, perennial word of God. In reading or listening to it, they felt that they were doing so in the same way as the original audience. This way of reading the scriptures[2]—that you are there—will be found in the Book of Deuteronomy, with which we will begin.

The Meaning of Social Justice

In regard to Social Justice, we are taking it in the sense of the principles by which each person obtains an equitable share in the resources and relationships within a society. Social Justice is not the same as biblical justice.[3] Biblical justice finds its meaning within rights and duties that emerge from a community covenant[4] relationship with God and other members of the community. Social Justice may obtain its principles from other sources, for example, the nature and dignity of the human person.

1

Social Justice in the Torah

The Meaning of *Torah*

The Hebrew word itself is usually translated in the Bible as "law." However, this definition is very different from modern connotations of "laws." These are ordinarily decrees and obligations promoted by a government or ruling society. *Torah*, however, consists of the responses and duties that flow from a covenant with God. The Ten Commandments start with the statement, "I am the LORD your God who brought you out of the land of Egypt, out of the house of slavery" (Exod 20:1–2). These words express God's loving initiative to intervene and liberate his people. Following this statement, we find a list of the responses and duties of gratitude that God expects from his people. These begin with the Ten Commandments and are followed by other regulations. At the end, the people state their agreement: "All the words the LORD has spoken we will do" (Exod 24:3). Then, Moses takes the book of the covenant containing all these words. He reads it to the people. Once again they state their agreement. Finally, Moses sprinkles the blood of sacrifice on the altar and on the people and says, "See the blood of the covenant that the LORD has made with you in accordance with all these words" (Exod 24:8).

Torah, however, also designates all the biblical texts in which covenant rules are found, explained, or even amplified. Primarily, these are the Pentateuch, the first five books of the Bible: Genesis, Exodus, Leviticus, Numbers and Deuteronomy. The whole Hebrew Bible can also be called *Torah*. However, among all these books, the Book of Deuteronomy holds a special place.[5] It is the only book that claims for itself the title of being the Torah: "The book of this Torah" (28:61; 30:10). I am choosing to begin from this book, not only for that reason, but also because it makes the claim (at least indirectly) that it is adding or improving on the Sinai Covenant in Exodus. The writer notes at the sealing of the covenant in Deuteronomy: "These are the words of the covenant that the LORD commanded Moses to make with the Israelites in the land of Moab, *in addition to* the covenant that he had made with them at Horeb" (29:1). Also, Deuteronomy is the cherished traditional book of the Torah for the Hebrew and Jewish people. It is the book (as we will point out in the chapter on Matthew) that Matthew chooses as a model for his Gospel.

Deuteronomy describes how Moses spent 40 days and 40 nights with God receiving this message. Then, he spoke all these words to all Israel (31:1). After this, "Moses wrote down this law, and gave it to the priests" (31:9). Finally, he commanded the Levites, "Take this book of the law and put it beside the ark of the covenant of the LORD your God" (31:26).

Consequently, when people visited this central place of worship (later, the Temple), they would always recall that the Book of Deuteronomy was in the most sacred place beside the holy ark. They knew that the perpetual light of the seven-branched oil lamp was a sign of God's presence not only through the holy ark, but also through the book of the covenant that was put beside it. They would also actually *see* it when the book was taken out at the feast of booths every seventh year and read publicly to all the people (31:9–13). To listen to this reading would be to listen to the same living voice of God that spoke to Moses on Mount Sinai.

Finding the Lost Book of the Torah
During the Reform of King Josiah

The actual Book of Deuteronomy as we have it now is the product of many revisions and additions through the centuries. However, the precious core of this book goes back to the unusual story of its finding. The reigns of King Manasseh and Amon

(687–640 B.C.) represented the culmination of the evil of many previous kings. The Bible notes that Manasseh "erected altars for Baal, made a sacred pole, as king Achab had done, worshiped all the host of heaven and served them." He even placed their images in the sacred Temple area: "The carved image of Asherah that he made he set in the house of which the LORD said to David and his son Solomon, 'In this house; and in Jerusalem, which I have chosen out of all the tribes of Israel, I will put my name forever'" (2 Kgs 21:7). Baal (meaning "lord") was a god of nature and fertility. Asherah was his female consort, which some even considered to be associated with Yahweh. The "carved image" was her symbol, that of a pole or tree. The "hosts of heaven" were the sun, moon, and stars.

King Amon was assassinated by his servants. His son Josiah (640–609 B.C.), then only eight years old, took his place. From his subsequent actions, it is likely that he was educated by priests close to the royal court and grew up to be profoundly religious. As a devout young man in his late twenties, he was determined to repair and restore the Temple. To that end, he directed the high priest Hilkiah to take the peoples' Temple offerings and give them to workers to begin the work. During its course, Hilkiah reported to the king's secretary, Saphan, "I have found the book of the law (literally, "the book of the Torah") in the house of the LORD" (22:8). Saphan then read the book to King Josiah.

After the king heard the words of the book, he tore his clothes in grief for he realized that God's commandments in this book had not been kept; he feared divine punishment for himself and his people. So, he told the high priest and Saphan, "Go inquire of the LORD for me and for all Judah concerning the words of this book" (22:13). So, they went to the prophetess Huldah, the wife of Shallum son of Kikvah, son of Harjasa, keeper of the wardrobe. The unusual nature of this consultation and its crucial importance emerge from the fact that there had been only two other prophetesses by name in the Hebrew Bible. Each of these appeared at important historical junctures: Miriam, sister of Moses, had led the people in song and dance after their victory over Egypt at the Red Sea. Her importance was such that God declared through Micah the prophet, "I brought you up from the land of Egypt before Moses, Aaron (their brother) and Miriam" (Mic 6:4). Deborah was a prophetess and even a leader of Israel during the time of the Judges (Judg 4:4).

Hulda declared to them, "Thus, says the LORD, 'I will indeed bring disaster on this place and on its inhabitants—all the words of the book that the king of Judah has read, because they have abandoned me and made offerings to other gods'" (2 Kgs 22:15–17). These words announced that the coming destruction of Jerusalem and the sufferings in exile would be caused by proliferation of worship to other gods instead of the one Yahweh. Consequently, this became a message to Jews returning to Israel more than a century later and for all time: Monotheism, complete worship to Yahweh alone, must be the center of their religion—if they wished to avert the same punishment. However, she sent this message to Josiah, "Thus says the LORD, the God of Israel: 'Regarding the words that you have heard, because your heart was penitent, and you humbled yourself before the LORD....I have also heard you....you shall be gathered to your grave in peace; your eyes shall not see all the disaster that I will bring on this place'" (22:18–20). After the king received this message, he gathered together all the people. Following this,

> He read in all their hearing all the words of the book of the covenant that had been found in the house of the LORD. The king stood by the pillar and made a covenant before the LORD, keeping his commandments, his decrees, and his statutes, with all his heart and all his soul, to perform the words of this covenant that were written in this book. All the people joined in the covenant. (23:2–3)

At the core of this covenant was total commitment to Yahweh as their one God, according to the central prayer, "Hear O Israel, the LORD is our God, the LORD alone" (Deut 6:4). The spirit was complete dedication *with all one's heart and soul,* the repeated theme of Deuteronomy. *One God* meant that their worship should no longer be spread and shared with the worship of other gods, especially fertility deities. The king immediately took action in this regard. He ordered the priests to remove from the Temple the vessels for worship of the Baals and Asherahs and had them burnt. He removed those priests who cooperated in that worship. He took the image of Asherah from the Temple, burnt it into dust, and threw the dust into a cemetery for added desecration. "He broke down the houses of the male temple prostitutes that were in the house of the Lord, where the women did the weaving for Asherah" (2 Kgs 23:7). The translation *male prostitutes* is of the literal Hebrew "holy ones," men dedicated to Baal and acting out his part (quite realistically) in fertility dramas. The women "weaving for Asherah" were making clothes for the goddess's image and probably wearing them when they likewise acted out her role.

King Josiah reestablished the Passover, with the orders "Keep the passover to the LORD your God as prescribed in this book of the covenant" (23:21). The writer then notes, "No such Passover had been kept since the days of the judges." These "days" were centuries before, showing how radical the king's restoration and renewal was. Josiah was so completely dedicated to Yahweh that the writer concludes with a statement unlike anything else in the Hebrew Bible: "Before him, there was no king like him, who turned to the LORD *with all his heart, with all his soul, and with all his might, according to the law of Moses; nor did any like him arise after him*" (23:25). We have little information on what else King Josiah did, but the prophet Jeremiah holds him up as an example to Jehoiakim, Josiah's son, with these words: "Did not your father eat and drink and do justice and righteousness? Then it was well with him. He judged the cause of the poor and the needy; then it was well. Is not this to know me? Says the Lord" (22:15–16).

Despite all this, King Josiah had a tragic ending. When only thirty-one years old, he went north to the pass of Megiddo to meet Neco the Pharaoh of Egypt who then killed him in battle. Few details are given. The much later Book of Chronicles was not satisfied with this and changed the ending: King Josiah personally led his forces in battle against the Egyptians' mighty army. He went in a chariot but in disguise. However, an Egyptian archer mortally wounded him and he was brought back to Jerusalem where he died and was buried. There, "All of Jerusalem and Judah mourned for Josiah. Jeremiah also uttered a lament for Josiah, and all the singing men and singing women have spoken of Josiah in their laments to this day" (2 Chr 35:24–25).

The Heart of the Torah in Deuteronomy

God's Total Unconditional Love

Although God is almighty and "will fight for you" (1:30), he carries Israel tenderly like a loving parent: "In the wilderness, where you saw how the LORD your God carried you, just as one carries a child, all the way you traveled until you reached this place" (1:31). He has a long history of taking the initiative, intervening to care for his people: "Because he *loved* your ancestors, he chose their descendants after them" (4:37). As a result, he declares, "*Take to heart* that the LORD is God in heaven above and on the earth beneath; there is no other" (4:39). The repeated words, "there is no other" (also 4:35; 5:7), are an invitation to undivided and total response.

The unconditional nature of this love is especially shown in his choice of his people. God did not choose them for their goodness, their greatness, or their large population:

> It was not because you were more numerous than any other people that the LORD set his heart on you and chose you—for you were the fewest of all peoples. It was because the LORD loved you and kept the oath that he swore to your ancestors. (7:7–8)

The expression "set his heart" is one of the few in which the English translation has *heart* and the Hebrew does not. However, it corresponds to the strong verb *hashaq,* meaning "to be attached" or "devoted to." The emphasis is on the oath God made to care for his people and his reliability to keep it. Accordingly, his *faithful* nature is noted and the fact that he "maintains covenant." Literally, these last words are that he "keeps *hesed.*" We have seen that this *hesed* is one of the supreme qualities of God, his covenant choice to maintain a family relationship to his people. In fact, God chooses this people because of their neediness and tendency to fail:

> Know, then, that the LORD your God is not giving you this good land to occupy because of your righteousness; for you are a stubborn people. Remember and do not forget how you provoked the LORD your God to wrath in the wilderness; you have been rebellious against the LORD from the day you came out of the land of Egypt until you came to this place. (9:6–7)

The great secret of life, not only about God but also about human beings, is to *remember* (14 times in Deuteronomy) when this love has been shown and *not to forget* (9 times). At first glance, this love seems exclusive, directed to one people. However, Deuteronomy stresses that Yahweh "executes justice for the orphan and the widow, and...loves strangers, providing them food and clothing" (10:18). Earlier legislation in Exodus also enjoined this justice but did not have the word *love* (24:17–22). In imitation of God, as his family, "You shall also love the stranger, for you were strangers in the land of Egypt" (10:19).

The Perpetual Nature of This Love

The writer has a special way to present this love: In this book, Moses addresses *another generation* that had not come out of Egypt with him and was not at Sinai. There, God spoke in a thunderous voice from a fiery mountain and inscribed a covenant on two stone tablets. The present people are now the children of those who were originally there. Moses makes a final address to them before their entry into the Promised Land, because God has not permitted him to go any farther. He says,

> The LORD our God made a covenant with us at Horeb (Mt. Sinai). Not with our ancestors did the LORD make this covenant, but with us, who are all of us here alive today. The LORD spoke with *you* face to face at the mountain, out of the fire. (5:2–4)

Moses insists that God's covenant is not ancient history that took place forty years ago with their ancestors. The covenant was made and is being made today with all those who are now here alive. The Lord spoke with *you* face to face. God is always making his covenant. So *you are there!* The word *today* means "now and ever." To leave not a shadow of doubt about this, Deuteronomy uses the expression, "this day" or "today," continually, some 77 times in all! God's covenant continues for a thousand generations (7:9). Our great national debt has made us familiar with numbers in the billions and trillions, but the Hebrews only counted to ten thousand or ten thousand times ten thousand. *A thousand generations* meant "forever."

But how to accomplish *being there,* and yet not physically there at all. For the Bible this was accomplished through images in memory. These were not just "pictures" but also part of the reality itself that was stored away. To remember, then, was to reexperience here and now. Moses does everything possible to make these images as deep and as vivid as possible. We note above that God spoke at the mountain, out of the *fire.*

The Sinai mountain burning in fire with God's voice coming out of the fire like thunder and accompanied by lightning is the most powerful image in Deuteronomy. It is repeated 30 times in the book, each time with special details for reinforcement. By way of background, every Hebrew home was dark inside, without windows. Oil lamps provided light along with warmth and were never extinguished. They were visible signs of life within. God spoke with Moses from a burning bush out of a fire that could not be extinguished—a symbol of inexhaustible energy. In the anteroom of the Ark of the Covenant, there was a seven-branched lampstand with an oil flame burning day and night as a sign of God's continuous energy and presence. Likewise, God's thundering voice out of the fiery Mount Sinai was a voice continuously proclaiming his covenant to every generation. In our modern age, we think more of words as conveying information; the ancients focused on the energy in them and behind them. (And, of course, words are sound waves of energy.)

Some of the progression in the fire image in Deuteronomy helps to sharpen the image: God led them on the way in a fire at night and in a cloud by day (1:33). The flames over Mount Sinai went up to the sky (4:11). God's voice came out from the fire

(4:12, 33; 5:4). The result was a full sensory experience in both seeing and hearing (4:36). God himself is a devouring fire (4:15). There was a fiery cloud in the background of thick darkness (5:22). It seemed like the whole mountain was on fire (5:23). The fear that the raging fire would consume them (5:25). The people's request to have Moses come down to speak to them out of fear of the fire and God's voice (18:16–18). The important matter was to remember, reexperience, and never forget.

The above section on how Deuteronomy listened to the scripture as the living, perennial voice of God must be kept in mind all through this book as a necessary guide. Deuteronomy teaches how to listen not only for what originally happened but also what is always happening—today, yesterday, and tomorrow. This is the way that Jesus and the early church read the scriptures.

The Loving Response to God's Covenant Initiative

The first response is to God himself, and the second will be through Deuteronomy's unique program of eliminating poverty in the land of Israel. The first will be illustrated in the great central prayer of Judaism, the *Shemah Israel* (Hear O Israel). The purpose of this prayer is to provide a unique way of remembrance, continuity, and teaching: "so that you and your children and your children's children may fear the LORD your God all the days of your life, and keep all his decrees and commandments...so that your days may be long" (6:2). Just as Yahweh always remembers his people, so will they also remember him:

> Hear, O Israel: the LORD is our God, the LORD alone. You shall love the LORD your God with all your heart, and with all your soul, and with all your might. Keep these words that I am commanding you today in your heart. (6:4–6)

The central theme of this prayer is complete loving dedication to Yahweh, *the Lord alone,* not any other form of worship. We have seen the serious nature of this in the reform of Josiah and the radical cleansing of a Temple cluttered with fertility cults and other forms of worship. In the *Shemah,* heart and memory are closely linked: "Keep these words...in your heart." The heart is the storehouse of memory. The Wisdom teacher of Proverbs tells his students to write his words on the (school) tablets of their hearts (3:3). This prayer was at the core of education: "Recite them to your children" (so they will memorize it). This matter of a living tradition through instruction of children is found five times in this book. The phrase "with all your heart and with all your soul" is a theme song of total devotion. It is repeated nine times in Deuteronomy.

Even in the worst possible scenario, if the people betray their God and are punished by exile, God will not abandon them. They can still return "with all their heart and soul" and "God will...have compassion on you, gathering you again from all the people among whom the LORD your God has scattered you" (30:3). The word used for *compassion* in this text is *rahum,* God's deepest womb love. All through the book, *hesed,* covenant love, is used for God's faithfulness, but it is his deep womb/heart compassion that forgives and brings them back. Only here and in 13:17 is the root used. When God does bring them back, he will give them a brand new beginning and birth, interior instead of exterior: "The LORD God will *circumcise* your heart and the heart of your descendants, so that you will love the LORD your God with all your heart and soul that you may live" (30:6).

The prayer instructs that these words be the subject of conversation at home and also at work and traveling, which was usually with other people. It should be the first prayer when rising in the morning and the last words when going to sleep. The words were to be so strongly engraved on the memory that they would be like a tattoo on the hand or a mark between the eyes. As a sign of home dedication, the words were to be written over the house entrance. Later, Judaism applied these words literally. The words were written inside of tiny leather pouches that were placed over the heart, between the eyes, and wrapped around the wrists during times of prayer.

The *Shemah* has been recited many millions of times over the course of history. It would be hard to underestimate its power and influence as the central prayer of Judaism. In compliance with the text, Jewish people said this prayer morning and evening, at the synagogue, and often during the day. It was the special prayer of Jesus, who pointed to it as a summary of the Torah along with love of one's neighbor (Mark 12:28–34; Matt 22:34–40; Luke 10:25–28). Parents taught it to children as their first words. Everyone hoped it would be the last prayer on their lips.

The great Rabbi Akiba made them his last words. He was tortured by the Romans for his faith and died in the second century A.D. On the last day of his life, when the evening hour for praying the *Shemah* arrived, he became smiling and happy. The Roman officer in charge asked him for the reason. The rabbi replied that he had always wanted to live out the words "to love God with all his soul (life)" and now he had the opportunity to really do so. Since his time, millions have died with this prayer on their lips. This was especially true in history's darkest hour when German Nazis murdered some 6 million Jews in the horrible death camp ovens. Consequently, the words have a special holiness and aura about them that is hard to equal in human language. This is because so many human lives have been behind those words at their moment of death, when they did not stop praying despite unimaginable sufferings.

The opening word, *Shemah,* literally means "Hear." It conveys the idea of total surrender and openness to God in all of life. There is no Hebrew word for *obey.* Actually, the English word *obedience* comes from the Latin verb *obaudire* meaning "to hear, listen, or observe." Everything, including love and service of other people, was looked upon as personal service and dedication to God. This love and service were not merely idealistic but also very practical. It meant openness to all God's commandments, especially those concerning people in need of help. The Jewish supreme ideal was imitation of God, especially in that area: "(God) executes justice for the orphan and the widow, and who loves the strangers, providing them food and clothing. You also shall love the stranger, for you were strangers in the land of Egypt" (Deut 10:18–19).

The rabbinic *midrash* was a scripture commentary drawn from oral teaching over the centuries but first put in writing around the sixth century A.D. In regard to "with all your heart" it teaches, "Don't let your heart be divided, that is, not wholly one—in your love of God." In regard to "With all your soul (life)," the *midrash* teaches that all of life must be behind this love, even if it means risking one's life. The words *with all your might* were interpreted as "referring to riches or possession." Serving God with love must have priority over all earthly possessions and wealth. The whole purpose of the *Shemah* was to inculcate a complete vibrant life, not subservience.

The Deuteronomy Program for the Elimination of Poverty

By way of background, Deuteronomy is written for people living or going to live on the land. The Ten Commandments were originally addressed to a people on a journey through the desert. However, they never entered the land because of their lack of faith. Moses addressed their children who were about to enter and live in the promised land. God's goodness in giving them the land now becomes an additional initiative of God in addition to bringing them out of Egypt. The word *land* occurs some 158 times in Deuteronomy, more than in any other book in the Bible except Jeremiah (which is twice as long). The land is considered a special gift or inheritance (mentioned 20 times) from God.

Because we are dealing with an agricultural economy, based on each family with its own plot of land, the Deuteronomy program for eliminating poverty is closely connected to the land. Any loss of land or the lack of people to work it means disaster. As a result, landless strangers, widows, or orphans often will live on the brink of survival. This book has a deep concern about protecting property and ownership. Even in the Ten Commandments, the Deuteronomic version of the tenth commandment adds the "field" of one's neighbor as something not to be coveted (5:20, compare Exod 20:17). Old landmarks indicating property from one's ancestors deserved special protection: "You must not move your neighbor's boundary marker, set up by former generations, on the property that will be allotted to you in the land that the LORD your God is giving you to possess" (19:14). In the solemn

16

curses at the end of the covenant, pronounced by the Levites, we have the following: "'Cursed be anyone who moves a neighbor's land marker.' All the people shall say, 'Amen'" (27:17).

The Deuteronomy program ideal was, "There will, however, be no one in need among you, because the LORD is sure to bless you in the land that the LORD your God is giving you as a possession to occupy" (15:4). However, a condition is attached to the blessing: "If only you will obey the LORD your God by diligently observing this entire commandment that I command you today" (15:5).

The matter of the remission of debts is in the text below. The first and most radical way to eliminate poverty was through periodic debt remission every seven years.[6] Nowhere else except in Deuteronomy is there found such a remarkable provision. With an agricultural economy, there is always danger of losing crops through weather failure, pestilences, or other causes. There are no banks to keep money, and it is difficult to store crops. Consequently, there is frequent need to borrow money to obtain seed for the next crop or to tide one over. Lenders prefer to have the security of the land as the best guarantee. In ancient times, this meant handing over the title of the land beforehand as security. Failure to pay back the loan meant that there was no way to repossess land that often was the sole means of support.

> Every seventh year you shall grant a remission of debts. And this is the manner of the remission: every creditor shall remit the claim that is held of a neighbor, not exacting it of a neighbor who is a member of the community, because the LORD's remission has been proclaimed. (15:1–2)

Because the human tendency was to avoid lending money because of this, a following text encouraged loans to help those in need:

> If there is among you anyone in need, a member of your community in any of your towns within the land that the LORD your God is giving you, do not be hard-hearted or tight-fisted toward your needy neighbor. You should rather open your hand, willingly lending enough to meet the need, whatever it may be. Be careful that you do not entertain a mean thought, thinking, "The seventh year, the year of remission, is near."(15:7–9)

This seventh year was not a variable for each person. It was a regular calendar event which everyone celebrated at a special time, during the feast of booths every seven years. Moses commanded them, "Every seventh year, in the scheduled year of remission, during the festival of booths, when all Israel comes to appear before the LORD your God at the place that he will choose, you shall read this law before all Israel in their hearing" (31:10–11). Thus, people could never forget that this was the time for the remission of debts.

We will later see that this text on remission of debts was taken seriously by the Qumran community near the time of Jesus. Also, in Matthew we will note the close connection to Deuteronomy, especially in the Lord's Prayer petition on debt forgiveness, which uses the same terminology as remission of debts in Deuteronomy 15:1–2.

Another means of raising money to pay debts was through selling one's self as a slave for a number of years, as seen also in Leviticus 25:39 and Amos 2:6. By way of background, most Hebrew slavery was caused by debt. In agricultural economies, because of the unpredictability of weather, people often had to borrow until the next harvest. To do so, they had to place a pledge in advance either of the land they owned or of their own personal service as a slave until the debts were paid. Loss of land through foreclosure or personal freedom because of this kind of debt was the principal road to poverty that so many people were forced to take. Often, debt slavery lasted many years or even a lifetime. Deuteronomy provides a much more liberal limitation of this than Exodus 21:2–11.

> If a member of your community, whether a Hebrew man or a Hebrew woman, is sold to you and works for you six years, in the seventh year you shall set that person free. And when you send a male slave out from you a free person, you shall not send him out empty-handed. Provide liberally out of your flock, your threshing floor, and your wine press, thus giving to him some of the bounty with which the LORD your God has blessed you. Remember that you were a slave in the land

of Egypt, and the LORD your God redeemed you; for this reason I lay this command upon you today. (15:12–15)

This was another means of reducing poverty: The periodic release of these "debt slaves" meant that they could return to assist their families. It also kept people from being indentured for a whole lifetime. Further treatment of the slave status will come when we treat of Social Justice and relationships in Deuteronomy.

Another avenue of moving toward elimination of poverty was through interest-free loans: "You shall not charge interest on loans to another Israelite, interest on money, interest on provisions, interest on anything that is lent" (23:19).

In an agricultural economy, farmers were forced to seek loans for emergency needs to support their families. It was not the time to make money off them besides. The honor of the borrower must be always respected. If security was needed, lenders should not enter the person's house but wait outside until it was brought out to him or her (24:10–11).

Relieving the Poverty of the Landless

In this category were especially the following: 1) Levites, because they were the priestly tribe, and God had commanded that they have no inheritance but God himself (12:12). Part of their support came from sharing in the offerings made in the Dwelling Place or Temple. Frequent appeals are made to support them (14:27; 12:19). 2) Widows, often left destitute, because women had no inheritance for themselves, as it went to the sons. 3) Orphans, because inheritances only went to natural children, unless the orphans were formally adopted. 4) Aliens or strangers or non-Israelites who lived among the Hebrews but had no ancestral land that was handed down to them.

Help to these people was not considered part of charity or left to kind gifts; it was a matter of strict justice in imitation of God's own just care for those in need: The Lord "executes justice for the orphan, and the widow, and who loves strangers, providing them food and clothing. You shall love the stranger, for you were strangers in Egypt" (10:18–19). With strangers especially, the natural tendency was to just tolerate them at most. But here twice, we have the verb *love*. In Exodus the command is not to abuse or oppress them (22:21; 23:9). The matter of justice is so important that negligence of these people deserves the solemn community curse at the end of the covenant: "'Cursed be anyone who deprives the alien, the orphan, and the widow of justice.' All the people shall say, 'Amen!'" (27:19). The final motivation is one of identification with these people and imitation of God (10:19).

The above general declaration of Social Justice was accompanied by practical applications. Here, an important connection was made between religion, liturgy, and justice. Every year, all families had to offer a tithe of grain, oil, wine, and livestock (or their money equivalent), at the Dwelling Place, later the Temple (14:22–27). The Levites obtained a share of this. However, only in Deuteronomy, there was a special designation for the tithe on the third year. The people did not bring it to the central holy place but stored it in their towns. This was so "The Levites, because they have no allotment or inheritance with you, as well as the resident aliens, the orphans, and the widows in your towns, may come and eat their fill so that the LORD your God may bless you in all the work that you undertake" (14:28).

The three pilgrim festivals each year, Passover, Pentecost and booths, were also special times of seven-day rejoicing and sharing with their families, slaves as well as "Levites, strangers, orphans, widows" (16:11, 14–16). A repeated motivation was, "Remember that you were a slave in Egypt, and diligently observe these statutes" (16:12). This remembering about Egypt is a constant matter, 46 times in all!

In addition there was constant provision for sharing in every field or harvest:

> When you reap your harvest in your field and forget a sheaf in the field, you shall not go back to get it; it shall be left for the alien, the orphan, and the widow, so that the LORD your God may bless you in all your undertakings. When you beat your olive trees, do not strip what is left; it shall be for the alien, the orphan, and the widow. When you gather the

grapes of your vineyard, do not glean what is left; it shall be for the alien, the orphan, and the widow. (24:19–21)

We find an example of this ancient form of charity in the biblical world in the Book of Ruth. She said to her mother-in-law Naomi, "Let me go to the field and glean among the ears of grain" (2:2). There, she gleaned so well that she even found a future husband!

"Not by Bread Alone" (Deut 8:3)—
God's Food Program for Equal Sharing

Remember the long way that the LORD your God has led you these forty years in the wilderness, in order to humble you, *testing* you to know what was in your heart, whether or not you would keep his commandments. He humbled you by letting you hunger, then by feeding you with manna, with which neither you nor your ancestors were acquainted, in order to make you understand that *one does not live by bread alone, but by every word that comes from the mouth of the* LORD. (8:2–3)

The account above is a shortened form of a long account in Exodus of God's distribution of manna to the Israelites in the Sinai desert. The hungry people complained to God that they were dying of hunger. God promised to send them bread they could gather up for each day. As in Deuteronomy, it is a test as to whether they will follow God's commands: "In that way I will test them, whether they will follow my instruction or not" (Exod 16:4). Accordingly, on the morning God promised, the people found a white breadlike substance on the ground. Moses said to them:

This is what the LORD has commanded: "Gather as much of it as each of you needs, an omer to a person according to the number of persons, all providing for those in their own tents." The Israelites did so, some gathering more, some less. But when they measured it with an omer, those who gathered much had nothing over, and those who gathered little had no shortage; they gathered as much as each of them needed. (16:16–18)

The italicized first sentence above is literally, "This is the *word* which the Lord has commanded." Thus, it corresponds literally to "the (word) which comes from the mouth of the Lord" in Deuteronomy 8:3 and also the all-important word of God in creation. In the first chapter of Genesis we have the expression "And God said" eight times. God does not want to just "rain bread from *heaven*" (Exod 16:4). He wants people to be co-creators with him on *Earth* to make that bread shared by everyone. In view of the account that follows, each day God provided enough bread to be shared equally if the people follow his procedure.

The people went out to gather bread in the morning, "some gathering more, some less." Perhaps the elderly and children were only able to gather a little, while the young and sturdy gathered large amounts. At the end of the day they divided it up equally. As a result, "those who gathered much had nothing over, and those who gathered little had no shortage; they gathered as much as each of them needed." Thus, we have a great miracle of sharing and distribution according to the axiom, "From each one according to their ability; to each one according to their need."

Moses then said, "Let no one leave any of it over until morning." Here, we note the effects of not following God's command through Moses. Those who distrusted and hoarded for the future wake in the morning and find worms eating their bread. In memory of this whole event, God commanded that some of the manna be placed beside the Ark of the Covenant (16:32–33). In Hebrew and Jewish tradition, this miracle of distribution was regarded as even greater than the bread itself. We will later see how St. Paul recalls it as a model of equal sharing for his ecumenical collection (2 Cor 8:13–15). The Acts of the Apostles recalls the Deuteronomy plan of eliminating poverty and the ideal of sharing according to each one's need and the ability of others to help (4:34–37).

Social Justice and Relationships, Personal Rights

Again, we can only make relative comparisons in view of the patriarchal system that pervaded the ancient biblical world. We will select the categories of women and slaves.

22

Not for Men Alone: Women's Influence on Deuteronomy

While hardly a textbook for women's liberation, Deuteronomy has some surprises relative to the patriarchal world that surrounded it. There is an air of mystery about the finding of the lost book of the Torah. King Josiah tears his garments when he first hears the book read. He then tells the high priest Hilkiah to go inquire from the Lord the meaning of the book. However, the high priest does not do this personally, as might be expected in such an important matter. Instead, he goes to a prominent woman, the prophetess Hulda (very few of these in the Bible!). She explains the significance of the book and tells the high priest to bring word to King Josiah (2 Kgs 22:11–13). This opens the possibility of her influence or some other women's on parts of that book.

Of course, we will not find material for a modern women's liberation movement, but we will discover some movements toward equality that would be ahead of the times. In reading through Deuteronomy, we see that this book is meant to improve on or even supersede others. It is *this book of the Torah.* Even what it omits, that is in other sources, can be very important. A modern woman might read in Exodus covenant laws that a father could sell his daughter (21:7) but not his son and be understandably shocked. However, no such law is found in the Deuteronomic version of the covenant.

Women, the Decalogue, and the Covenant (Some Examples)

Hopefully, when people hang up the Ten Commandments in schools and other places, they will not use the version in Exodus 20. There, the ninth and tenth commandments read together: "You shall not covet your neighbor's house; you shall not covet your neighbor's wife, or male and female slave, or ox, or donkey or anything that belongs to your neighbor" (20:17). There, we find lumped together in typical patriarchal fashion: the household, wife, slaves, ox, donkey, and other possessions. We notice the striking difference in Deuteronomy 5:21: "Neither shall you covet your neighbor's wife" is a separate commandment, followed by "Neither shall you desire your neighbor's house, or field, or male or female slave, or ox or donkey, or anything that belongs to your neighbor." Also the differentiation is brought out by two different verbs, *covet* in regard to the wife and *desire* in regard to the house, slaves, animals, and possessions.

In regard to debt slavery, Exodus puts together the fate of a woman and her husband in regard to slaves who love their masters and want to remain with them after the six years of service before the seventh year of required freedom (21:5–6). However, Deuteronomy distinguishes carefully and gives the same right to a woman: "You shall do the same with a female slave" (15:16–17).

In ancient times, men were the ones who made covenants on behalf of themselves and their tribes or families. But in Deuteronomy, women are present with an active part. After the community blessings and curses pronounced by all the people, the writer notes: "These are the words of the covenant that the LORD commanded Moses to make with the Israelites in the land of Moab in addition to the covenant that he had made with them at Horeb" (29:1). Among the people standing assembled are the tribal leaders, the elders, officials, the men of Israel also with *women and children*" (29:10–11). At the renewal of the covenant every seven years, the same was true. All the Torah was read to the people, men, women, and children, as well as aliens residing in the towns (31:12).

Slaves—"Remember that you were a slave in the land of Egypt" (5:15)

This remembering and identification is a repeated theme in 16:12; 24:18, 22. God identifies himself at the beginning of the Decalogue as the one "who brought you out of the land of Egypt that house of slavery" (5:6). So, we would expect a much better treatment of slaves in this book. In comparison with the Exodus Decalogue, Deuteronomy's version adds specifically that both male and female slaves should *rest* on that day (5:14) in addition to prohibiting their work. In Exodus, the motivation for the Sabbath is based on creation (20:11) and God's own rest. In

Deuteronomy, the motivation is based on God's role as a liberator: "Remember that you were a slave in the land of Egypt, and the LORD your God brought you out of there with a mighty hand and an outstretched arm; therefore the LORD your God commanded you to keep the sabbath day" (5:15).

Among other things, slaves accompany and participate with the family in the joyful pilgrim feasts of Pentecost and booths (16:11, 14). When the time comes at the seventh year that they must be liberated, they should be sent away with abundant gifts: "When you send a slave out from you as a free person, you shall not send him empty-handed. Provide liberally out of your flock, your threshing floor and your wine press....Remember that you were a slave in the land of Egypt, and the LORD your God redeemed you" (15:13–15).

The most unique feature in Deuteronomy is the treatment of runaway slaves:

> Slaves who have escaped to you from their owners shall not
> be given back to them. They shall reside with you, in your
> midst, in any place they choose in any one of your towns,
> wherever they please; you shall not *oppress* them. (23:15–16)

This statement is most surprising especially in view of the strict laws forbidding this in the ancient world, including the Roman and Greek eras. The question of runaway slaves and state laws was even one of the causes of the American Civil War. Why is it here in Deuteronomy? We have seen the liberation from Egypt motif in the Decalogue. *The Hebrew people were a nation that sprang up from runaway slaves!* A key connecting word is *oppress*. The Book of Exodus opens with the story of an *oppressed* people. Pharaoh oppressed them as slaves. At the burning bush God says to Moses, "I have also seen how the Egyptians oppress them" (3:9).

The Role of a King

A future king is not above the covenant but subject to it, equally with other people:

When he has taken the throne of his kingdom, he shall have a *copy of this law* written for him in the presence of the Levitical priests. It shall remain with him and he shall read in it all the days of his life, so that he may learn to fear the LORD his God, diligently observing all the words of this law and these statutes, neither exalting himself above other members of the community nor turning aside from the commandment, either to the right or to the left, so that he and his descendants may reign long over his kingdom in Israel. (17:18–20)

Italicized above are the words "copy of this law." The Septuagint Greek translated this as *Deuteronomion touto,* from which we get the title of this book. The second Book of Kings describes King Josiah as listening to this book with all the people and making a covenant to keep it along with them (23:1–30). Jeremiah later praises him to his son Shallum with these words: "Did not your father eat and drink and do justice and righteousness? Then it was well with him. He judged the cause of the poor and needy; then it was well. Is not this to know me? says the LORD" (22:15–16).

The Book of Numbers and God's Equitable Division of the Land

We have seen how the central issue of the Torah in Deuteronomy is the gift of the land as God's initiative and the people's covenant response to this. However, the book is in a time warp with present, past, and future coming together in a way that is often confusing. Theoretically, the people are listening to Moses by the Jordan, yet some provisions in the book hint at longtime occupation already. For example, the care to respect "boundary markers set up by former generations" (19:14). Also, there is a final covenant curse warning against moving a neighbor's landmark (27:17). The Book of Numbers fills in this gap by showing how God divided the land.

A helpful understanding of this comes from the story of King Ahab's attempt to take the vineyard of Naboth (1 Kgs 21:1–16). The king had cast an envious eye on this adjoining vineyard and wanted to buy it or exchange it for another. But Naboth refused to sell or exchange it, saying with an oath, "I will not give you my ancestral inheritance." This refusal is emphasized in the story by repeating it three times. The king kept repeating these words to himself, for he knew that he had no power in such a matter. Not even a king could change the ancient laws on hereditary land. He even lost sleep over it and refused to eat.

Queen Jezebel noticed this and took matters into her own hands. She arranged a false accusation to a court that Naboth had cursed God and the king. As a result, the court condemned him to death, and the king seized the vineyard. At this point God intervened through the prophet Elijah saying, "Go down to meet King Ahab of Israel, who rules in Samaria; he is now in the vineyard of Naboth, where he has gone to take possession" (21:18). Because of this serious crime, Elijah tells him that his dynasty will crumble.

From this story we see the importance of each particular ancestral land. It is a designated sacred gift from God that cannot be alienated (except often through sinful intrigue). The enormity of the crime is so great that the great prophet Elijah intervenes with a message from God that this will cause the fall of the king's dynasty.

This tradition about the land is either told or reconstructed by the Book of Numbers. God instructed Moses and Eleazar the priest to make a census of all of the new generation of Israel that was to enter the promised land (Num 26:1–4). Then, God said to Moses:

> To these the land shall be apportioned for inheritance according to the number of names. To a large tribe you shall give a large inheritance, and to a small tribe you shall give a small inheritance; every tribe shall be given its inheritance according to its enrollment. But the land shall be apportioned by lot; according to the names of their ancestral tribes they shall inherit. Their inheritance shall be apportioned according to lot between the larger and the smaller. (Num 26:52–56)

God carefully delineated the boundaries of Israel in Numbers, chapter 34. Moses then told the people, "This is the land that you shall inherit by lot" (34:13). Then, the representatives of each tribe and the heads of the families further divided the land by lot, finally concluding with the statement:

These are the inheritances that the priest Eleazar and Joshua son of Nun and the heads of the families of the tribes of the Israelites distributed by lot at Shiloh before the LORD, at the entrance of the tent of meeting. So they finished distributing the land. (Josh 19:51)

The equal distribution of the land was of supreme importance for agricultural economies. Their very existence depended upon it. There were professional tradespeople, yet the average farmer tried to be a jack-of-all-trades to save unnecessary expenses. Any threat to the land is a threat to life. So, if they perceive that one family has overabundance and they have not enough, this is evil in itself.

Putting together the views on the land in Deuteronomy and Numbers, we have the following: Biblical justice is built on three pillars: 1) scarcity of the land—this particular geographic area; 2) the land is an inherited designated gift of God that should never be alienated; 3) it is a land "equally" (land can never be perfectly shared) divided by divine lot to tribes and then to families. In regard to number 2, the geographical area is not theirs through conquest but by means of a promise made to Abraham and repeated to Isaac, Jacob (Israel), and their descendants.

The Priestly Tradition in Leviticus and the Biblical Jubilee Year

This book was often called in early rabbinic tradition "The Priests' Manual." However, it goes beyond this to the people and the land. The book aims to show that ethical and religious "uncleanness" caused the pollution and consequent loss of the land and the exile. The predominant vocabulary in this book witnesses these views: The word *holy, hagios,* is found 76 times. *Clean, katharos,* or *cleanse* occurs 71 times. *Unclean* appears a large 115 times.

A comparison between Deuteronomy and Leviticus helps to understand the latter. In Deuteronomy, we have a biblical liberation theology of God intervening to free his people from Egyptian slavery and oppression. In response, they are asked to "liberate" the oppressed and the landless. In Leviticus, God liberates them from the moral degradation of Egypt so they can be a holy people: "For I am the LORD who brought you up from the land of Egypt, to be your God; you shall be holy, for I am holy" (11:45). Also, "You shall not do as they do in the land of Egypt, where you lived, and you shall not do as they do in the land of Canaan, to which I am bringing you. You shall not follow their statutes" (18:3 also 19:35–36)

As regards the land, it must be freed from pollution and restored to its original state. The priestly tradition of creation (Gen 1–2:4) emphasizes the pristine *goodness* of creation. At the end of each of the seven days, God saw that what he did was *good;* on the last day, *very good.* The first humans do not *own* the Garden of Eden but are its custodians under God's direction. The fact that the Levites were not permitted to own any land helped them appreciate this as an ideal. In Leviticus, the land itself needs to purify and reestablish itself by a sabbatical vacation when no sowing or reaping may be done (25:6). In Deuteronomy, God gives the land as an inheritance and gift. In Leviticus, God retains ownership and title but lends it out: "The land shall not be sold in perpetuity, for the land is mine; with me you are but aliens and tenants" (25:33).

The above theology of the land lies behind the year of the Jubilee:

> You shall count off seven weeks of years, seven times seven years, so that the period of seven weeks of years gives forty-nine years. Then you shall have the trumpet sounded loud; on the tenth day of the seventh month—on the day of atonement—you shall have the trumpet sounded throughout all your land. And you shall hallow the fiftieth year and you shall proclaim liberty throughout the land to all its inhabitants. It shall be a jubilee for you: you shall return, every one of you, to your property and every one of you to your family. (25:8–10)

The liberty or freedom mentioned above was not only in regard to land being restored to original owners but also to indentured workers as well. For Leviticus, the word *slave* had a taint of evil connected to it because of slavery in the "corrupted" land of Egypt. So, the actual word is avoided. People belong to God, not earthly masters, so technically it is forbidden to sell or own slaves (25:43). Those who become dependent or give their services to pay debts are to be regarded as hired workers not as slaves. In the fiftieth year, they return home free from any claims against them (25:39–43).

There are no definite indications in the prophets that the Jubilee year was ever enforced. However, we will see later that it had a great influence on the dedicated community at Qumran near the time of Jesus. We will also study how Luke makes the Jubilee an important theme for his Gospel. (Incidentally, the original American Liberty Bell in Philadelphia carries the inscription from the Jubilee year proclamation, "Proclaim liberty in the land," with chapter and verse reference.)

The priestly code also called for the highest ethical responsibilities to others that would go along with an interior cleansing of the heart:

> You shall not hate in your *heart* anyone of your kin; you shall reprove your neighbor, or you will incur guilt yourself. You shall not take vengeance or bear a grudge against any of your people, but *you shall love* your neighbor as yourself: I am the LORD. (19:17–18)

Thus, purity of the heart, removing hatred, is important for the priestly ethic. The words "You shall love" are the same as the opening words of the *Shemah* in regard to God. The expression "As yourself" appeals to creation theology in which God creates man and woman to be "as himself," to his own image and likeness (Gen 1:27). This love is for another as sharing the same divine image.

In our study of the New Testament, we will find the profound influence of this text on the Gospels and the early church as they follow the lead of Leviticus in the matter of the heart and the link with the *Shemah*.

Also, of great interest to those of us who are getting younger day by day: "You shall rise before the aged and defer to the old; and you shall fear your God: I am the LORD" (Lev 19:32). The connection to God is not immediately evident until we recall that God is the "ancient one" in Daniel 7:13, because he is the eldest of all beings! (From Josephus, *Against Apion,* 2, 28.) Therefore, an older person becomes more like God!

Leviticus rises to new heights in the Hebrew Bible in its attitude to outsiders and strangers: "The alien who resides with you shall be as the citizen among you; *you shall love the alien as yourself,* for you were aliens in the land of Egypt: I am the LORD your God" (Lev 19:34). This attitude will also have a profound influence on the teachings of Jesus. The great prophets Isaiah, Jeremiah, and Ezekiel were all priests and deeply influenced by the lofty ethics of the priestly tradition. This influence will come out in our next chapter on the prophets and Social Justice.

The Renewal of the Torah After the Return from Exile

The central justice theme of Deuteronomy had a great influence[7] on other texts as the Bible traditions were put together after the exile. This renewal is really the work of the prophets, especially Isaiah II and III, Jeremiah, and Ezekiel. Here, however, we will look at the covenant renewal according to Deuteronomy (31:10) that took place in the time of Nehemiah, in the fifth century B.C. The evil of the loss of land through debts continued through history, perhaps not recorded often because it was so common.

After the Jews returned from exile in Babylon, there was a great outcry of the people to the governor Nehemiah because so many had lost their lands through debts. Some said, "We are having to pledge our fields, our vineyards, and our houses in order to get grain during the famine." Others said, "We are having to borrow money on our fields and vineyards to pay the king's tax....we are forcing our sons and daughters to be slaves....our fields and vineyards now belong to others" (Neh 5:3–5).

After hearing this, the governor called a great assembly and brought charges against the guilty nobles and officials. He demanded, "Restore to them, this very day, their fields and vineyards, their olive orchards, and their houses and the interest...you have been exacting from them" (5:11). He then required them to take a public oath that they would do so, and they did as they promised.

At the end of the Book of Nehemiah, there is a renewal of the covenant during the seventh month after the seventh year as prescribed in Deuteronomy 31:10: "All the people gathered together into the square before the Water Gate. They told the scribe Ezra to bring the book of the law of Moses, which the LORD had given to Israel. Accordingly, the priest Ezra brought the law before the assembly, both men and women and all who could hear with understanding. This was on the first day of the seventh month" (Neh 8:1–2).

A central part of that covenant follows:

> The rest of the people, the priests, the Levites…join with their kin, their nobles, and enter into a curse and an oath to walk in God's law, which was given by Moses the servant of God, and to observe and do all the commandments of the LORD our Lord and his ordinances and his statutes. We will not give our daughters to the peoples of the land or take their daughters for our sons; and if the peoples of the land bring in merchandise or any grain on the sabbath day to sell, we will not buy it from them on the sabbath or on a holy day; and we will forego the crops of the seventh year and the exaction of every debt. (10:28–31)

In the last verse above, we find a unique combination of two previous texts that protect the poor. The first is Exodus 23:10–11 that requires a sabbatical year for the land. With no sowing or reaping, the poor of the people and even the animals will have enough to eat. The second is Deuteronomy 15:1–11 regarding the forgiveness of debts on the seventh year. Even though Nehemiah has undergone much editing, the inclusion of the above texts shows that the spirit of Deuteronomy is still remembered and appealed to.

Summary and Prelude to the Prophets

The Torah is founded on two great initiatives of God. The first is that of *oppression* in Egypt, "that house of slavery." It provokes a loving response in practically designated ways for the relief of the oppressed without land—the widows, orphans, strangers, Levites. A connected second initiative is the gift of the land of Israel as an inheritance. God equally divides this limited land as a designated gift to tribes and families. The loss or danger of loss to the land is protected in special ways, especially by a seventh-year remission of debts and freedom of debt slaves. The priestly tradition sees liberation from Egypt especially in terms of relief from evil and wickedness. Thus, it asks for the highest degree of ethical response to God, especially in love of neighbor and strangers as well as special consideration for slaves.

In view of this message, the prophets will have a limited role as innovators. They will mainly function as mouthpieces of the living voice of God calling for a radical return to the core of the covenant in the Torah. Each of the prophets will add a special flavor to that message in view of their personal characteristics and situation, but the essence will be the same.

Our first chapter prepares the way for the last chapter of the United Nations Millennium Declaration. Fundamental is the view of our planet as a place of limited resources where a basic justice demands an equal sharing of resources.

2

The Prophets and Social Justice

ISAIAH, PROPHET OF RADICAL REFORM

Among all the prophets of Israel, Isaiah holds a primary place. He is preeminently the great *prophet of justice*. *Justice* is mentioned on almost every page, more often than in any book of the Bible, and more than by all the other prophets combined. The New Testament quotes him more frequently than any other book of the Bible. The opening announcement of Jesus' ministry in Matthew, Mark, and Luke comes from the living voice of God relayed from Isaiah and John the Baptist. Matthew writes, "This is the one of whom the prophet Isaiah spoke when he said, 'The voice of one crying out in the wilderness: "Prepare the way of the Lord, make his paths straight"'" (3:3).

The Call and Mission of Isaiah

We know little more about Isaiah's origins and life than his opening words, "The vision of Isaiah which he saw concerning Judah and Jerusalem in the days of Uzziah, Gotham, Achaz and Hezekiah, kings of Judah." His prophetic ministry began around 738 B.C. and lasted until about 701 B.C. He was married and had at least two children (7:3; 8:3). His prophetic call came at a time of serious crisis for Judah. Israel had two kingdoms at this time; the south, called Judah, and the north, Ephraim, or Israel. The northern kingdom had formed an alliance with Syria to depose the Davidic king of Judah and set up a new dynasty. The purpose was the formation of an alliance to counter the growing power of Assyria. The story of Isaiah's prophetic call already contains some of the dominant themes in his prophecies:

> In the year that King Uzziah died, I saw the Lord sitting on a throne, high and lofty; and the hem of his robe filled the temple. Seraphs were in attendance above him; each had six wings: with two they covered their faces, and with two they covered their feet, and with two they flew. And one called to another and said: "Holy, holy, holy is the LORD of hosts; the whole earth is full of his glory." (6:1–3)

The "high and lofty throne" was the space between the two fifteen-foot-high cherubim, one on each side of the ark. The fact that the Lord's robes filled the Temple points to a colossal image of God. The burning creatures or seraphim had to cover their faces and body to protect themselves from the radiant glory in their midst. They chanted to one another, "Holy, Holy, Holy," in acknowledgment of God's complete separation from all that is impure or mundane. He is *Lord of hosts* (a term used 56 times in chapters 1–39), an expression of power as head of the heavenly "armies" of angels. Yet at the same time, this glory extends to the whole Earth. Then, continuing:

> The pivots on the thresholds shook at the voices of those who called, and the house filled with smoke. And I said: "Woe is me! I am lost, for I am a man of unclean lips, and I live among a people of unclean lips; yet my eyes have seen the King, the LORD of hosts!" (6:4–5)

The thunderous voices of the seraphim shook the whole Temple as the smoke from the altar of incense filled the atmosphere. Isaiah felt completely unworthy before such an overwhelming manifestation of the divine presence. He had seen "the King, the LORD of hosts." These two expressions of power are meant to contrast with the weak earthly kings who were trying to overthrow the Davidic dynasty that was supported by God's promises. The revelation of God's holiness and power will influence all Isaiah's prophecies in their sharp contrasts between human evil and God's holiness. A favorite title of God in Isaiah's prophecies is "The Holy One of Israel," found 29 times in his book. The use of this title enables him to stress justice so firmly and sharply in contrast to human weakness. The Temple atmosphere of this vision leads us to believe that Isaiah himself was a priest.

Then, one of the seraphim brought a live coal from the incense fire and purified his lips saying that his guilt was taken away and his sin forgiven. Then, God asked, "Whom shall I send? Who will go for us?" Isaiah replied, "Here am I; send me" (6:8). Then, God warns him that his words will polarize and bring many to judgment instead of repentance (6:9–13). This repentance will be the message brought out especially in the early prophecies of chapters 1–5.

The Way of Justice in Isaiah

God's Opening Challenge—a Lawsuit Against His People

"Hear, O heavens, and listen, O earth; for the LORD has spoken: I reared children and brought them up, but they have rebelled against me. The ox knows its owner, and the donkey its master's crib; but Israel does not know, my people do not understand" (1:1–2).

In this scathing introduction, God declares that seemingly dumb animals, such as an ox and a donkey, know where to go for their source of nourishment but his people do not know. All through Isaiah, a central theme will be to *know the Lord* in a deep sense. This knowing will involve every facet of life but will be summed up in justice. Later in preparing a way for the Lord's return, it will be called a way of justice (40:14), a description later taken over by Matthew to describe the way of John the Baptist and Jesus (21:32; 3:15). Justice is so close to God's nature that he will declare, "I the LORD love justice" (Isa 61:8).

Isaiah's presentation consists of various stages, although not in strict, logical order:

1. Judgment time is near—*that day* or *day* of God. *That day* is repeated 69 times in Isaiah. *Day* or *that day* occurs 9 times in chapters 1–5. God's intervention as a judge is coming soon because evil has reached a climax.

2. A description of evil works and the sorry condition of the people, e.g.:

> Ah, sinful nation, people laden with iniquity, offspring who do evil, children who deal corruptly, who have forsaken the LORD, who have despised the Holy One of Israel, who are utterly estranged! Why do you seek further beatings? Why do you continue to rebel? The whole head is sick, and the whole heart faint. From the sole of the foot even to the head, there is no soundness in it, but bruises and sores and bleeding wounds. (1:4–6)

In a city that was once faithful and "full of justice," now, "they do not defend the orphan and the widow's cause does not come before them" (1:23). In regard to the land, the rich gobble up the lands of the poor: "Ah, you who join house to house, who add field to field, until there is room for no one but you, and you are left to live alone in the midst of the land" (5:8).

3. Invitation to change and assurance of forgiveness:
"Wash yourselves; make yourselves clean; remove the evil of your doings from before my eyes....Come now,...says the Lord: though your sins are like scarlet, they shall be like snow; though they are red like crimson, they shall become like wool" (1:16–18).

4. Justice as a sign of repentance:
"Cease to do evil, learn to do good; seek justice, rescue the oppressed, defend the orphan, plead for the widow" (1:16–17).

5. Hope for the future:
If there is true repentance, Jerusalem will once more be a "city of justice" (1:26). And someday it will be a center where the world's nations will come to learn justice, avoid war, and establish peace. As a result, "nation shall not lift up the sword against nation, neither shall they learn war any more" (2:4).

So far, what we have heard is God's plea for a return to the core of the Sinai covenant, if we take the central issues of the land and those deprived of land such as the widows, oppressed, and orphans. However, another covenant with the king begins when Israel entered the land and finally evolved into a kingdom.

The King's Justice and the Covenant

God made a promise to David through Nathan the prophet in these words: "He shall build a house for my name, and I will establish the throne of his kingdom forever. I will be a father to him, and he shall be a son to me" (2 Sam 7:13–14). The relation of father to son is one of trust and delegation. The king will be responsible to establish God's covenant justice on Earth. The biblical writer states that "David administered justice and equity to all his people" (2 Sam 8:15). When the queen of Sheba visited Solomon, David's successor, she declared, "Blessed be the LORD your God, who has delighted in you and set you on the throne of Israel! Because the LORD loved Israel forever, he has made you king to execute justice and righteousness" (1 Kgs 10:9).

In practice, the Bible praises few kings for their justice. We have already seen that the prophet Jeremiah's praise of King Josiah for his justice is an exception (22:15). However, the birth of every new successor raised hopes for a future reign characterized by justice and peace. At a time when the Davidic dynasty was threatened, God announced through Isaiah that a young woman had conceived and would bear a son called Immanuel, meaning "God is with us" (7:14). As time goes on, future successors are idealized as symbols of hope. Thus, Isaiah announces:

> For a child has been born for us, a son given to us; authority rests upon his shoulders; and he is named Wonderful Counselor, Mighty God, Everlasting Father, Prince of Peace. His authority shall grow continually, and there shall be endless peace for the throne of David and his kingdom. He will establish and uphold it with justice and with righteousness from this time onward and forevermore. The zeal of the LORD of hosts will do this. (9:6–7)

We notice above that divine titles are given to the king in view of his father-son relationship with God. Because of this title, his role is to establish the kingdom in justice and righteousness. This is why Isaiah tells King Achaz that his child will be called Immanuel, meaning "God is with us" (7:14).

Hopes for Justice Through Future Ideal Kings

Even though the Davidic dynasty seems like a small stump to its enemies, God promises that "A shoot shall come out from the stump of Jesse" (11:1). These shoots will be future successors, gifted with divine qualities of wisdom and understanding—rulers characterized by justice:

> His delight shall be in the fear of the LORD. He shall not judge by what his eyes see, or decide by what his ears hear; but with righteousness he shall judge the poor, and decide with equity for the meek of the earth; he shall strike the earth with the rod of his mouth, and with the breath of his lips he shall kill the wicked. Righteousness shall be the belt around his waist, and faithfulness the belt around his loins. (11:3–5)

Also, once Israel's oppressors lose their power, "then a throne will be established in steadfast love *(hesed)*, in the tent of David, and on it shall sit in faithfulness a ruler who seeks justice, and is swift to do what is right" (16:5). Psalm 72, a psalm for a king's inauguration, is a beautiful prayer that the king's reign be characterized by justice for the poor and needy:

> Give the king your justice, O God, and your righteousness to a king's son. May he judge your people with righteousness, and your poor with justice. May the mountains yield prosperity for the people, and the hills, in righteousness. May he defend the cause of the poor of the people, give deliverance to the needy, and crush the oppressor. (72:1–4)

A king was literally "an anointed one," *Messiah* in Hebrew, translated into Greek as *Christos*. This title was derived from the ceremony in which he was designated through an anointing with oil. The idealization of future kings gave rise to a belief that there would be a great future king, a Messiah, who would finally establish God's kingdom on Earth. It was this hope that gave rise to the New Testament and expectations in regard to Jesus.

Israel in Exile, the Servant of the Lord, and Hopes for Justice

Isaiah, chapters 40–55, is often called *2 Isaiah* because these chapters are addressed to people in exile in Babylonia in the sixth century B.C. God announces that their term of suffering is over, and they shall soon return to Israel. God's herald calls out to prepare the way for them to travel: A voice cries out: "In the wilderness prepare the way of the LORD, make straight in the desert a highway for our God" (40:3). In exile, there was no king to promote justice, but God is still a God of justice and knows "the path of justice" for them to take (40:14). He will do this not through a king or power but in a new way through his *Servant,* a word referring to faithful Israelites, singular or plural:

> Here is my servant, whom I uphold, my chosen, in whom my soul delights; I have put my spirit upon him; he will bring forth justice to the nations. He will not cry or lift up his voice, or make it heard in the street; a bruised reed he will not break, and a dimly burning wick he will not quench; he will faithfully bring forth justice. (42:1–3)

Here, we have an image of servants of God who suffer but are not overcome or crushed and who bring about justice in a humble, nonviolent way. Yet, God's spirit is in them to accomplish this as a witness to the world. But how will God do this? They are living in a foreign country dominated by alien gods. Their own Temple and Dwelling Place of God has been destroyed. This process will be described in 52:13 to 53:12. The Temple had been a place to offer sacrifices for themselves and others in order to bring about peace and reconciliation. This chapter applies Temple terminology to faithful people who accept their sufferings and offer them to God to bring his justice and forgiveness to others. In this way, they become living Temples.

This happens despite the fact that the typical *Servant of the Lord* appears to be only a failure and loser: "He was despised and rejected by others; a man of suffering and acquainted with infirmity; and as one from whom others hide their faces, he was despised, and we held him of no account" (53:3). Yet, all this is changed because they have been able to accept this suffering and that of others and offer it like a Temple sacrifice to God:

> Surely he has borne our infirmities and carried our diseases; yet we accounted him stricken, struck down by God, and afflicted. But he was wounded for our transgressions, crushed for our iniquities; upon him was the punishment that made us whole, and by his bruises we are healed. (53:4–5)

Because his offering is like a Temple sacrifice, the Servant is described as a lamb willing to give its life for others: "The LORD has laid on him the iniquity of us all" (53:6). "Like a lamb that is led to the slaughter" (53:7). Because of this, the outcome will be a great surprise: "The righteous one, my servant, shall make many righteous, and he shall bear their iniquities" (53:11).

The image of the Servant of the Lord contributes a valuable inner dimension to the quest for justice. Those who live according to their faith despite external opposition can help bring justice to others not only by their example but also by the offering of their lives to God as a sacrifice and intercessory prayer.

The Returned Exiles and Justice for Those Excluded

The last chapters of Isaiah, 56–66, are often called *3 Isaiah* because their message is addressed to those exiles who have already returned. They came back to Israel with great fervor, rebuilt their Temple, and sought to influence for the better those who had remained in the land. However, some were overzealous in a way that led to exclusivism. Immediately, this section opens with a warning: "Thus says the LORD: Maintain justice and do what is right, for soon my salvation will come and my deliverance be revealed" (56:1).

The question of exclusivism involves two groups: First the *foreigner* (stranger or alien), people who were non-Israelites, but who lived in their midst and followed their laws. We have seen in Deuteronomy how they enjoyed many privileges, such as those of the Sabbath rest and the various benefits for the poor. They functioned as paid laborers because they could not own land (Deut 24:14). The second group were *eunuchs*. They were specifically excluded from the assembly of Israel along with illegitimate children, Moabites, and Ammonites (Deut 23:1–3).

In the planning and rebuilding of the Temple after the exile, some purists wanted foreigners and eunuchs to be excluded from temple worship. However, God's word directs that the two groups should have a privileged place: "Do not let the foreigner joined to the LORD say, 'The LORD will surely separate me from his people'; and do not let the eunuch say, 'I am just a dry tree'" (Isa 56:3).

> For thus says the LORD:…To the eunuchs who keep my sabbaths, who choose the things that please me and hold fast my covenant, I will give, in my house and within my walls, a monument and a name better than sons and daughters; I will give them an everlasting name that shall not be cut off. (56:1–5)

In regard to foreigners:

> And the foreigners who join themselves to the LORD, to minister to him, to love the name of the LORD, and to be his servants, all who keep the sabbath, and do not profane it, and hold fast my covenant–these I will bring to my holy mountain, and make them joyful in my house of prayer; their burnt offerings and their sacrifices will be accepted on my altar; *for my house shall be called a house of prayer for all peoples*. Thus says the Lord GOD, who gathers the outcasts of Israel. (56:6–8)

The words italicized above will be quoted by Jesus as his reason for cleansing the Temple to make it open for all believers without discrimination (Mark 11:17).

True Liturgy, Worship, and Openness to the Poor and Oppressed

The returned exiles came back joyfully to rebuild the Temple and enjoy the beautiful liturgies and worship. However, some became so wrapped in their devotions that they did not turn outwardly to those in need. God speaks through Isaiah to warn them:

> Is not this the fast that I choose: to loose the bonds of injustice, to undo the thongs of the yoke, to let the oppressed go free, and to break every yoke? Is it not to share your bread with the hungry, and bring the homeless poor into your house; when you see the naked, to cover them, and not to hide yourself from your own kin? Then your light shall break forth like the dawn. (58:6–8)

God will answer prayers only when liturgy is accompanied by this outreach in justice to others: "Then you shall call, and the LORD will answer; you shall cry for help, and he will say, Here I am" (58:9).

AMOS, SHEPHERD AND PROPHET

The first words of this book inform us that Amos[8] was a shepherd from a little town of Tekoa in Judea about ten miles south of Jerusalem. His prophetic activity, however, took place in the northern kingdom of Israel. He describes his call as follows:

> Then Amos answered Amaziah, "I am no prophet, nor a prophet's son; but I am a herdsman, and a dresser of sycamore trees, and the LORD took me from following the flock, and the LORD said to me, 'Go, prophesy to my people Israel.'" (7:14–15)

Amaziah was a priest in the northern shrine of Bethel. He tried to force Amos to leave Israel and return to Judah. At this time, around 750 B.C., Israel was enjoying a temporary prosperity under King Jeroboam II. This king was able to temporarily throw off the yoke of the Syrians at a time when Assyria was temporarily weak but rapidly regaining strength.

As a shepherd, Amos lived most of his life outdoors. The great events of his life were sunrise and sunset. He felt God's presence as he watched the stars at night and welcomed the sun as well as the rain. All shepherds love open spaces and freedom. Amos implores the people to "seek the Lord and live" (5:6).He is "the one who made the Pleiades and Orion, and turns deep darkness into the morning, and darkens the day into night, who calls for the waters of the sea, and pours them out on the surface of the earth" (5:8).

This awareness of the beautiful harmony of God's creation intensified his shock as he came near wealthy cities like Samaria and Bethel. The sight of so much injustice made him certain that God could not endure it much longer and that a day of the Lord, a day of reckoning was at hand:

> Thus says the LORD: For three transgressions of Israel, and for four, I will not revoke the punishment; because they sell the righteous for silver, and the needy for a pair of sandals— they who trample the head of the poor into the dust of the earth, and push the afflicted out of the way; father and son go in to the same girl, so that my holy name is profaned. (2:6–7)

"Selling the righteous for silver" means debt slavery for failure to meet obligations. The trampling of the poor and afflicted refers to unjust decisions of judges and elders at the "gates" of the city where such judgments take place. With a shepherd's special sensitivity about the land he announces God's judgment on those who accumulate extra homes and property while others have not sufficient on which to live: "I will tear down the winter house as well as the summer house; and the houses of ivory shall perish, and the great houses shall come to an end, says the LORD" (3:15).

Amos is especially concerned about the contrast between religion and justice. People came to religious shrines trusting that God would hear their prayers despite injustice to the poor. God says:

> I hate, I despise your festivals, and I take no delight in your solemn assemblies. Even though you offer me your burnt offerings and grain offerings, I will not accept them; and the offerings of well-being of your fatted animals I will not look upon.

Take away from me the noise of your songs; I will not listen to the melody of your harps. But let justice roll down like waters, and righteousness like an ever-flowing stream. (5:21–24)

These poetic texts contrast the noisy music of religious songs to the pleasing melody of justice that is constant and flowing like a stream. The Hebrew text brings this music out with plays on sounds and words.

A God of Impartiality to All People on Earth

A distinct feature of Amos is God's impartiality. If God expects people to be just and impartial, it is because he is so himself. He has chosen Israel in a covenant relationship, but that does not mean automatic protection. God has intervened to bring Israel out of Egypt, but he has also worked in the history of other people, even in their traditional enemies, such as the Philistines and Arameans (Syrians):

Are you not like the Ethiopians to me, O people of Israel? says the LORD. Did I not bring Israel up from the land of Egypt, and the Philistines from Caphtor and the Arameans from Kir? (9:7)

Amos even ends with a prophecy of the restoration of Judah to whom all the nations of the Earth will be joined. This restoration took place centuries after Amos's time. While it was probably added to Amos's original prophecies, the early church never read scriptures making those distinctions about composition. We will see later in the New Testament that at the council of Jerusalem, James quotes this prophecy as referring to the entry of Gentile converts into the church (Acts 15:15–17).

MICAH, THE FARMERS' PROPHET

Micah, like Isaiah, prophesied in Judah in the late eighth century. He was from Moresheth-gath, a rural agriculture area about twenty-five miles southwest of Jerusalem. While Isaiah was very much concerned with the Davidic succession and its future, Micah's interests were almost entirely focused on the land and justice. Among his earliest prophecies were the following:

> Alas for those who devise wickedness and evil deeds on their beds! When the morning dawns, they perform it, because it is in their power. They covet fields, and seize them; houses, and take them away; they oppress householder and house, people and their inheritance. (2:1–2)

However, the prophet predicts that those who take land from others violently will experience violence in return from the Assyrians who will soon invade the land:

> On that day they shall take up a taunt song against you, and wail with bitter lamentation, and say, "We are utterly ruined; the LORD alters the inheritance of my people; how he removes it from me! Among our captors he parcels out our fields." Therefore you will have no one to cast the line by lot in the assembly of the LORD. (2:4–5)

This text refers to the change in the ancient apportioning of the land that we described in Numbers in the last chapter. This precious ancestral land, divided by lot and given to them by God, will be given to others by the Assyrians. The people complained about such a dire prophecy: "one should not preach of such things; disaster will not overtake us" (2:6). Despite this, Micah continued to preach the word of God. His prophecies were read and reread through the centuries. Jeremiah a hundred years later notes their fulfillment (26:18–19). Matthew will refer to Micah in pointing to Bethlehem as the place where the Messiah will be born (5:2–6).

HOSEA, PROPHET OF DIVINE LOVE

While all the prophets convey the core message of the covenant, each of them makes a special contribution toward its understanding. In our opening page, we noted that Social Justice in the scriptures must be studied in a covenant context with its divine initiative and the people's response. No other prophet conveys God's deep personal love in so strong a way as Hosea. Social Justice does not consist of principles alone but of shared relationships that are the moving forces behind principles.

Hosea, like Isaiah, was a prophet in the late eighth century but a native of the northern kingdom of Israel. The first image of divine love is that of the love between man and woman:

> When the LORD first spoke through Hosea, the LORD said to Hosea, "Go, take for yourself a wife of whoredom and have children of whoredom, for the land commits great whoredom by forsaking the LORD." So he went and took Gomer daughter of Diblaim, and she conceived and bore him a son. (1:2–3)

We do not know whether this was an actual marriage or a symbolic one. In either case, the prophet's action represents God's experience with Israel. He has taken her as a bride, yet she has proved faithless and ungrateful by leaving God and going after fertility gods as her lovers. She will suffer the consequences of this betrayal. But, despite her infidelity, God will seek her out, forgive her, and take her back again as if they were newlyweds once more: "Therefore, I will now allure her, and bring her into the wilderness, and speak tenderly to her (literally, "speak to her heart")" (2:14). The "wilderness" was the "time of courtship" in the Sinai peninsula when God first made a covenant with Israel. Then, God says:

> I will take you for my wife forever; I will take you for my wife
> in righteousness and in justice, in steadfast love, and in mercy.
> I will take you for my wife in faithfulness; and you shall
> know the LORD. (2:19–20)

God presents himself with all his primary covenant qualities: justice, steadfast love, mercy, and faithfulness. *Steadfast love* translates the Hebrew *hesed* for covenant responsibility; *mercy* renders *rahamim,* compassionate womb-love, from the root *rehem,* womb. When God pronounced his name *Yahweh* to Moses, these were the eminent attributes of his nature (Exod

47

34:6). As a result, the bride will really "know the Lord" as a deep personal response.

A second image of divine love is that of the tender love of a father toward a young son:

> When Israel was a child, I loved him, and out of Egypt I called my son. The more I called them, the more they went from me; they kept sacrificing to the Baals, and offering incense to idols. Yet it was I who taught Ephraim to walk, I took them up in my arms; but they did not know that I healed them. I led them with cords of human kindness, with bands of love. I was to them like those who lift infants to their cheeks. I bent down to them and fed them. (11:1–4)

The response to all this loving care of God is not simply liturgy and prayers. God declares, "I desire steadfast love, *hesed,* and not sacrifice, the knowledge of God rather than burnt offerings" (6:6). Hosea has a special understanding of covenant love in terms of a deep personal and loving commitment. We will later see in Matthew that this verse from Hosea is a special Gospel theme. The second term, *knowledge* or the verb *know,* is a favorite with Hosea. *Knowing* in Semitic languages often has a deep personalistic sense. God declares that he *knows* Ephraim (5:3). The response of Israel as spouse of Yahweh is to "know the LORD" (2:20). In an appeal for repentance, Hosea writes, "Let us know, let us press on to know the LORD" (6:3). The verb *know* fits into Hosea's marriage symbolism. The Hebrew text of Genesis 4:1 reads literally, "(Adam) knew his wife Eve, and she conceived and bore Cain."

We do not find in Hosea the lists of practical social justice seen in Isaiah and Amos. Hosea has it summed up in a total response of love with the words "know the Lord." When this happens, everything else will follow, because justice is God's central activity. The Lord "loves justice" (Isa 61:8). So, Hosea will only name justice in general as a return for God's love, because justice includes all else: "Sow for yourselves justice; reap steadfast love; break up your fallow ground; for it is time to seek the LORD, that he may come and rain righteousness upon you" (10:12). Also, "But as for you, return to your God, hold fast to love and justice, and wait continually for your God" (12:6).We will see later in the

New Testament that Hosea's image of God as a loving spouse has a great influence on portraying Jesus' message in terms of love.

JEREMIAH, THE PASSIONATE AND DARING PROPHET

Jeremiah is the longest book in the Bible, second in importance only to Isaiah in the New Testament. In Matthew, when Jesus asked his disciples who people thought he was, one of the answers was, "Jeremiah or one of the prophets" (16:14). In Jewish and Christian tradition, Jeremiah was one of the most popular prophets. We know more about him as a person than about any other prophet. We can identify with his struggles and temptations as a human being when faced with the burdensome vocation of a prophet. As regards Social Justice, Jeremiah will add a special dimension. Justice never comes about quietly and peacefully, without a struggle. To bring about justice requires risk, suffering, and sometimes death because justice will be opposed by powerful interests. Jeremiah is an example of this struggle and will have a profound influence on the New Testament.

His Prophetic Call and Mission

Jeremiah was born of a priestly family around 650 B.C. in a town called Anathoth near Jerusalem. However, he could not function as a priest because King Solomon had previously removed his family from the priestly office. Jeremiah describes his call to be a prophet in these words, "Now the word of the LORD came to me saying, 'Before I formed you in the womb I knew you, and before you were born I consecrated you; I appointed you as a prophet to the nations'" (1:4–5). Jeremiah replied, "Ah Lord GOD, truly I do not know how to speak, for I am only a boy." God then said, "Do not say, 'I am only a boy'; for you shall go to all to whom I send you, and you shall speak whatever I command you. Do not be afraid of them. For I am with you to deliver you" (1:6–8) God then reassured him by touching his mouth and saying, "Now I have put my words in your mouth. See, today I appoint you over nations and over kingdoms, to pluck up and to pull down, to destroy and over-throw, to build and to plant" (1:9–10). Jeremiah's hesitancy and fear remained all during his life as he faced a mission of enormous difficulty. He only went ahead because of the assurance of God's presence and God's word speaking through him.

When Jeremiah first began to preach, he received an enthusiastic reception. He supported King Josiah in the great reform beginning with the discovery of a lost book of the Torah—which we described in our last chapter. In his prophecies, we notice the influence of Deuteronomy with its focus on inner reform from the heart. In the same manner, Jeremiah also relayed God's word on turning the heart (3:10; Deut 30:10), on circumcising the heart (4:4; Deut 10:16), on total service with all the heart (29:13, Deut 30:2).

However, toward the end of his life, King Josiah began to attempt military alliances with surrounding superpowers, such as Egypt, Assyria, and Babylon. We have already seen that King Josiah was killed in attempting to meet the Pharaoh of Egypt. After Josiah's death, this flirting with political alliances increased. However, it was very dangerous because Israel was a small nation surrounded by great military powers. To be on the wrong side could mean disaster and exile. Even being on the right side meant becoming a servile vassal subject to heavy tribute.

Even before Josiah's death, Babylonia was gradually extending its power over the Middle East. The Babylonian king offered Judah the choice of becoming a vassal and thus exempt from attack. Instead, the king persisted in joining alliances with Egypt and other countries who banded together against Babylon. There was great pressure from patriotic and military factions for this view. Their argument was that God's presence in the Temple gave them security from any attack even though they were so tiny in comparison to Babylon. They also enlisted the help of false prophets. These men kept preaching to the people that the Temple, with its sacred Ark of the Covenant, made them invincible.

The Temple Sermon and Return to the Core of the Covenant

Jeremiah had to publicly confront the views of leaders and false prophets with the basic teachings of the covenant. The Lord told him to stand at the gate of the Temple area and tell the people who entered these words:

> Do not trust in these deceptive words: "This is the temple of the LORD, the temple of the LORD, the temple of the LORD." For if you truly amend your ways and your doings, if you truly act justly one with another, if you do not oppress the alien, the orphan, and the widow, or shed innocent blood in this place, and if you do not go after other gods to your own hurt, then I will dwell with you in this place, in the land that I gave of old to your ancestors forever and ever. (7:4–7)

The false prophets had continually repeated, "This is the temple of the LORD," as a sign of God's unconditional protection for his people. In contrast, Jeremiah repeats the basic core of the covenant around which the Temple was built. This meant elimination of oppression of the alien, orphan, and widow as well as violent shedding of blood. However, the king and his generals were looking to military solutions in an alliance between religion and power politics. This kind of alliance has always been the greatest obstacle to justice. The king, as we have seen in Deuteronomy and Isaiah, was obliged to direct the work of justice. But if most of the resources of a small country were given over to the military, justice could not be done. In addition, there was the great deception in which people were encouraged to believe that fighting against "God's enemies" was heroic service of God. Throughout history, unholy alliances between religion and the military have caused terrible sufferings and the loss of resources that could be given to the pursuit of justice.

Later, King Zedekiah made an attempt to keep part of the covenant during the siege of Jerusalem by the Babylonians in 588, hoping to win God's favor. He and all his officials, along with the people, made a covenant to free Hebrew debt slaves according to Deuteronomy 15:12–18.

However, when there was a temporary withdrawal of Babylonian troops to face an Egyptian threat, they changed their mind, broke the covenant, and took back the slaves (34:8–22).

Reactions to Jeremiah—Suffering, Temptation, and Threats to His Life

Government and military leaders considered Jeremiah unpatriotic and even a revolutionary threat when the Babylonians besieged Jerusalem in the time of Zedekiah, son of Josiah. However, Jeremiah stood by God's message. He even went out to the walls of Jerusalem and told the soldiers not to resist the Babylonians so the city would be spared destruction. Finally, the king ordered Jeremiah to be arrested. The military wanted him put to death, but the king placed him in a cistern to temporarily save his life (chapter 38). Even the people of Jeremiah's hometown in Anathoth rejected him and plotted to put him to death (11:18–23). On one occasion, he was even publicly disgraced by being fastened to stocks near an entrance to the Temple area (20:1–6).

Jeremiah's greatest suffering was the feeling that he was all alone in this struggle. His preaching received little response from the government leaders and the people. He could not even count on the support of a family because God told him not to marry and raise children in view of the imminent peril of the city's destruction:

> The word of the LORD came to me: "You shall not take a wife, nor shall you have sons or daughters in this place. For thus says the LORD concerning the sons and daughters who are born in this place....They shall die of deadly diseases." (16:1–4)

With almost everyone against him, Jeremiah was tempted to leave his preaching ministry. Biblical people did not consider it wrong to complain to God. On the contrary, they felt they could complain to him as a friend. So Jeremiah accused God of "seducing" him into such a difficult vocation: "O LORD, you have enticed me, and I was enticed; you have overpowered me, and you have prevailed. I have become a laughingstock all day long; everyone mocks me. For whenever I speak, I must shout out, 'Violence and destruction!' For the word of the LORD has become for me a reproach and derision all day long" (20:7–8).

On the other hand, he felt such a divine impulse to preach that he could say,

> If I say, "I will not mention him, or speak any more in his name," then there is something like a burning fire in my bones (heart); I am weary with holding it in, and I cannot. For I hear many whispering,…"Denounce him! Let us denounce him!" All my close friends are watching for me to stumble. "Perhaps he can be enticed and we can prevail against him and take our revenge on him." But the LORD is with me like a dread warrior; therefore my persecutors will stumble, and they will not prevail. (20:9–11)

Jeremiah knew how much his people had suffered because of the intransigence of military leaders pretending they trusted in God's help. He was not a hard-nosed prophet, but a deeply sensitive man under compulsion to deliver God's message of peace. When he heard false prophets speak, he was overcome by his feelings: "Concerning the prophets: my heart is crushed within me, all my bones shake" (23:9). He has a clear imagination of the horrors of war that will come to Israel from rejecting his message. This imagination is so vivid that it causes his heart to knock and tremble:

> My anguish, my anguish! I writhe in pain! Oh the walls of my heart! My heart is beating wildly; I cannot keep silent; for I hear the sound of the trumpet, the alarm of war. Disaster overtakes disaster, the whole land is laid waste. (4:19–20)

Elsewhere he exclaims, "My joy is gone, grief is upon me, my heart is sick. Hark the cry of my poor people far and wide in the land" (8:18). However, this heart sickness is not only for his own people but also even for the Moabites, traditional enemies overrun by the armies of Babylon: "Therefore I wail for Moab; I cry out for all Moab" (48:31). Despite all this sadness and grief, Jeremiah maintains deep inner confidence: "You (God) alone know me; you see me and test me—my heart is with you" (12:3). God's words are so important for him that he "eats them" and makes them his own as a source of inner joy: "Your words were found, and I ate them, and your words became to me a joy and the delight of my heart; for I am called by your name, O LORD, God of hosts" (15:16).

God's New Heart Covenant and Hope for the Future

Over the centuries, Jeremiah has been read again and again as a message of hope. Even when God's people were in exile or suffering under impossible circumstances, this book gave them courage to go on. (It is interesting that the root of *courage* is the Latin *cor* meaning "heart.") People are often tempted to despair because of their own weakness or repeated failures. Jeremiah's message proclaims that nothing is impossible with God. Change can come about through God's gift of a "new heart" that reverses human weakness:

> I will give them a heart to know that I am the LORD; and they shall be my people and I will be their God, for they shall return to me with their whole heart. (24:7)

Because of many attacks on their small country over the years, the Hebrew people became scattered all over the world. Jeremiah was confident that God would bring them back again.

> I will bring them back to this place, and I will settle them in safety. They shall be my people and I will be their God. I will give them *one heart and one way*....I will make an everlasting covenant with them, never to draw back from doing good for them; and I will put the fear of me in their *hearts,* so that they may not turn from me. I will rejoice in doing good to them, and I will plant them in this land in faithfulness, *with all my heart and soul.* (32:37–41)

Despite its being the longest book in the Bible, the Book of Jeremiah is especially read and cherished. The most influential passage is God's promise of a new inner covenant of the heart. First, God declares it will be a *new* covenant, unlike the one made by Israel at Mount Sinai after they came from Egypt:

The days are surely coming, says the LORD, when I will make a *new covenant* with the house of Israel and the house of Judah. It will not be like the covenant I made with their ancestors when I took them by the hand to bring them out of the land of Egypt—a covenant that they broke, even though I was their husband. (31:31–32)

Then, God shows how different and new it will be in comparison with the past:

This is the covenant that I will make with the house of Israel after those days, says the LORD: I will put my law within them, and I will *write it on their hearts;* and I will be their God and they shall be my people. No longer shall they teach one another, or say to each other, "Know the LORD," for they shall all know from the least of them to the greatest;…for I will forgive their iniquity, and remember their sin no more. (31:33–44)

This unusual message explains the true nature of a heart covenant. It is designed to contrast with the covenant of God written on stone tablets. That external law required readers, intermediaries, teachers, and interpreters. It could also be forgotten. But here God writes an internal message on the heart, which will always remain. Even the *least,* a child, will be able to understand and experience it as a complete loving gift from God. Finally, sins will not only be forgiven but also even *forgotten* as well.

Jeremiah's new heart covenant will have an important place in the New Testament. In the Hebrew Bible, the expression "new covenant" is only found in 31:31 above. The New Testament Letter to the Hebrews uses the expression "new covenant" in comparison with the former covenant in four places specifically quoting Jeremiah. Early liturgical formulas of the Eucharist will describe the cup as a new covenant in blood (1 Cor 11:25). Luke also has the same words in his institution narrative (longer Greek version): "And he (Jesus) did the same with the cup after supper saying, 'This cup that is poured out for you is the new covenant in my blood'" (22:20).

EZEKIEL, THE PSYCHIC PROPHET, HIS HEART TRANSPLANT, AND SOCIAL REFORM

The Background of Ezekiel and His Prophecies

The opening words of his book provide important information: He was a priest and had come to Babylon among the first exiles; he received his opening vision and call to be a prophet during his fifth year of exile, around 593 B.C. The vision took place about five years before the destruction of Jerusalem by the Babylonians. When the first exiles arrived there, their physical conditions were not harsh. Ezekiel had his own house in which people visited and consulted with him (3:24; 8:1; 14:1). The prophet Jeremiah had warned the people that the exile might be long. He advised them to settle down, build houses, plant gardens, marry, and raise children (29:5). In Babylon, they had the freedom to do these things. Away from the Temple, Ezekiel could no longer function as a priest, but his vision of a future Temple influenced his prophecies and writings.

In contrast to physical well-being, the psychological burden of the exiles was very heavy. Their God in the Temple had not protected them from exile. In those days, many people thought in terms of national gods and their territories. They were now in a foreign land under foreign gods. Would their own God prove unable to help them here? Or were they "losers," abandoned and deserted? Their Babylonian captors often taunted them for trusting in a helpless God. The Psalmist writes, "By the rivers of Babylon—there we sat down and wept when we remembered Zion....For there our captors asked us for songs, and our tormentors asked for mirth, saying, 'Sing to us one of the songs of Zion'" (137:1–3).

Ezekiel felt very much alone in this atmosphere, which was accentuated when he lost his wife around six years after he came to Babylon. God told him not to mourn or perform the usual funeral customs as a sign of the coming loss of Jerusalem (24:16–18). He spent a great deal of time at home in prayer and received many visions and revelations from God to perform

56

unusual symbolic actions. As a result, many people considered him a strange eccentric and made him the butt of jokes. Some of his visions were so unusual that later Jewish teachers warned their students about them and forbade the reading of certain parts of Ezekiel until they were thirty years old!

Ezekiel's Inaugural Vision and Call

The prophet pondered and prayed for enlightenment in view of this great crisis for his people in exile. The great question was that of the divine presence and covenant. Had God deserted his people here in a foreign land far away from the Temple in Jerusalem? What should the prophet say to people tempted to come to terms with Babylon and her victorious gods? One day, an answer came to him in the form of an unusual vision that defies any attempt at accurate description. Something like a chariot of fire came down from the sky, propelled by four living creatures, each with four faces, one face like a human being, another like a lion, another like an ox, and a fourth like an eagle.

The living creatures seem to symbolize God's presence in all living creatures, whether humans, wild beasts (lion), domestic animals (ox), or birds (eagle). These symbols were an assurance that God was in all creation, not just locally in the Temple. There were wheels beside the creatures and something like a wheel inside and perpendicular to an outside wheel, so they could move in any direction. These wheels pointed to God's ability to move anywhere he wishes. Above the heads of the creatures was a crystal sky, and on top of this, the glory of God dwelt in a fiery cloud (1:1–26).

The impact of this vision on Ezekiel was that God's presence was not limited to the Ark of the Covenant in Jerusalem but was with Ezekiel and his people in exile. Then, the prophet heard God's voice saying:

> O mortal, eat what is offered to you; eat this scroll, and go, speak to the house of Israel...and he gave me the scroll to eat....Then I ate it; and in my mouth it was sweet as honey....He said to me: Mortal, all the words that I shall speak to you receive in your heart and hear with your ears;

then go to the exiles....Say to them, "Thus says the Lord
GOD"; whether they hear or refuse to hear. (3:1–11)

The eating of the scroll was the external sign of God's word
entering his heart and becoming part of his whole being. Hence-
forth, the presence of God dominated his whole life. He often
referred to this as "the Spirit." The breath/Spirit of God is so
prominent in his life that Ezekiel is often called "the pneumatic
prophet." The Spirit is mentioned 25 times in Ezekiel. About half
of these are regarding Ezekiel in phrases like "the Spirit entered
into me" or "lifted me up." Among the prophecies about the
Spirit, God brought him in a vision to a field of dry bones, representing those "dead" in exile. There, God "breathed" his Spirit on
them to give them life and bring them back to their own land
(37:1–14). In regard to the Temple, Ezekiel had the vision of a
new Temple built through the work of the Spirit. Underneath the
altar, he saw a mysterious fountain flowing into an ever deepening
stream going down to the Dead Sea and making it a new Garden
of Eden and source of life (47:1–12).

Renewal of the Covenant and Social Reform Through a New Heart

An impediment to this renewal was the feeling of many people that they were suffering and even dying for the sins of their
parents and ancestors. They quoted this proverb, "The parents
have eaten sour grapes and the children's teeth are set on edge"
(18:2). The word of the Lord assured Ezekiel that this was not so.
Every person is responsible for his or her own deeds, not those of
the past. This teaching on individual responsibility is a special
contribution of Ezekiel and the key to renewal. God declares,

> If a man is righteous and does what is lawful and right—if he
> does not eat upon the mountains or lift up his eyes to the
> idols of the house of Israel, does not defile his neighbor's wife
> or approach a woman during her menstrual period, does not
> oppress anyone, but restores to the debtor his pledge, com-
> mits no robbery, gives his bread to the hungry and covers the

naked with a garment, does not take advance or accrued interest, withholds his hand from iniquity, executes true justice between contending parties. (18:5–8)

Within that statement, we find the basic core of the Sinai covenant to which other prophets referred. This covenant is concern for the oppressed, the poor and hungry, those in debt, and the execution of justice in courts. Ezekiel likes to repeat key teachings three times. So we have it here, again in regard to a son, then a grandson in 18:10–18. To these teachings are added parts of the Ten Commandments and part of the priestly tradition in Leviticus. This latter is evident above in the law of ritual purity for menstrual women. The second repetition in 18:10–13 opens and closes with respect for life and blood, a special priestly emphasis (Lev 17:4).

But how will the people be able to do all these things if they have failed in the past? The ethical teaching above ends with the designation of a new path: "Get yourselves a new heart and a new spirit" (18:31). In Ezekiel, God answers through the gift of a new heart. We have seen that Jeremiah already spoke of a new heart covenant, but Ezekiel has a new covenant in the form of a heart-transplant operation. A triple repetition for emphasis is found in 11:19–20; 18:31; 36:26–27. For example:

A new heart I will give you, and a new spirit I will put within you; and I will remove from your body the heart of stone and give you a heart of flesh. I will put my spirit within you, and make you follow my statutes and be careful to observe my ordinances. Then you shall live in the land that I gave to your ancestors; and you shall be my people, and I will be your God. (36:26–27)

The Spirit is mentioned throughout the Bible, but here, as in Isaiah, we find the Spirit in an ethical context as the transforming agent of the heart. God teaches Ezekiel this heart-transplant imagery as a powerful means of meditation and a source of hope that God can transform the human heart to keep his commandments, especially in regard to compassion and love for the poor and oppressed. Interestingly, an actual heart-transplant surgical operation has only been in use for a few decades, yet the imagery was known for thousands of years and used very effectively. The following elements in the prophecy bring out its full meaning:

1) Three times, the verb *give* or *put* is used, but they are translations of the one Hebrew verb. The triple form emphasizes that the work of renewal is God's alone, through the Spirit.

2) There is a real transplant in the image of removing the heart of stone and substituting the heart of flesh. In the Bible, the heart is where God acts to transform the will and human activity. A "heart of flesh" is not a mere image but has ethical implications. It means a sensitive heart enabling people to listen to God and obey his commandments. Such obedience involves returning to the inner core of the covenant about justice and responsibility to others.

3) "Then you shall live in the land that I gave to your ancestors." This ending is vital because the land is God's inheritance gift to his people. It was passed down from parents to children. Because the land was limited, God divided it equally among the tribes and then among their families so there would be a sufficient allotment for everyone. The biblical principle of justice consisted in equal sharing of land and resources, not generous gifts from the rich.

In the New Testament, we will see that Ezekiel's image of the Spirit-transformed heart will have a great impact on Paul the Apostle.

JOEL, THE IMAGE OF A NEW WORLD SOCIAL ORDER

Nothing is known of the author of this book, and the time of its composition is also uncertain. So far, the texts we have studied concern actions and responsibilities within human history. However, Joel is predominantly eschatological. He describes a coming day of judgment and visionary future events that God will initiate outside present human history. This type of literature is called apocalyptic. We have not studied books that are mostly apocalyptic like Daniel and Zechariah because Social Justice is about this world, not the next. However, some New Testament passages explained Jesus' mission in terms of these apocalyptic texts. This is especially true of Joel 2:28–32. We will later study how Paul and especially Luke takes this prophecy as a central theme in his Gospel and the Acts of the Apostles as a basis for God's plan that "Everyone who calls on the name of the Lord shall be saved" (Acts 2:21).

Joel begins with a description of a frightful locust plague that comes like an army to devastate the land. This plague is symbolic of actual armies or of the forces of evil that prelude a coming last day of the Lord. In response, the priests sound an alarm for all the people to come for public prayer and repentance. If the people respond, God promises a victory over the invading armies, abundant crops, and a brilliant future. During this visionary future, God says that there will be a great surprise in the universal working of the Spirit in breaking down traditional walls of separation:

> Then afterward I will pour out my spirit on all flesh; your sons and your daughters shall prophesy, your old men shall dream dreams, and your young men shall see visions. Even on the male and female slaves, in those days, I will pour out my spirit. I will show portents in the heavens and on the earth, blood and fire and columns of smoke. The sun shall be turned to darkness, and the moon to blood, before the great and terrible day of the LORD comes. Then everyone who calls on the name of the LORD shall be saved. (2:28–32)

In this great outpouring of the Spirit, first of all, gender barriers are broken. Only three prophetesses are named in the Hebrew Bible: Hulda, Miriam, sister of Moses, and Deborah. Then, age hierarchies are destroyed: Both young and old will see visions. Finally, class boundaries between slaves and free persons are broken. All of these will happen at the end of this age, signaled by the failure of the sun and moon. The final result will be that "everyone who calls on the name of the LORD shall be saved" (2:32).

MALACHI AND THE FINAL DIVINE MESSENGER

Malachi is the last book in the Hebrew canon of prophets. We know nothing about the author; perhaps *Malachi* just means literally in Hebrew "my messenger." The book ends with God's promise to send a messenger before the coming last day of the Lord. The New Testament opens with a fulfillment of this promise in the appearance of John the Baptist as God's chosen messenger of the last times.[9]

In this book, the writer wants to show his audience why their prayers and sacrifices will not be accepted unless accompanied by sincere repentance. Of special interest regarding Social Justice is the passage on faithlessness or treachery in 2:10–16. It begins with the theme of one father and family: "Have we not all one father? Has not one God created us? Why then are we *faithless* to one another, profaning the covenant of our ancestors?" (2:10). *Faithless* (to covenants) is a key repeated word (five times) in this section. Judah has been faithless as well as Israel by breaking their marriage bonds with God and going off to strange gods as if to a new spouse. But there is another type of faithlessness that hits at the heart of the family of the one God: "And this you do as well: You cover the LORD's altar with tears, with weeping and groaning because he no longer regards the offering or accepts it with favor at your hand" (2:13). And why does not God favor them?

> Because the LORD was a witness between you and the wife of your youth, to whom you have been *faithless,* though she is your companion and your wife by covenant. Did not one God make her? Both flesh and spirit are his. And what does the one God desire? Godly offspring. So look to yourselves, and do not let anyone be *faithless* to the wife of his youth. For I hate divorce (putting away), says the LORD....So take heed to yourselves and do not be *faithless.* (2:14–16)

This passage counteracts the provision of divorce in Deuteronomy as purely a matter of a husband's viewpoint: "Suppose a man enters into marriage with a woman, but she does not please him because he finds something objectionable about her, and so he writes her a certificate of divorce, puts it in her hand, and sends her out of his house" (24:1).

In Malachi, there are striking differences: marriage is a *personal* covenant in parallel with the covenants with Judah and Israel. "The Lord was a witness" of this covenant. In view of the creation story, the woman belongs not to the man but to the God who made her. The God of hosts *hates* this patriarchal "putting away" of a spouse. In this passage, we find the strongest words in the Hebrew Bible supporting women's rights, even though they are still under a patriarchal umbrella.

Another basic matter of covenant comes in response to the people's question, "Where is the God of justice?" (2:17). God responds that he is sending his messenger to prepare the way for judgment. At this time, he says. "I will be swift to bear witness against the sorcerers, against the adulterers, against those who swear falsely, against those who oppress the hired workers in their wages, the widow and the orphan, against those who thrust aside the alien, and do not fear me" (3:5).

As in other prophets, we find the elements of the ancient core covenant in justice for the wage earners, oppressed, widows, and aliens. The people have changed in their neglect of this covenant, but God has not changed. His message is, "Return to me, and I will return to you, says the LORD of hosts" (3:7).

Malachi closes with God's promise to send the prophet Elijah before the day of the Lord to turn the hearts of parents and children to one another. The Gospels later will portray John the Baptist as this Elijah returning with this message of re-turning to God.[10]

JONAH, THE COMIC PROPHET

The Book of Jonah is not a collection of prophecies like the others we have studied. It is really comic literature written for entertainment and as a humorous way to move readers to renounce stereotyped narrow views of God and break the walls of separation from "enemies"—people of diverse ethnic and religious cultures. The New Testament considers Jonah very important.

Jesus mentions him nine times in the Gospels and the "Sign of Jonah" four times.

> Now the word of the LORD came to Jonah son of Amittai, saying, "Go at once to Nineveh, that great city, and cry out against it; for their wickedness has come up before me." But Jonah set out to flee to Tarshish from the presence of the LORD. He went down to Joppa and found a ship going to Tarshish; so he paid his fare and went on board, to go with them to Tarshish, away from the presence of the LORD. (1:1–3)

Right from the first verse we have strange paradoxes. God has never called upon any prophet to preach to any nation but Israel. To Jonah, the call is so ridiculous that he immediately tries to avoid it by taking a ship to Tarshish. Tarshish was a port in Spain, which was regarded in ancient times as the very end of the world. Yet God is determined in his desire to reach other people and "sends a storm" to finally cause the sailors at Jonah's instigation to throw him overboard as the guilty cause of the storm. In his mercy, "the LORD sent a large fish to swallow up Jonah and Jonah was in the belly of the fish three days and three nights" (1:17).

The event symbolized an interior death experience for Jonah. He prayed to God and repented for what he had done. Consequently, the "whale" threw up Jonah on the shore. There, God called Jonah a second time, saying, "Get up, go to Nineveh, that great city, and proclaim to it the message that I tell you." This was, "Forty days more, and Nineveh shall be overthrown" (3:1–4). Jonah obeyed but presumed they would not repent and that God would destroy them.

To Jonah's astonishment, "the people of Nineveh believed God; they proclaimed a fast, and everyone, great and small, put on sackcloth" (3:5). Everyone from the king down kept this fast, prayed to God, and turned from their evil ways. As a result, "When God saw what they did, how they turned from their evil ways, God changed his mind about the calamity that he had said he would bring upon them; and he did not do it" (3:10).

When Jonah saw this, he was furious because God had changed his mind about destroying Nineveh. He prayed to God:

> O LORD! Is not this what I said while I was still in my own country? That is why I fled to Tarshish at the beginning; for I knew that you are a gracious God and merciful, slow to anger, and abounding in steadfast love, and ready to relent from punishing. And now, O LORD, please take my life from me, for it is better for me to die than to live. (4:2–3)

This description of God comes from the three essential attributes of God that were revealed to Moses when God passed by, pronouncing his name *Yahweh,* Lord (Exod 34:6–7). These attributes are "gracious," *hanun;* "merciful," *rahum,* womb-compassionate, from *rehem,* womb; "steadfast love," *hesed,* mindful of covenants. They describe a God of complete impartial justice, loving all people of every race and every belief and even enemies of Israel. This concept is simply too much for Jonah who wants to quit life right at this point. He does not want to live in a world not governed by the laws of "justice" in which he grew up. But God loves Jonah, his stubborn reactionary, and has a little lesson for him too. The Lord said to him, "Is it right for you to be angry?"

Meanwhile, Jonah built himself a shelter from the hot sun out of a bush near the city and sat down to watch what would happen to the city. He was still waiting for it to be struck by God, perhaps by an earthquake, in punishment for its sins. On the next day, however, he found that the bush had dried up and he was in danger of being scorched by the blazing sun. Once again he asked that he might die. God said to him, "Are you angry about the bush?" He replied, "Yes, angry enough to die." God's response, the last line of the book, needs no further comment than the words themselves:

> Then the LORD said, "You are concerned about the bush, for which you did not labor and which you did not grow; it came into being in a night and perished in a night. And should I not be concerned about Nineveh, that great city, in which there are more than a hundred and twenty thousand persons who do not know their right hand from their left, and also many animals? (4:9–11)

Summary

The prophets take the basic covenant requirements of justice found in the Torah and preach them to everyone—the people and the rulers alike. Thus, they may be called mediators of the covenant. The program for the elimination of poverty found in Deuteronomy does not remain hidden on a scroll but is continually taught to people in different areas and in different generations. The New Testament is not really "new" but a return to the radical message of justice taught by the prophets.

3

Social Justice in the Psalms and Wisdom Literature

THE PSALMS, LOVE SONGS OF THE COVENANT

The Psalms contain the essence of the prayer life and aspirations of the Hebrew people. On the cross, Jesus died with their words on his lips. Psalms is, along with Isaiah, the most quoted book in the New Testament. Through the centuries, Christians have continued to draw energy, inspiration, and nourishment from them. As they stand, they are a collection with many contributions from different authors at different times. Some were originally private prayers but were later adapted for community and liturgical use. They have a wide variety in their content. Some are dominated by praise, others by sorrow, thanksgiving, pleas for forgiveness or even help in any possible situation. They take in all the dimensions of life because devotion to God involves the total concerns of individuals and community. They are written in poetry and in song so that people can fully express all their emotions and needs as they pray to God.

Justice and the Psalms

The Psalms do not merely contain references to justice; the bulk of them are love songs of covenant justice. In the opening pages of this book, we noted that Social Justice in the Bible must be understood in terms of biblical justice. This means justice centered about covenant initiatives on the part of God and responses on the part of his people. In addition, the way that God acts inspires a like response in his people. God is just, therefore people should be just to one another, fulfilling their responsibilities toward each and recognizing the other's rights. The vocabulary of the Psalms reflects this primary intention. The words *just* (or *upright*) are found 66 times in the 150 Psalms. *Justice* (or *righteousness*) occurs 48 times. God himself "loves justice" (37:28; 33:5). In addition, he especially favors and guides those who are just: "The eyes of the LORD are open to the righteous, and his ears are open to their cry" (34:15).

Basic Covenant Qualities in the Psalms

The roots of all covenant qualities go back to the revelation name *Yahweh*, the sacred unpronounced name in Hebrew that lies under *Lord* found in many modern translations. In the Psalms, it is found around 800 times as the primary address to God. From the burning bush near Sinai, God revealed himself to Moses with the mysterious words of uncertain meaning, "I AM WHO I AM," or "I will be what I will be" (Exod 3:14). However, there is a hint of interpretation when Moses asked God just before this, "Who am I that I should go to Pharaoh, and bring the Israelites out of Egypt?" God replied, "I will be with you" (3:11-12). In view of this response, God *will be who he will be* in the events in which he is asked to intervene. In each one of these, he will reveal something of who he is. "I will be with you" is a frequent refrain through the first five books of the Bible.

Likewise, in the Psalms there will be dozens of occasions in which God intervenes and thus reveals a new facet of his nature under titles like redeemer, protector, forgiver, rock, fortress, savior, and many others. These titles have given rise among Muslims to a special devotion to "the 99 names of Allah" that are found in the scriptures. These titles are memorized and recited as a prayer. Many, if not most, are found in the Psalms. Primary, of course, is God's intervention to save his people from slavery in Egypt. This intervention is central to the introduction to the Ten Commandments with the words "I am the LORD your God who brought you out of the land of Egypt, out of the house of slavery" (Deut 5:6).

Among God's attributes and qualities, those that flow from his name *Yahweh* and his intervention on behalf of his people are most important. The first is that of his covenant love, *hesed,* translated *steadfast love* in the NRS version we are using. The term occurs some 120 times in the Psalms. Flowing from this is his *faithfulness* (39 times) in keeping his promises. The two qualities, faithfulness and steadfast love, are mentioned together seven times. Corresponding to these qualities are trust, faith, and love on the part of his people, even in the most difficult circumstances. Love with all one's heart as in the *Shemah* is found seven times.

Second is Yahweh's mercy or compassion, *rahum,* from the root *rehem* meaning "womb." This quality denotes a more emotionally felt love, especially in forgiveness or in loving compassion. Then, there is Yahweh's graciousness or favor, taking the initiative without obligation. The root verb is *hanan* and the noun *hēn,* from which the English name Hannah or Anne is derived. The New Testament Greek will have *charis,* meaning "favor" or "grace." Often, several of these prime attributes are combined. For example, in Psalm 86:15, "You, O Lord, are a God merciful and gracious, slow to anger and abounding in steadfast love and faithfulness."

Imitation of God's Covenant Qualities

This theme occurs all throughout the Psalms because imitation of God is the highest form of piety. One interesting example is the parallel descriptions in Psalms 111 and 112, which have been a part of Sunday vespers for many centuries. Both are alphabetic acrostic Psalms. The first is about God, and the second is imitation of God, sometimes in exactly the same words. Below is the text of each Psalm, with italicized words showing the parallels.

Psalm 111

Praise the LORD! I will give thanks to the LORD with my whole heart, in the company of the *upright,* in the congregation.
Great are the works of the LORD, studied by all who delight in them.

Full of honor and majesty is his work, and his *righteousness
endures forever.*

He has gained renown by his wonderful deeds; the LORD
is *gracious and merciful.*

He provides food for those who fear him; he is ever mindful
of his covenant.

He has shown his people the power of his works, in giving them
the heritage of the nations.

The works of his hands are faithful and just; all his precepts are
trustworthy.

They are established forever and ever, to be performed with
faithfulness and uprightness.

He sent redemption to his people; he has commanded his
covenant forever. Holy and awesome is his name.

The fear of the LORD is the beginning of wisdom; all those who
practice it have a good understanding. His praise endures
forever.

Psalm 112

Praise the LORD! Happy are those who fear the LORD, who
greatly delight in his commandments.

Their descendants will be mighty in the land; the generation
of the *upright* will be blessed.

Wealth and riches are in their houses, and *their righteousness
endures forever.*

They rise in the darkness as a light for the *upright; they are
gracious, merciful, and righteous.*

It is well with *those who deal generously and lend,* who
conduct their affairs with *justice.*

For the *righteous* will never be moved; they will be remembered
forever.

They are not afraid of evil tidings; their hearts are firm, secure
in the LORD.

Their hearts are steady, they will not be afraid; in the end
they will look in triumph on their foes.

*They have distributed freely, they have given to the poor; their
righteousness endures forever;* their horn is exalted in honor.

The wicked see it and are angry; they gnash their teeth and melt
away; the desire of the wicked comes to nothing.

Imitation of God's Exodus Liberation Qualities

In bringing his people out of Egypt, God intervened to save a homeless, landless people who had no one to help them. This intervention becomes part of a core covenant of response in the Torah and the Prophets that is applied to widows, orphans, the oppressed, foreigners, and others who had no land inheritance and lacked many other resources. In the Psalms, we find special attention is given to this core covenant. The following are examples on the part of both God and his people:

Psalm 9:18
> For the needy shall not always be forgotten, nor the hope of the poor perish forever.

Psalm 10:17–18
> O LORD, you will hear the desire of the meek; you will strengthen their heart, you will incline your ear to do justice for the orphan and the oppressed, so that those from earth may strike terror no more.

Psalm 15
> This Psalm describes the qualities of those who may abide in God's tent or dwell on his holy hill. Among them are those "who do not lend money at interest, and do not take a bribe against the innocent. Those who do these things shall never be moved" (15:5).

Psalm 68:5
> While God is the Father of his own covenant people, this is especially true of those who are most needy: "Father of orphans and protector of widows is God in his holy habitation."

Psalm 85:10–11
> When God's attributes are manifest in his faithful, "Steadfast love and faithfulness will meet; righteousness and peace will kiss each other. Faithfulness will spring up from the ground, and righteousness will look down from the sky."

Psalm 103:6
> The LORD works vindication and justice for all who are oppressed.

Psalm 107:41–42

>He (God) raises up the needy out of distress, and makes their families like flocks. The upright see it and are glad; and all wickedness stops its mouth.

Covenant Justice and the King

In Isaiah we saw how God's covenant with the people becomes the covenant with the king as "son of God" and administrator of his justice. The following excerpts from Psalm 72 illustrate this:

>Give the king your justice, O God, and your righteousness to a king's son.
>May he judge your people with righteousness, and your poor with justice.
>May the mountains yield prosperity for the people, and the hills, in righteousness.
>May he defend the cause of the poor of the people, give deliverance to the needy, and crush the oppressor.
>May he live while the sun endures, and as long as the moon, throughout all generations.
>May he be like rain that falls on the mown grass, like showers that water the earth.
>In his days may righteousness flourish and peace abound, until the moon is no more.
>May he have dominion from sea to sea, and from the River to the ends of the earth....
>May all kings fall down before him, all nations give him service.
>For he delivers the needy when they call, the poor and those who have no helper.
>He has pity on the weak and the needy, and saves the lives of the needy.

The Priestly Theme of Liberation from the Slavery of Egypt, Representing Evil

Our first chapter on the Torah discussed from Leviticus the priestly theme of liberation from evil. Isaiah also emphasized this liberation in his favorite title of God as "the Holy One of Israel" and the holiness and justice of people made to God's image. The Psalms take up this theme, with the word *holy* applied to God or the Temple some 50 times. The theme calls for a response in a holy people. The Psalms use a special word for a people who are "holy" or "saints." It is *hasid,* found 27 times. In the entire Hebrew Bible, it is seen elsewhere only seven times. In the Psalms, the contrast between God's absolute holiness and human injustice brings out sharply the challenge to imitate God.

PROVERBS AND LADY WISDOM

After the chapters on Social Justice in the Torah and the Prophets, we might be tempted to conclude that we need only to *just do it*. However, the Wisdom tradition in the Bible reminds us that action without listening first to the voice of experience is likely to end in unnecessary failure.

The Roots and Tools of Wisdom Literature

The roots of Wisdom literature are in the search for a meaningful, successful life. The tools of this search lie in a listening-and-observing attitude to God's work in creation and human nature. The Torah and the Prophets are less mentioned, but this does not mean they are less important. They are opposite sides of the same coin of God's revelation and need one another. On one side of the coin, God intervenes to save an enslaved people and adopt them with a family covenant. On the reverse side, he only does so because he has listened to the cries of a suffering people and observed their oppression:

> Then the LORD said, "I have observed the misery of my people who are in Egypt; I have heard their cry on account of their taskmasters. Indeed, I know their sufferings, and I have come down to deliver them from the Egyptians, and to bring them up out of that land to a good and broad land, a land flowing with milk and honey." (Exod 3:7–8)

Thus, God himself is the model of one who *listens* and *feels* the oppression and slavery of his people.

Solomon, Patron and Idealized Model of Wisdom Literature

The Book of Proverbs opens with this statement: "The proverbs of Solomon son of David, king of Israel." However, on reading Proverbs, we find other authors mentioned and indications that parts of the book were written centuries after Solomon who ruled in the tenth century B.C. Also, other Wisdom books have opening dedications to him, such as Qoheleth and Song of Songs. The author of Wisdom of Solomon, written more than eight centuries after his time, also writes in his name. King Solomon, like other kings and rulers through history, served as a patron of the arts and liked to have writers ascribe their works to him. As a young king, he established a tradition of wisdom that endured through the centuries. This tradition continues even in the New Testament in which Jesus appeals to the Wisdom tradition of God's goodness in all of creation in the Sermon on the Mount: "Consider the lilies of the field, how they grow; they neither toil nor spin, yet I tell you even Solomon in all his glory was not clothed like one of these" (Matt 6:29).

The Bible presents the young King Solomon as the idealized model for searchers after wisdom. As a young man, Solomon took over the kingdom from his father David. At that time, the Bible notes, "Solomon loved the LORD, walking in the statutes of his father David" (1 Kgs 3:3). On one festive occasion, Solomon went to Gibeon, a noted holy place about five-and-a-half miles north of Jerusalem. There, "Solomon used to offer a thousand burnt offerings on that altar" (1 Kgs 3:4). This number is more symbolic of total devotion to God than an actual figure. What follows shows that God was very pleased with his offering and planned to give him a special gift in return. Consequently, "At Gibeon, the LORD appeared to Solomon in a dream by night; and God said, 'Ask what I should give you'" (3:5).

In response, King Solomon reflected on his own situation as a young man called to hold enormous responsibilities, especially as an administrator of justice. He said to God,

> I am only a little child; I do not know how to go out or come in. And your servant is in the midst of the people whom you have chosen, a great people, so numerous they cannot be numbered or counted. Give your servant therefore an understanding mind to govern your people; able to discern between good and evil; for who can govern this your great people? (1 Kgs 3:7–9)

Behind the translation *an understanding mind* is the literal Hebrew *a listening heart.* This term means "a heart open to God's work and counsel," for the heart is where God directly operates. It also means a heart open to others, so Solomon can make good decisions to serve them well. God was very pleased that Solomon asked for such a gift. God replied to him,

> Because you have asked this, and have not asked for yourself long life or riches or for the life of your enemies, but have asked for yourself understanding to discern what is right, I now do according to your word. Indeed I give you a wise and discerning mind (heart)....I give you also what you have not asked, both riches and honor all your life. (1 Kgs 3:11–13)

The Bible then illustrates the meaning of a wise, *listening heart* in the above texts by a story of two mothers who came to the king for a difficult decision in an apparently impossible case. The case seemed impossible because the two opposing women were the only witnesses. They were two prostitutes who lived together. One night, each of them went to sleep with their newly born babies in bed with them. During the night, one of the babies died. In the morning, each mother claimed the living child as her own. They then went together to King Solomon for a judgment. Solomon's solution came from his gift of a sensitive, listening heart. He pretended to make a decision by ordering a soldier to take a sword and split the child in half to solve the problem. Then, he carefully observed which woman was more affected by the decision. Then, "the woman whose son was alive said to the king—because compassion for her son burned within her—'Please, my lord, give her the living boy; certainly do not kill him!'" The other woman, however, was willing to comply with the "decision." The king then said, "Give the first woman the living boy; do not kill him. She is the mother" (1 Kgs 3:26–28).

A close reading of the Hebrew text helps us toward a deeper understanding of the story. How can one possibly find out which woman's womb, *rehem,* in Hebrew, carried the living child? The English translation has it that "compassion for her son burned within her." Literally, the Hebrew says that her *womb compassion,* from the root *rehem,* went out to the son of her womb. Solomon, from a listening heart, was able to judge from this deep level. In reaction to the story, "All Israel heard of the judgment that the king had rendered; and they stood in awe of the king, because they perceived that the wisdom of God was in him, to execute justice" (3:28). Their awe was due to their perception that God was truly at work. His principal attribute, we saw in the last chapter, was *rahum,* compassionate womb love, and now this love was transmitted in the king's judgment.

The Bible describes this wisdom as a deep sensitivity to all of nature, which is rooted in God as the source and author of all life. Today, a dictionary describes a quality called broad-mindedness, but the Bible goes deeper and emphasizes "broadening of the heart": "God gave Solomon very great wisdom, discernment, and breadth of understanding as vast as the sand on the seashore, so that Solomon's wisdom surpassed the wisdom of all the people of the East and the wisdom of Egypt" (4:29–30). The expression "breadth of understanding" is a translation of the literal Hebrew "largeness of heart." It is interesting that even today "the wisdom of the East" and "the wisdom of Egypt" are phrases still in use.

As the result of this "largeness of heart" in wisdom, the Bible notes,

> He (Solomon) composed three thousand proverbs and his songs numbered a thousand and five. He would speak of trees, from the cedar that is in Lebanon to the hyssop that grows in the wall; he would speak of animals, and birds, and

reptiles, and fish. People...came from all the kings of the earth who had heard of his wisdom. (4:32–34)

The above references to Solomon's literary activity gave rise to his name being included in the Wisdom literature and also to his role as patron of wisdom and the arts. A large number of proverbs resulted from the exchanges that kings had with one another through ambassadors and delegations. The most famous of these was the visit of the Queen of Sheba:

When the queen of Sheba heard of the fame of Solomon... she came to test him with hard questions. She came to Jerusalem with a very great retinue, with camels bearing spices, and very much gold, and precious stones; and when she came to Solomon, she told him all that was on her mind (literally, "in her heart"). Solomon answered all her questions; there was nothing hidden from the king that he could not explain to her. When the queen of Sheba had observed all the wisdom of Solomon, the house that he had built...she said to the king, "Not even half had been told me; your wisdom and prosperity far surpass the report that I had heard. Happy are your wives! Happy are these your servants who continually attend you and hear your wisdom!" (10:1–8)

The writer concludes with these observations: "Thus King Solomon excelled all the kings of the earth in riches and in wisdom. The whole earth sought the presence of Solomon to hear his wisdom, which God had put into his mind" (10:23–24).

The "Listening Heart" in Proverbs: Women as Transmitters of Tradition

An important part of the wisdom quest is the tradition in human experience that goes back in time and is passed on to others. The ability to listen to tradition is the prime attitude of a wisdom seeker. The admonition to listen, hear, heed, or follow is on almost every page. The first contact with wisdom on the part of a child is through parents. And here, the primary teacher is the mother, especially through the early years of childhood but continuing all through life. Thus, through the centuries, women, especially mothers, are the great guardians and transmitters of tradition.

The Book of Proverbs begins with nine chapters that bear marks of women's traditions.[11] They culminate in Proverbs 8 and 9 with feminine wisdom as an attribute or personification of God. (*Wisdom* is *hokmah* [f.] in Hebrew and *sophia* [f.] in Greek). Proverbs ends with two instructions centering on women: the instruction of King Lemuel's mother and the poetic conclusion about the ideal woman or wife. For this reason, we will concentrate on Lady Wisdom as the highest contribution to women's dignity and equality in the Hebrew Bible.

The following prelude opens the book:

> The proverbs of Solomon son of David, king of Israel: For learning about wisdom and instruction, for understanding words of insight, for gaining instruction in wise dealing, righteousness, justice, and equity; to teach shrewdness to the simple, knowledge and prudence to the young—Let the wise also hear and gain in learning, and the discerning acquire skill. (1:1–7)

The concern for justice or righteousness pervades the entire book; those terms occur thirty times. Often, they reflect ordinary secular wisdom and security. However, they sometimes reach such heights of generosity that they are recalled in New Testament counsels for community ethical guidance. For example, "Hatred stirs up strife, but love covers all offenses" (10:12; 1 Cor 13:7). Also, "If your enemies are hungry, give them bread to eat; and if they are thirsty, give them water to drink; for you will heap coals of fire on their heads, and the LORD will reward you" (Prov 25:21–22; Rom 12:20).

The proverbs begin with the appeal "Hear, my child, your father's instruction, and do not reject your mother's teaching" (1:8). Both parents are teachers 12 times in the book. However, the first 9 chapters hint at a woman's voice or author. The contrasting images are Lady Wisdom and Dame Folly. Wisdom pours out thoughts like a fountain (1:23), which resembles a woman's gender descriptions: "Let your fountain be blessed and rejoice in the wife of your youth" (5:18). The author writes, "At the window of my house, I looked out through my lattice" (7:6). This description is an ancient portrayal of a woman looking out her window, but hidden from the view of outsiders. It was popular on Phoenician ivory pieces. It occurs in 2 Kings 9:30 and in Song of Songs 2:9. Also, this first part of Proverbs has a beautiful description of a woman's special gender distinctions in her breasts and womb: "Drink water from your own cistern, flowing water from your own well....let your fountain be blessed, and rejoice in the wife of your youth, a lovely deer, a graceful doe. May her breasts satisfy you at all times; may you be intoxicated by her love" (5:15–19).

The collection of Lady Wisdom in chapters 1–9 leads to a poetic description of God's personification as Wisdom in 8:1–36 beginning with the invitation:

> Does not wisdom call, and does not understanding raise her voice? On the heights, beside the way, at the crossroads she takes her stand; beside the gates in front of the town, at the entrance of the portals she cries out. (8:1–3)

Following this invitation, Wisdom appeals for people to listen to her words. They are righteous, better than *jewels, silver, or gold. Kings rule* by them. Relations with her are characterized by *love* for those who seek and find her (8:5–17). But most extraordinary of all, Wisdom was with God right from the creation of the Earth:

> The LORD created me at the beginning of his work, the first of his acts of long ago. Ages ago I was set up, at the first, before the beginning of the earth. When there were no depths I was brought forth, when there were no springs abounding with water. Before the mountains had been shaped, before the hills, I was brought forth....then I was beside him, like a master worker (or child); and I was daily his *delight, rejoicing* before him always, *rejoicing* in his inhabited world and *delighting* in the human race. (8:22–31)

The above description is poetic and does not lend itself to neat logical explanation. However, a look at the Genesis creation story helps to obtain a better perspective. At the beginning, the first day of creation, there are darkness and chaos; the first thing God does is create light. "God said, 'Let there be lights' and so it was....And God saw that it was good" (1:14–18). After the work of each of the days of creation, we have the same refrain: "And God saw that it was good." After the sixth day, the creation of human beings to his own image, we have a seventh refrain, "God saw everything that he had made, and indeed it was *very* good" (1:31).

So what we have above is a double aspect of God. He acts, then he sees or reflects on what he has done. This reflective activity is really Wisdom. It is presented as a model for how human beings should act, reflect, and learn. They will not always find the result to be *very good,* just as God reflected after the great flood and said in his heart, "I will never again curse the ground because of humankind for the inclination of the human heart is evil from youth; nor will I ever again destroy every living creature as I have done" (8:21).

Going back now to the poetic description, Wisdom's great joy is to be a "companion" of God, enabling him to see himself in his works of creation. At the end, Wisdom then delights to continue this action in the human beings God has created like himself. This delight is brought out by the repeated sequence in the corresponding Hebrew for the words that are italicized. The delight and rejoicing of Wisdom becomes a special gift of human beings.

The conclusion of chapters 1–9 is in the form of an invitation to become part of the house of Wisdom:

> Wisdom has built her house, she has hewn her seven pillars. She has slaughtered her animals, she has mixed her wine, she has also set her table. She has sent out her servant-girls, she calls from the highest places in the town, "You that are simple, turn in here!" To those without sense she says, "Come, eat of my bread and drink of the wine I have mixed." (9:1–5)

This description prepares the way for the end of the book with its description of the ideal, capable woman. It is preceded by the teachings of the mother of a king called Lemuel. She advises her son not to waste his strength with strange women or to dull his judgment with wine and strong drink that makes him forget the suffering of those in distress and poverty. Instead, she tells him, "Speak out for those who cannot speak, for the rights of all the destitute. Speak out, judge righteously, defend the rights of the poor and needy" (31:8–9).

Proverbs closes with an extraordinary tribute to an ideal woman of real strength (31:10–31). The author gives so much attention to this closing because it goes beyond an ideal woman to the type of a family household centered about wisdom and justice. It is carefully written in an acrostic poetic style to stress its importance. The poem is designed to link with the description of Lady Wisdom in the first nine chapters of Proverbs. Examples are the following verses: The woman is more precious than jewels just as the teachings of wisdom (v. 10; 8:3). Her husband trusts in her, as those who listen to the woman Wisdom (v. 11; 1:33). It is *her* household. She is not a submissive member of a patriarchal household (vv. 15, 21). She "buys a field," which is usually the husband's domain of business, and then plants a vineyard on it (v. 16). She ministers to the poor and hungry (v. 20).

Above all things, she is a teacher: "she opens her mouth in wisdom" (v. 26). The translation then reads that the "teaching of kindness" is on her tongue. Literally, the Hebrew reads, the "*Torah* of *hesed*." The last verse reads, "The woman who fears the LORD is to be praised." This "fear of the LORD" also introduces the Proverbs collection: The "fear of the LORD" is the beginning of wisdom, and this "fear" is repeated 17 times in the book. It sums up everything involved in reverential service of God.

THE BOOK OF JOB
DOES A JUST GOD ALWAYS REWARD JUST PEOPLE?

This is an ancient question found in the literature of other nations going back thousands of years. The biblical literature we have seen thus far expressly states that God loves justice and favors those who are also just like himself. In contrast, the wicked suffer the consequences of their evil deeds and injustice. At the time of the writing of Job, belief in an afterlife had not yet been clearly stated in the Bible, so the question must be answered in terms of this earthly life.

Job's Dilemma—A Just Man Who Loses Everything

> There was once a man in the land of Uz whose name was Job.
> That man was blameless and upright (literally, "perfect and
> just"), one who feared God and turned away from evil. There
> were born to him seven sons and three daughters. (1:1–2)

Job had everything a person could desire at that time: the
"ideal" family of seven sons and three daughters. His land hold-
ings were extensive enough to support thousands of livestock.
His sons had their own homes, and they enjoyed a cycle of feasts
moving from home to home. Then suddenly disaster struck.
Job's family and animals were carried off by Sabaean and
Chaldean raiders; lightning struck his fields, destroying his
crops, livestock, and servants. Finally, Job's health was
destroyed by such a loathsome disease that even his friends kept
a distance. Even his wife told him, "Do you still persist in your
integrity? Curse God, and die" (2:9). (Literally, the Hebrew has
bless God, to imply, but not state, the opposite.)

Job replied to his wife, "Shall we receive the good at the hand
of God and not receive the bad?" (2:10). This statement follows
his first reaction, before his disease: "Naked I came from my
mother's womb, and naked shall I return there; the LORD gave,
and the LORD has taken away; blessed be the name of the LORD"
(1:21). This initial acceptance did not keep him from making long
laments to God about his pain and suffering. Nor did it prevent
complaining to God about his treatment and asking for a just trial
to show why he deserved it. In the Bible, such complaining is part
of prayer and an expression of friendship. Job, as well as the
book's readers, must go through a long process before they can
really begin to accept God's mysterious ways.

The friends of Job appear on the scene to "help" him. They
encourage him to repent. They stress that his afflictions must be
the result of some sin, perhaps hidden. They hint that he may be
too self-righteous before God. Job persists in his innocence despite
every possible accusation. The matter of Social Justice toward
others is a central area of questioning (22:5–11). Job later
responds:

> If I have withheld anything that the poor desired, or have caused the eyes of the widow to fail, or have eaten my morsel alone, and the orphan has not eaten from it—for from my youth I reared the orphan like a father, and from my mother's womb I guided the widow. If I have seen anyone perish for lack of clothing, or a poor person without covering, whose loins have not blessed me, and who was not warmed with the fleece of my sheep; if I have raised my hand against the orphan, because I saw I had supporters at the gate; then let my shoulder blade fall from my shoulder, and let my arm be broken from its socket....the stranger has not lodged in the street; I have opened my doors to the traveler. (31:16–32)

In his defense to his friends, Job briefly states that the old axiom that the wicked are punished and the just always rewarded does not always work out in practice.

> It is all one; therefore I say, he destroys both the blameless and the wicked. When disaster brings sudden death, he mocks at the calamity of the innocent. The earth is given into the hand of the wicked; he covers the eyes of its judges—if it is not he, who then is it? (9:22–24)

Job's above statement is brief, but challenges the whole system. It hints at "contempt of court." However, despite everything, Job continues to trust in God. Despite all his friends' arguments he declares, "I have indeed prepared my case; I know that I shall be vindicated. Who is there that will contend with me? For then I would be silent and die" (13:18–19). Job's problem is his inability to get an immediate hearing, where he would be surely justified:

> Oh, that I knew where I might find him, that I might come even to his dwelling! I would lay my case before him, and fill my mouth with arguments. I would learn what he would answer me, and understand what he would say to me. (23:3–5)

Finally, God comes down in a whirlwind to answer Job. God reviews his extraordinary care of the whole universe, even nature, the animals and the fish of the sea. He does not condemn Job or say that he is wrong. God only finds fault that he has spoken too boldly in face of all the mysterious divine providence in the universe. However, God does rebuke Job's friends and asks Job to intercede for them and offer sacrifices that they may be forgiven.

Conclusion for Job

Job does not furnish any neat answers about the problem of a just, powerful God and the frequent suffering and pain of so many people dedicated to justice. However, the book represents a process toward answers that every reader must make. God is not an answering machine to offer the set solutions people would like to see. However, he is a friend, advocate, and answering person. Those who work for Social Justice must not do so from ulterior motives, rewards, utility, or fear of punishment. Such motives would make people into objects or a means to something else. Often, the best efforts will meet with failure, suffering, and pain especially when injustice and evil seem to triumph. God, indeed, is just and loves justice, according to the message of the prophets. But compassionate justice is long term, rejecting the control and power so necessary for short-term, quick results. Job echoes a Sermon on the Plain teaching: "Do good...expecting nothing in return" (Luke 6:35).

QOHELETH (ECCLESIASTES) THE MAVERICK TEACHER

Qoheleth is perhaps the most controversial book in the Bible. Countless scholars have tried to understand how it fits into the Bible. Because it is so different, it is likely that copyists or editors have even tampered with some texts to make the book more orthodox. Here we will examine the dominant, repeated themes of the author to see how they affect his whole presentation. The beginning and end of the book set off his principal concerns:

The words of the Teacher, the son of David, king in Jerusalem. Vanity of vanities, says the Teacher, vanity of vanities! All is vanity. What do people gain from all the toil at which they toil under the sun? A generation goes, and a generation comes, but the earth remains forever. The sun rises and the sun goes down, and hurries to the place where it rises. The wind blows to the south, and goes around to the north; round and round goes the wind, and on its circuits the wind returns. (1:1–6)

Amidst this repetitive cycle of nature, people come for a short time and then go: "The people of long ago are not remembered nor will there be any remembrance of people yet to come...after them" (1:11). The brevity, fragility, and unpredictability of life will be the reason why so much toil is a "chase after wind." The book ends on the same "vanity" note, before an editor's addition: "Vanity of vanities says the teacher; all is vanity" (12:8). The meaning of this *vanity* is the key to this unusual book. As in Job, there are no certain indications of a future life in Qoheleth.

The Meaning of Vanity, Chasing after Wind, and Toil

First of all, the word *vanity* may throw off the reader. A dictionary usually defines it in terms of "conceit" or "pride." However, the root lies in an expression like "in vain" or "futile." The word occurs 27 times in Qoheleth. Another associated word is "chasing after wind," found nine times. Of these, seven occur together with *vanity* as "vanity and chasing after wind." The basis for this vanity is the uncontrollable nature of life itself and the meaning of toil or work. The word *toil* occurs 26 times in addition to various synonyms in the 12 chapters. This toil can be of two kinds: The first is the toil for the end-product of achievement based on persevering hard work on one's own efforts. This type of toil is "chasing the wind." The writer, speaking like King Solomon, describes his quest for pleasure, money, possessions, women, and even wisdom.

Wisdom is a good example of the two types of toil. Qoheleth writes that he applied himself to be a recognized wise person and concluded that this was a "chasing after wind. For in much wisdom is much vexation" (1:17–18). However, if one is open to wisdom as a gift from God, this chase is an entirely different matter.

The author appreciates wisdom as a gift but not the obsessive toil of striving for wisdom through relentless human effort. The toil for real wisdom is that of gratefully receiving it and applying it in action. The first type of toil leads to vanity and frustration because the end product is unpredictable in view of the nature of life and human behavior. This human behavior is the prevalent tendency to evil in the world that manifests itself in competition and even opposition to wisdom. Life and toil can so quickly and unexpectedly be brought to an end by poor health and accidents.

The author applies this gift or grace motif to all of life in general in a first summary that is repeated and amplified several times:

> There is nothing better for mortals than to eat and drink, and find enjoyment in their toil. This also, I saw, is from the hand of God; for apart from him who can eat or who can have enjoyment? (2:24–25)

Applications to Life Situations

Taking Life as It Comes

Qoheleth focuses on receiving from life (and he always means God as its author) whatever comes at any time. Being totally responsive to the present moment, whether in joy or sorrow, is being close to God, the creator of life itself as the best teacher:

> For everything there is a season, and a time for every matter under heaven: a time to be born, and a time to die; a time to plant, and a time to pluck up what is planted; a time to kill, and a time to heal; a time to break down, and a time to build up; a time to weep, and a time to laugh; a time to mourn, and a time to dance; a time to throw away stones, and a time to gather stones together; a time to embrace, and a time to refrain from embracing; a time to seek, and a time to lose; a time to keep, and a time to throw away; a time to tear, and a time to sew; a time to keep silence, and a time to speak; a time to love, and a time to hate; a time for war, and a time for peace. (3:1–8)

Fundamental Values but Not Obsessions or Frantic Striving

On work: "So I saw that there is nothing better than that all should enjoy their work, for that is their lot; who can bring them to see what will be after them?" (3:22).

On friendship: "Again, I saw vanity under the sun: the case of solitary individuals, without sons or brothers. Two are better than one, because they have a good reward for their toil. For if they fall, one will lift up the other; but woe to one who is alone and falls and does not have another to help" (4:7–10).

On wisdom: "Wisdom is as good as an inheritance, an advantage to those who see the sun. For the protection of wisdom is like the protection of money, and the advantage of knowledge is that wisdom gives life to the one who possesses it. Consider the work of God; who can make straight what he has made crooked?" (7:11–13).

On excessive righteousness or religion and on too little of it: "In my vain life I have seen everything; there are righteous people who perish in their righteousness, and there are wicked people who prolong their life in their evildoing. Do not be too righteous and do not act too wise....Do not be too wicked, and do not be a fool; why should you die before your time?...Wisdom gives strength to the wise more than ten rulers that are in a city (7:17–19).

Enjoy simple living with its pleasures: "Go, eat your bread with enjoyment, and drink your wine with a merry heart; for God has long ago approved what you do. Let your garments always be white; do not let oil be lacking on your head. Enjoy life with the wife whom you love, all the days of your vain life that are given you under the sun, because that is your portion in life and in your toil at which you toil under the sun. Whatever your hand finds to do, do with your might; for there is no work or thought or knowledge or wisdom in Sheol, to which you are going" (9:7–10).

Laughter and a sense of humor: "Feasts are made for laughter; wine gladdens life, and money meets every need. Do not curse the king, even in your thoughts, or curse the rich, even in your bedroom; for a bird of the air may carry your voice, or some winged creature tell the matter" (10:19–20).

Be ready for many options in Life: "Send out your bread upon the waters, for after many days you will get it back. Divide your means seven ways or even eight. For you do not know what disaster may happen on earth" (11:1–2).

Keep yourself young: "Remember your creator in the days of your youth, before the days of trouble come, and the years draw near when you will say, 'I have no pleasure in them'" (12:1).

For Qoheleth, "keeping young" means thoroughly living each moment and losing the sense of time, worry, and concern that makes people old before their time.

Conclusion for Qoheleth

What do all of these values have to do with Social Justice? Perhaps Qoheleth would answer in this way: "If you make Social Justice a goal or achievement for which you obsessively toil trusting in human efforts, it will be 'chasing after the wind.'" Real justice and wisdom go together as a gift of God to which we must be open at every opportunity. Social Justice must begin with a choice of simple living and enjoying the beautiful gifts of each day, especially those that come from living and working with other human beings. Qoheleth is a preparation for the wisdom teachings of the Sermon on the Mount where Jesus advises believers to live fully each day: "Do not worry about tomorrow; for tomorrow will bring worries of its own" (Matt 6:34).

4

Social Revolution in the Desert: The Qumran Community

A Startling Discovery of Scrolls Lost for 2,000 Years

In 1946 or 1947, several Bedouins entered a narrow cave near the Dead Sea and found some old and tattered scrolls. Little did they realize that they had begun to discover a vast trove of scrolls whose contents would forever change the course of biblical studies and the knowledge of the Near East. After further exploration, some 1,000 scrolls were found along with many thousands of fragments. In general, there were two types of scrolls, biblical and nonbiblical.[12]

The biblical documents were about one quarter of the scrolls, with at least parts of every book of the Bible except Esther. What is remarkable about this finding is that previously, the earliest extant copy of the Hebrew Bible went back to only about A.D. 1000. Yet, some of the Qumran copies were written as early as around 200 B.C., a time gap of about 1,200 years. Despite this gap, there was an extraordinary fidelity in the transmission of most of the texts. At the same time, there was a variety in some biblical versions, showing that at the time of Jesus, people did not all read a standard text. The fixed canon and version of the Hebrew Bible only came around A.D. 1000. The Qumran books also proved that the ancient Greek translation of the Hebrew made in pre-Christian times often had better readings because it was made from older Hebrew texts at their disposal.

The other three quarters of the scrolls were nonbiblical. Of these, one part comprised Jewish texts already known, such as

Jubilees, The Testaments of the Twelve Patriarchs, 1 Enoch, and others. The other parts consisted of writings almost completely unknown except for secondhand references in Philo and Josephus, which were sometimes quite extravagant. This group of scrolls became the most exciting find for Christian scholars. Previously, there existed no contemporary writings outside the Gospels that could give firsthand accounts of Jewish beliefs and practices in Israel around the lifetime of Jesus. But now, the detailed rules and records were found of an ascetic Jewish community that dwelt near the Dead Sea from around 200 B.C. to A.D. 100.

The impact of such a find can hardly be overstated. It had often been claimed that Christianity sprang from mixed Greek and Hebrew backgrounds. Now, this claim can no longer be held. The many parallels between Jesus, the early church, and the Qumran community indicate that there is much in common between them. First we will discuss the origin of the community and then its practices.

The Origins of the Qumran Community

The name *Qumran* refers to a *Wadi* (seasonal creek) *Qumran* flowing into the northwest end of the Dead Sea. Nearby is a site called *Kirbet Qumran,* meaning "ruins of Qumran," which seems to have been a dwelling center or at least a community center for a group that numbered at times around a hundred or more people. The scrolls were found in the cliffs of the nearby mountains. They seem to have been hidden there at a time of crisis, perhaps during the Jewish War with Rome. The community called themselves the *Yahad,* meaning "unit," but do not tell us why. Perhaps it was because they bound themselves to God and to one another to keep the Mosaic covenant in a perfect way. Because they were a "priestly" community, the words of Psalm 133:1–3 must have been very meaningful: "How very good and pleasant it is when kindred dwell together in unity (*yahad*)! It is like the precious oil on the head, running down upon the beard of Aaron, running down over the collar of his robes."

The exact origins of the community are difficult to ascertain. That is because the references are scattered in the scrolls, and the people mentioned are identified only by the roles they play rather than by name. Thus, the founder is probably the "Teacher of Righteousness," a charismatic leader with revelations from God about the interpretation of the law of Moses and the meaning of the scriptures. The "Man of the Lie" would be the leader of an opposing group. The "Wicked Priest" seems to be a ruler in Israel, at first favorable to the founder but later opposing him, attempting to execute him and then driving the community into exile. In exile, they became estranged from the Temple and bitterly opposed to the priests in charge of it.

Community Lifestyle at Qumran

The exiled priests, Levites, and lay people considered themselves the embodiment of the desert community of Israel, and many settled in the desert region near the Dead Sea where Moses had spoken to a new generation before crossing the Jordan and entering the promised land. This story is told in the Book of Deuteronomy, which the community took as their primary guide. Estranged from the Jerusalem Temple, the community felt that they were the desert marching camp of Israel, which had the dwelling place of God in their midst. In this way, they were a new Temple in themselves. Their sacrifices took the form of entire devotion to the law of Moses plus a vow to share their possessions with one another and the total community as an offering to God. There are indications that other scattered groups in Israel were formed on the model of chapters, with at least ten persons to a chapter and at least one priest. They were organized in this way to make sure that they could alternate in studying the Torah on a 24-hour basis. They made their livelihood in ordinary pursuits such as agriculture, raising animals, trades, and making precious copies of the Torah. "Sharing possessions" did not necessarily mean giving up any private property. It could mean that the income of their property was placed in deposit with others.

Each *Yahad* had at least one priest as an instructor. Its members were Levites and lay people. They met together for common meals and study of the Torah. This study was especially for one-third of each night and was devoted to reading of the Torah, biblical interpretations, and prayers. Entry into the *Yahad* was accomplished through personal conversion to perfect observance of the Torah. Married men and women are mentioned in some of the documents in which there is instruction about marriage and divorce. Upon entry, candidates handed over for deposit a certain amount of their possessions and devoted the first year to intense study of the Torah. After a second year, the sharing of possessions was completed. There was a hierarchy of age and position in the community. The younger and less advanced were supposed to respect and obey those above them, especially the priest members who were their instructors and guides. However, all community decisions were by a majority vote. The *Yahad* looked forward to a coming day of the Lord, a day of visitation when their enemies would be conquered, and they, in turn, would be rewarded with life everlasting.

A Community of Justice

Candidates to the community made two commitments. The first was an oath to keep the law of Moses perfectly. The Rule has these words:

> Everyone who enters into the community of the *Yahad* should enter in full view of all the members. He shall make a binding oath to return to the Law of Moses (according to all he commanded) with all his heart and with all his mind, to all that has been revealed from it to the Sons of Zadok—priests and preservers of the covenant—seekers of his will and the majority of the men of their covenant. (5:7–10)

For the law of Moses, the primary book was that of Deuteronomy. The words "With all your heart and...soul" point to the *Shemah,* the great central prayer of that book (6:5). The "mind" in this case, by comparison with other texts, refers to the knowledge

92

and practice of all the laws. "The heart" means total devotion. The study of the Torah was of such importance that the first year of membership was devoted to its study. After that, one-third of the community was always engaged in its study.

In Deuteronomy, we have seen the program for the elimination of poverty. These directions were to be followed with scrupulous care. In fact some laws that were unique to that book and little known elsewhere were kept, such as the remission of all debts after seven years in chapter 15. The Jubilee Year is found in the priestly code of Leviticus, chapter 25. This ideal of returning all properties every 50 years to the original owners was rarely followed in the rest of the Bible. However, the *Yahad* texts show that the community kept to its observance.

The second commitment was to the *Yahad* and fellow covenanters:

> All those voluntarily offering themselves to his (God's) truth will bring all their knowledge, and their strength and their wealth into the community of God in order to refine their knowledge in the truth of God's statutes and marshal their strength in accordance with his perfect ways and all their wealth in accordance with his just counsel. (1:11–13)

In addition to sharing this wealth with one another, they also set apart at least two days' income each month for the poor and needy. This was given to the overseer and judges to be distributed as follows:

> They will strengthen the hand of the poor and destitute, the old man, the afflicted, the captive of a foreign people, the virgin, the youth who has no one to care for him. (CD 14:12–19)

This sharing with those in need had a theological as well as humanitarian motive. Because men and women were created in God's image, any deficiency is a reflection on God's image. Helping the poor and unprotected meant restoring the damaged image of God. This sharing of wealth was a special mark of the community that was often connected with their aspiration to be "perfect ones" or part of the "perfection of the way." The Levitical injunction to love one's neighbor as one's self was broadly interpreted to apply not only to "one's brother" but also to support for the "poor, the needy and the alien."

The ideal of a community of justice was not only in reference to external possessions and goods. There was a strong sense of personal respect and concern for one another. At community meetings, each person had the right to speak, and no one could interrupt the speaker while he or she was speaking. All decisions in reference to the whole community had to be made by a majority vote. The central part of the day was the community sacred meal. The priests gave the blessings, but regardless of rank, everyone had equal food portions at the table.

The covenanters were very concerned about the Levitical command to love one another as one's self (Lev 19:18). Hence, they were to care for one another's welfare and progress: "They shall all comprise a *Yahad* based on truth, real humility, love, and righteous intent, caring for one another in this manner in a holy society bound as comrades in eternal fellowship." This was made practical by correcting one another and settling disputes before sunset of each day. No one should bring up anything to the whole community unless it was previously done in private before witnesses:

> Each man should reprove his brother in truth, humility and kindness, not speaking to him in anger. He is to rebuke him on the day of the offense, so he does not continue in sin. No one should bring a charge against a brother to the whole community unless he has previously rebuked him before witnesses. (5:25–61)

Although women are not specifically mentioned in the Rule, there is no indication that they were excluded. Outside the Rule, other texts with marriage regulations show that they were part of at least some scattered community groups. In addition, there is a scroll fragment of a liturgy of thanksgiving describing women as praying aloud with the elders and others. This would have been quite unusual for the times. Later, even Paul the Apostle has troubles with those opposing such "freedom" of women in Corinth liturgies (1 Cor 11:1–16).

In regard to women's vows or oaths, the Book of Numbers (30:8) prescribed that husbands or fathers had the right to annul them. However, this is not the case in the Damascus version of the Rule (16:10–12). A husband or father could only do so if the promises made were in opposition to the covenant. If there was any doubt on the matter, the vows or oaths were to stand. This was an important provision of women's rights.

Philo, Josephus, Pliny, and the "Essenes"

The Qumran movement was not simply an offbeat, isolated Jewish community living in the "end time." It became well known through writers with widespread influence at that time.[13] Philo was a renowned Jewish scholar who lived in Alexandria, Egypt, about the time of 30 B.C. to A.D. 40. He is the best source for understanding Hellenistic Judaism in the period close to Jesus' life and the Gospels. He had no firsthand contact with Qumran but investigated it through others and wrote extensively about it. Josephus was a Jewish commander in Galilee who was captured by the Romans early during the Jewish war with Rome around the year A.D. 66. After the war, he devoted himself to writing a history of the war and a history of his own people. Both writers attempted to impress the Greek and Roman world with the story of the Jewish people and their literature as well as customs. Pliny the elder was a Roman scholar and author who lived between A.D. 23 and 79, and thus was a contemporary of Jesus. Their writings describe the Essenes. There has been some discussion whether these are the same as the Qumran group. Most scholars believe they are. The differences may be due to the attempts of Philo and Josephus to describe them in ways appealing to the Greeks and Romans.

Philo describes the Essenes in terms of three great virtues: love of God, love of virtue, and love of humanity. In regard to virtue, he writes as a summary:

> Such are the athletes of virtue which this philosophy produces, a philosophy which undoubtedly lacks the refinements

of Greek eloquence, but which propounds like gymnastic exercises, the accomplishment of praiseworthy deeds as the means by which a man ensures absolute freedom for himself.

We note above the attempts to liken the community to a Greek philosophers' group. They are like ascetics and athletes in a gymnasium, so they can accomplish good deeds and become free men. However, Philo gives most time to their "love of humanity" when he discusses their common lifestyle:

> Indeed there is no house which does not belong to them all, for as well as living in communities, their homes are open to members of the sect arriving from elsewhere. Secondly, there is but one purse for them all and a common expenditure. Their clothes and food are also held in common, for they have adopted the practice of eating together. In vain one would search elsewhere for a more effective sharing of the same roof, the same way of life and the same table. This is the reason: whatever they receive as salary for their day's work is not kept to themselves, but is deposited before them all, in their midst, to be put to the common assistance of all those who wish to make use of it. As for the sick, they are not neglected on the pretext that they can produce nothing, for thanks to the common purse, they have whatever is needed for treatment, so there is no fear of great expense on their behalf. The aged for their part, are surrounded with respect and care.

Elsewhere, Philo writes that there were no marriages, women, or children. However, the Qumran documents indicate that there were married people and women at Qumran, as we have previously noted. In other texts, Philo praises their frugality and simplicity of lifestyle. However, the *Yahad* has no praise for frugality or poverty as such. They would prefer an abundance they could share with others and those in need.

The writings of Josephus have special value because he claimed that he knew the Jews personally. However, he is especially interested in presenting an ideal picture of the Jews after the disastrous war with Rome. So, his descriptions in regard to the Essenes tend to be exaggerated. Like Philo, he emphasizes their brotherly love for one another. He also focuses on their self-control, asceticism, and celibacy even more than Philo. Josephus writes,

> They despise riches and their communal life is admirable. In vain would one search among them for one man with a greater fortune than another. Indeed it is a law that those who enter the sect shall make public their property to the order so neither the humiliation of poverty nor the pride of wealth is to be seen anywhere among them. Since their possessions are mingled there exists for them all, as for brothers, a single property.

In regard to this commonness of wealth, he also writes,

> Their goods are common to them and the wealthy man does not enjoy the benefit of his property more than the one who possesses nothing at all....they live among themselves and serve each other. They choose noble men to collect the income and gather various products of the land and (they choose) priests to make the bread and the food.

A number of details about Qumran are found only in Josephus: He mentions the white clothes they wore, especially at meals. Along with Philo, he states that they elected the officials, who supervised the common property. Josephus has interesting details about the common meals: The food is carefully measured out so that there are equal and abundant servings of bread for each person. According to Qumran ideals, any deficiency detracts from the fullness of God's image in everyone. In this way, love of God and love of neighbor came together.

Pliny the Elder

His writings about the Essenes, although brief and exaggerated, show that their reputation had spread even as far as Rome. Significantly, he notes their exact location near the Dead Sea. He describes them as "without women, without money and without contact with others." In his flair for the extraordinary, Pliny states that the Essenes were an eternal community that has existed for "thousands of centuries." However, they are continually being renewed by the large number who daily enter in order to be reborn. They enter in order to repent for their past lives and to escape the economic worries of this world.

Qumran and Its Bearing on the New Testament and Social Justice

Here, we cannot go into the numerous studies and books examining the similarities between the Qumran community and the New Testament. However, we will make some observations in regard to Social Justice. In some ways, the *Yahad* provides almost a "missing link" between the ancient Torah, the Prophets, and the New Testament. I use the term "missing link" because we saw in Deuteronomy and, to a certain extent, Leviticus a radical program for the elimination of poverty. This included, among other provisions, the forgiveness of debts every seven years and the Jubilee Year for the return of ancestral properties. Yet, we saw little evidence of their practical application of it in history.

Suddenly after 2,000 years, we find the documents of a community that put them carefully into practice in their daily lives. This practice is described in a detailed community Rule showing how it is to be done. All of this is involved in repentance with one's whole heart to follow the "way of the LORD" in the Torah and Prophets. In fact, the text of Isaiah, "In the wilderness prepare the way of the LORD" (40:3) is like a theme song for Qumran. Members of the community separate themselves from the world to prepare a *way of the truth* in accord with Isaiah 40:3: "In the wilderness prepare the way of the LORD, make straight in the desert a highway for our God" (Rule 8:13–15). The community instructor guides those who have chosen *the way*, which is a *secret way* to be followed by those who follow the *way* of Isaiah 40:3. Then follows a series of *precepts of the way* that the instructor is to teach.

By way of examples, the Qumran community helps us to understand the radical nature of the opening invitation to repent that begins the preaching of John the Baptist and Jesus. The desert theme of Isaiah in preparing the way of the Lord is identical with that of Qumran: "This is the one of whom the prophet Isaiah spoke when he said, 'The voice of one crying out in the wilderness: "Prepare the way of the Lord, make his paths straight"'" (Matt 3:2–3). Like Qumran, Matthew's favorite book is Deuteronomy. The Yahad emphasized brotherhood and covenant through the Levitical precept to love one's neighbor as oneself. Matthew will focus on this theme three times as a fulfillment of the law and prophets (7:12; 19:19; 21:39–40). Luke takes the revived Jubilee year of Qumran and makes it a central theme for his Gospel (4:16–20). The sharing of possessions, as at Qumran, became an important feature of the early church at Jerusalem: "The whole group of those who believed were of one heart and soul, and no one claimed private ownership of any possessions, but everything they owned was held in common" (Acts 4:32).

PART II
SOCIAL JUSTICE
IN THE NEW TESTAMENT

Prelude to Part II

We return to the opening statements of Part I: Jesus stated that he had come to fulfill the Law and the Prophets (Matt 5:17). Therefore, Social Justice in the New Testament grows out of the models presented in the Hebrew Bible. We have seen that justice, in the agricultural economics of the Old Testament, refers primarily to the land. First, it is a limited land. Second, it is a sacred gift or inheritance from God. Third, it was "equally" divided by divine lot to tribes and families. Fourth, when anyone has abundance by whatever means, while others do not have enough, this is *evil in itself*. This is in opposition to some modern mythological views that there are unlimited lands and resources on our planet. Therefore, one person's overabundance does not hurt others, especially if they give generous gifts to those in need.

Social Justice in the Bible moves toward equality in land and resources. Therefore, there were definite provisions to protect the precious ancestral land so it would not be alienated. This was done, for example, by the remission of debts every seven years and the freedom of debt slaves also after six years. The Jubilee year was another, but longer range, provision.

As for people who did not live from the land, the Torah and the Prophets likewise provided for them. This provision flowed from the primary ethic of imitation of God. The God of the Hebrew Bible introduces himself as liberator of the oppressed in the Sinai covenant: "I am the LORD your God who brought you out of the land of Egypt, out of the house of slavery" (Deut 5:6). Because God intervened to care for an oppressed people, they too should care for those oppressed. Examples were widows, orphans, aliens, and others who were landless. This is not merely a generic principle. The Torah had definite prescriptions for the elimination of poverty. Among them was a special tithe every three years for the poor and a sabbatical year for the land when its produce could be used for that purpose.

The New Testament will be "new" in the sense of a radical return to the core of justice in the Torah as preached by the prophets. Jesus will build his preaching on that precious root and add to it with his own teachings.

5

Mark:
Breaking Down Dividing Walls
in the Roman Empire

"My house shall be called a house of prayer for all the nations." (11:17)

"Now when the centurion, who stood facing him, saw that in this way he breathed his last, he said, 'Truly this man was God's Son!'" (15:39)

We are accustomed to the usual order of Matthew, Mark, Luke, and John. However, most biblical scholars agree that Mark was written in Greek before Matthew, although Matthew does contain many older materials. Mark's community was suffering under oppressive Roman persecution.[14] The author knows that many believers wondered whether it really made a difference if they stood up for their beliefs and values even if it meant risking their lives. To motivate them, Mark provides the example of Jesus' suffering and death to fulfill his prophetic call. This is so the audience can realize that they too can achieve the extraordinary effect of winning over other Roman centurions in the same way that Jesus did on the cross. In this way, they can fulfill Jesus' promise of an all-inclusive worship of the one God when he stated his purpose was to create a "house of prayer for all the nations."

Mark's Audience and Roman Oppression

The time in history was soon after or during the Jewish War with Rome, A.D. 66–70, when the Jewish Temple was destroyed. The Gospel references to the Temple's destruction point to this (13:1–37). The Gospel audience was mostly Gentile Christian with a minority of Jewish Christians. We know this because Mark translates many original Aramaic words into Greek—*Abba* is a notable example. In the 60s of the first century, there had been persecution under Nero. After the war with Rome, authorities could not always distinguish neatly between Jews and Christians. They readily assumed that Christians were among those who rebelled against them in that long, bitter struggle. Many early Christians expected the imminent end of the world and return of Jesus. In Mark, the Temple's destruction intensified this hope. For them, it was a possible sign that the end of the world was near. Just before the Transfiguration story, Mark cites Jesus' saying: "Truly I tell you, there are some standing here who will not taste death until they see that the kingdom of God has come with power" (9:1, also 13:30).

The destruction of the Temple was the occasion for many Christian prophets to declare that Jesus was soon returning in power to overcome their Roman oppressors. Jesus warned about this and stated, "Beware that no one leads you astray. Many will come in my name and say, 'I am he!' and they will lead many astray" (13:5–6). These prophets described a Messiah of power who would crush the Romans and open their prisons and liberate them from suffering, persecution, and even death. Mark's Gospel response is to present Jesus as deliberately setting aside power and voluntarily embracing suffering in order to win over others. His death was a sacrifice and a supreme victory that even brought about the conversion of a hardened executioner, a Roman centurion. This story of conversion symbolized the opening of the Roman Gentile world to the Gospel and their inclusion in Jesus' new house of prayer for all the nations. The disgrace of the cross and the apparent victory of the Roman military had been reversed by God.

As for the end of the world, Mark separates it from the destruction of Jerusalem. Only after that destruction, people "will see the Son of Man coming in clouds with great power and glory" (13:26). This will not be a local sign like the Jerusalem disaster but will be manifest to the whole world: "Then he will send out the angels, and gather his elect from the four winds, from the ends of the earth to the ends of the heavens" (13:27). No one, prophet or otherwise, will be able to predict when the end will be: "But about that day or hour no one knows, neither the angels in heaven, nor the Son, but only the Father. Beware, keep alert; for you do not know when the time will come" (13:32).

The Imminent Return of Jesus and Its Effects

Christians should not expect to be liberated from suffering by a proximate return of Jesus in power. On the contrary, their sufferings and witness will be the very means of winning over others and hastening the return of the Lord. So, Jesus says, "As for yourselves, beware; for they will hand you over to councils; and you will be beaten in synagogues; and you will stand before governors and kings because of me, as a testimony to them" (13:9). In other words, their experience will duplicate that of Jesus. For he was brought before the high priest and Council, then put on trial before King Herod and Governor Pontius Pilate as a testimony or witness (the meaning of the term *martyr*).

Jesus stood up for what he believed in—his mission to preach the good news of the kingdom. This constitutes a sacrifice, which means doing what God wants, even as far as death. Such a sacrifice is the most effective witness to others and is what believers can duplicate. "And the good news will first be preached to all nations" (13:10). The effective witness of the suffering of believers will be the means of bringing the Gospel to the world, and then the end will come. This end of time and the return of Jesus will be made possible by their voluntary suffering, like that of Jesus.

In response to this challenge, nothing less than a total response is required: "You will be hated by all because of my name. But the one who endures to the end will be saved" (13:13).

This total response is typified before the Temple discourse by the story of the widow's mite.

> He (Jesus) sat down opposite the treasury, and watched the crowd putting money into the treasury. Many rich people put in large sums. A poor widow came and put in two small copper coins, which are worth a penny. Then he called his disciples and said to them, "Truly I tell you, this poor widow has put in more than all those who are contributing to the treasury. For all of them have contributed out of their abundance; but she out of her poverty has put in everything she had, all that she had to live on." (12:41–44)

Literally, the text means that she put in her whole "life," *bios*. Thus, she illustrates the heroism in the coming discourse of those who give everything, even their lives. This story is balanced at the other end of chapter 13 in the form of a literary enclosure: the Bethany woman put in *all she could*, the precious ointment, which symbolized her whole life. This contrasts with the criticism of those who were angry that the ointment was not sold and the proceeds given to the poor (14:3–9). Her example is so meaningful that Jesus says, "Truly I tell you, wherever the good news is proclaimed in the whole world, what she has done will be told in remembrance of her."

Only with the above preparation can we understand the Gospel beginnings. The Gospel beginnings foreshadow the cross.

The Voice Crying in the Wilderness

The symbol of Mark the evangelist is the roaring lion in a wilderness area as the Gospel opens with a clarion call for repentance:

> As it is written in the prophet Isaiah, "See, I am sending my messenger ahead of you, who will prepare your way; the voice of one crying out in the wilderness: 'Prepare the way of the Lord, make his paths straight.'" John the baptizer appeared in the wilderness, proclaiming a *baptism of repentance* for the *forgiveness* of sins. And people from the whole

Judean countryside and all the people of Jerusalem were going out to him, and were baptized by him in the river Jordan, *confessing their sins.* (Mark 1:2–5)

We noted the same theme text at the end of our the last chapter. The Qumran community felt they were called to repentance by the same voice of God through Isaiah. Italicized above are the same basic elements in Mark that we noted in Isaiah, chapters 1–5: repentance/change; washing/cleansing; forgiveness. Jesus repeats and adds to this, "The time is fulfilled, and the kingdom of God has come near; repent, and believe in the good news" (1:15). The "time" parallels the "day" or "day of the Lord" in Isaiah. The coming "kingdom of God" is found as part of the opening "voice of the wilderness passage" in Isaiah: "See, the Lord GOD comes with might, and his arm *rules* for him; his reward is with him, and his recompense before him" (40:10). The presentation of God as *King* occurs in Isaiah's opening call, "My eyes have seen the King, the LORD of hosts" (6:5).

The modern reader may sometimes be confused by the number of chapter/verse notations that we are making. The biblical authors originally wrote on scrolls, which were expensive and difficult to make. To save space, there were no vowels in the Hebrew text, and the words and sentences flowed on without spaces. Vowel markers were only added around the seventh century A.D. No chapter and verse divisions were made until many centuries after the whole Bible was completed. Consequently, the location of texts in the Bible was in accord with the message of the particular section. For example, Ezekiel 37:1–14 would be called "the passage about the dry bones." When a particular scripture was quoted, e.g., "the voice crying in the wilderness," *it was presumed that the listener or readers knew the rest of the passage also,* so it would not be necessary to locate and quote each part. There was no need of proof by specifically quoting each reference.

With all this in mind, it is enough for Mark to quote Isaiah's words of repentance and a voice crying in the wilderness. Mark presumes that the audience understands that Isaiah's whole message of repentance goes back to the core of the covenant behind the words of Jesus and the Baptist. This is confirmed by the fact that Mark has more references to Isaiah than any other prophet and Isaiah, as we have seen, is the great prophet of justice. Mark does emphasize Jesus' actions much more than his words. But, sometimes, even a few words of Jesus have many teachings of the Torah and prophets behind them.

Jesus' Baptism and Call

> And just as he was coming up out of the water, he saw the heavens torn apart and the Spirit descending like a dove on him. And a voice came from heaven, "You are my Son, the Beloved; with you I am well pleased." (1:11)

The "tearing open" of the heavens is an ancient way of expressing an opening of access to God. In the Bible, such communication is destined for the person to whom God wishes to speak; it is not available automatically to others. In Mark, this is a private matter in which God reveals to Jesus that he is his Son in a special manner. In fact, during the whole Gospel no one really confesses who Jesus is until the Roman centurion has a revelation after the splitting of the Temple veil which guarded access to God. Then, the centurion can state, "Truly this man was God's son!" (15:39).

The stage for this final confrontation with Rome is set soon after Jesus' baptism and temptation. Mark describes these with a few telling words: "Now after John was arrested, Jesus came to Galilee proclaiming the good news of God." (1:14). With the arrest of the Baptist, a prelude to execution, Jesus' own life is threatened also as a collaborator with him. The Roman puppet, King Herod, orders the arrest. The Romans had given him the title "king of the Jews" even though he was actually only half-Jewish. Besides that, his jurisdiction was only over Galilee. The Roman governor Pilate was in direct control over Judea. Jesus' proclamation of a coming kingdom was a personal threat to Herod and ultimately to Rome.

Despite this threat to himself, Jesus does not waver but instead goes out beyond the Jordan with his ministry of preaching repentance. The fact that Jesus goes ahead despite the risk to his life already puts himself under the shadow of the cross. This gives a special dimension to his mission of justice that will be evident to the

Gospel audience. The words of people risking their lives because of their convictions have a special power and influence behind them.

Jesus centered his teaching in Galilee, a region filled with turmoil because of injustice. It is estimated that Herod the king held almost one half the land as royal domain, leasing it to sharecroppers or renters. Mark's parable of the owner who leased out his vineyard to sharecropping tenants (12:1–9) would have been a familiar story to a Gospel audience in Roman times. At the heart of the Roman system of oppression was heavy taxation. When Jesus was a child, around 5 B.C., there was a tax revolt headed by Judas the Galilean. In punishment, Josephus tells us, thousands of Jews were crucified.

Although Jesus' appeal for radical return to the covenant was at the heart of the message, Mark gives us few specifics. Instead, he sketches Jesus' teaching in the form of general principles in his household instructions, along with an appeal to personally follow and imitate the Master. Jesus does not repeat the directions of the Deuteronomic program to relieve poverty nor the specific teachings of the prophets. Jesus knew that these were familiar to his audience. Few people directly broke laws, but some religious teachers were adept in pointing out ways to circumvent them. Mark provides one such example: Of course everyone knew the fourth commandment to honor one's parents and support them in their needs. However, if you knew the neat legal stratagem of declaring your goods as "Corban"—offering to God—this meant that they could be set aside for God and need not be given for any other purpose, even for helping parents (7:9–13).

Another area was that of debts. One of the principal means by which the rich grew richer and the poor grew poorer was through gaining property, possessions, or debt slaves through the failure of people to repay debts. On paper, the Torah enjoined the release of debts every seven years to prevent this from happening (Deut 15:1). This law could not be "broken," but there were ways of making an end run around it. This was a practice called *prosbol*.[15] It involved turning over the title of a loan to a court during the seventh year and then returning it afterward. This is only found in late rabbinic literature but is attributed to Hillel who lived near the time of Jesus. This does not mean necessarily that Hillel was the actual author. Yet, even though the Law was frequently circumvented, it showed at least that the precepts of the Torah were a live issue and could not be ignored.

The Healing Ministry—Removing the Social Stigma of Sickness

The healing of Simon's mother-in-law opens a cycle of miraculous cures in Mark:

> That evening, at sundown, they brought to him all who were sick or possessed with demons. And the whole city was gathered around the door. And he cured many who were sick with various diseases, and cast out many demons; and he would not permit the demons to speak, because they knew him. (1:32–34)

Jesus' preaching of repentance was accompanied by a healing ministry to the sick. Repentance involved turning the whole person to God and restoration to normal activity. After Jesus cured Simon's mother-in-law, she returned to her usual responsibilities: "She began to serve them" (1:31). Healing also meant dealing with what people considered the root causes. These were often the evil spirits, demons or personal sins. So, Mark writes above that Jesus "cast out many demons" (1:34) and forgave the paralytic's sins (2:9–10).

Social Justice involves compassion and care for others as equals. Yet, those who were sick were often regarded as being seriously deficient human beings, lacking in conformity to the divine image. We have seen in Leviticus that those with disabilities such as the blind, lame, or those with mutilated body parts were not allowed to approach the altar (21:16–21). While this was true for Levites, at least part of the same attitude was true for any sick person. In the group of healings above, we note that only after Sabbath sundown the people carried their sick to Jesus. While the sick were cared for on that day, it was certainly not the best day of the week for those who were not well. The oils and herbs needed for healing could not be bought on the Sabbath, and the work involved in making a healing ointment would be best postponed to another day.

Mark shows that Jesus made healing accompany preaching so that the sick became a priority rather than an unwilling burden. The description of Jesus' miracles was really a model for successors: "He appointed twelve, whom he named apostles, to be with him, and to be sent out to proclaim the message and to have authority to cast out demons" (3:14–15). Later, he sent them out two by two and "gave them authority over the unclean spirits" (6:7). Mark describes the result of their mission as follows:

> So they went out and proclaimed that all should repent. They cast out many demons, and anointed with oil many who were sick and cured them. (6:12–13)

Social Barriers of Ritual Cleanness or Uncleanness

Although Mark's audience was mainly Gentiles, as they learned more and more about the scriptures, they were concerned about compliance with the numerous biblical laws regarding ritual purity that pervaded every phase of life. Being "clean" had usually nothing to do with cleanliness and ethics. In fact, it was most praiseworthy to anoint and bury the dead. Yet, to do so meant becoming "unclean," which resulted in a disqualification from taking part in many social and religious gatherings. Some forms of uncleanness were also "contagious"—touching another person or object placed them in the same state.

The origins of such customs are hard to define. Some were due to health reasons, but many originated in a fear or "taboo" about excessive closeness to the divine in matters that were on the edge of life and death. For example, blood is especially sacred as the carrier of life. Hence, many laws were especially concerned about women in their closeness to the mysteries of life at childbirth and each month. In regard to food, all meat had to be "kosher," not mixed with any blood. There were also many classes of food that were unclean, most notably pork. Pigs could not be raised in Israel. Because Gentiles did not keep such observances, any table fellowship with them was impossible and even contact with them brought about uncleanness (Acts 11:2). The source of most of these regulations is the Book of Leviticus.

These were customs of everyday life in Israel and, in themselves, usually helped people to remember God by obediently following these biblical laws. However, they did create a kind of pyramid or hierarchy, with the priests and those who were "purest" on top. At the lowest rank were those whose business or occupation made them likely to be more "unclean." Near the bottom were women, not because of their gender but because of their involvement in the sacredness of blood. The legal times were at least 40 days for childbirth and 7 days during each menstrual period. This last time was extremely "contagious," which meant that caution was needed even in necessary contacts.

In practice, all this concern with cleanness led to considerable discrimination against those more likely to be unclean. For the Gospel audience, Jesus' behavior set a pattern to follow. A leper dared to come up to him, kneel down, and beg for a cure. Jesus then does what no one else would dare attempt by touching him and thus incurring the dread uncleanness. Yet, the reverse happens. The leper becomes whole, and Jesus tells him to go to the Temple and offer the necessary sacrifices to prepare for return to society (1:40–44).

The greatest barrier of uncleanness was the religious and racial one between Jews and Gentiles. Jesus himself had very little direct contact with Gentiles in his earthly life. However, the Gospel, written around forty years after his death, does not distinguish between past and future. The evangelist saw Jesus reaching out even to the future in symbolic actions. The story of the Gerasene demoniac and the 2,000 drowned pigs illustrates this (5:1–20). Those who are alert for the hidden humor do not worry about "poor drowned animals." Just as today, someone who says "Down with the pigs," is not necessarily talking about animals.

The story takes on meaning in view of its scriptural background. Pigs were very much the favorite food animals of the Romans and other peoples. The drowning recalls the disaster of the Egyptian armies who sought to follow and slaughter the Israelites as they crossed the Red Sea. Jesus' exorcism of the demoniac signifies his power over the Roman "legion" that is within. The Gospel audience can be assured of future victory despite overwhelming odds. They listen with confidence to Jesus' words as he sends them (as cured like the demoniac), "Go home to your friends and tell them how much the Lord has done for you and what mercy he has shown you" (5:19).

Reaching Out to Outcasts and the Marginalized

> As he was walking along, he saw Levi son of Alphaeus sitting at the tax booth, and he said to him, "Follow me." And he got up and followed him. And as he sat at dinner in Levi's house, many tax collectors and sinners were also sitting with Jesus and his disciples—for there were many who followed him. (2:14–15)

Here, Jesus extends discipleship and friendship to someone who externally was the least likely candidate. As employed by Roman authority, Levi had frequent contact with the Gentiles, rendering him suspect of uncleanness. His cooperation with foreign rulers was in the most sensitive area of tax collecting, in which oppression was especially evident and in which dishonesty often prevailed. Yet, Jesus took Levi as an equal and friend at table fellowship along with many of Levi's colleagues. Immediately, this act occasioned sharp criticism of the scribes (professional writers and teachers) from among the Pharisees. These latter devoted themselves to perfect observance of the law and priestly spirituality, although they were laymen. They asked Jesus' disciples why their master ate with "tax collectors and sinners." Eating together was a sign of close fellowship and association, in this case with people who might very well be not only unclean but also dishonest. Jesus replied to them, "Those who are well have no need of a physician, but those who are sick; I have come to call not the righteous but sinners" (2:17).

Creating Table Fellowship with Outsiders—Bread for the World

There is a whole major section in Mark devoted to the meaning of bread for the Gospel audience. Within this, there are two multiplications, one for 5,000, the other for 4,000 people.[16] The atmosphere of a hungry multitude in a deserted locality with no means to find food reminds the Gospel readers of Israel in the desert in Exodus 16. There, we noted the focus on God's word in the manner of gathering the bread. Obedience to this word initiated a great miracle of equal distribution and sharing. Likewise, in Jesus' loaves story, the production of the bread is not the central element. The focus is on Jesus' word. In response to him, some people do offer what they had, a mere five pancake-shaped loaves they had kept in their traveling belts. With these Jesus begins (as in the Exodus story) a great miracle of sharing and distribution. The story is even much more important than the mysterious origin of the bread.

However, Mark's Gentile Gospel audience has a problem. They cannot identify entirely with the Jewish people who received that bread. Before they can do that, they must be able to know that the barriers to table fellowship with many Jewish Christians have been removed. Among these barriers were regulations about the types of food that were eaten and how they were prepared according to biblical laws. Chapter 7 deals with these difficulties, opening with the observations of scribes and Pharisees and their question to Jesus, "Why do your disciples not live according to the tradition of the elders, but eat with defiled hands?" (7:5). This defilement is not a matter of dirt but of contact with Gentiles that would make them unclean.

Jesus answers with a principle that is above all laws: "Listen to me, all of you, and understand: there is nothing outside a person that by going in can defile, but the things that come out are what defile" (7:14–15). The disciples have great difficulty with this principle in view of all the customs and biblical laws involved. So, they ask Jesus again on this matter—but privately in the house. Jesus repeats his answer but with more specifics added: "It (the food) enters not the heart but the stomach, and goes out into the sewer." Then, the writer himself adds the revolutionary statement, *"Thus he declared all foods clean"* (7:19).

Once this declaration is made, the stage is set for a Gentile woman to appear on the scene and ask for her daughter (and home) to be cured of an "unclean spirit"—a demon whose presence had that effect. Jesus answered, "Let the children be fed first, for it is not fair to take the children's food and throw it to the dogs" (7:27). (*Dogs* was an epithet for the Gentiles.) This statement summarized a feeling of superiority in God's blessings for Israel. The woman replied humbly that even dogs eat the children's crumbs falling from the table. Jesus is pleased with this reply and heals her daughter *from a distance*. This is the only healing of a Gentile in Mark—but at a distance. The Gentile audience in another generation would understand Jesus' words as crossing time and space to reach them with assurance that Jesus' bread is equally theirs also.

With this in mind, the second multiplication story is told with hints that Jesus' one bread is to be multiplied and shared for the Gentiles as well. Thus, it is Jesus himself (at the woman's request) who takes the initiative with personal compassion, not the disciples as in the first multiplication. The number of loaves and baskets are *seven,* a number signifying completeness and universality (Gen 2:2). The people number *four thousand,* as in the *four* winds from the ends of the Earth (Mark 13:27). In the first story, Jesus took the loaves and *blessed* according to Jewish custom (6:41). In the second account, Jesus took the loaves and *gave thanks (eucharistēsas)*. This would be more in accord with Greek usage, whereas the Greek translation of the *blessing, eulogēsen,* in 6:41 reflects its Jewish background.

Compassionate Justice in the Household

Marriage and Women's Rights

An *oikodespotēs* or *paterfamilias* was the powerful patriarchal ruler of the household in the Jewish and Roman world. However, one is mentioned by name only once in Mark 14:14 as the owner of the house where Jesus celebrates his last supper. There will be more about him in Matthew's Gospel in which our discussion will be much broader. However, the position of the father as household head comes up in Mark's shorter collection on household ethics in 10:1–31. First, on marriage:

> Some Pharisees came, and to test him they asked, "Is it lawful for a man to divorce his wife?" He answered them, "What did Moses command you?" They said, "Moses allowed a man to write a certificate of dismissal and to divorce her." But Jesus said to them, "Because of your hardness of heart he wrote this commandment for you. But from the beginning of creation, 'God made them male and female. For this reason a man shall leave his father and mother and be joined to his wife, and the two shall become one flesh.' So they are no longer two, but one flesh. Therefore what God has joined together, let no one separate." (10:2–9)

This "command" of Moses is found in Deuteronomy 24:1, which allows a husband to give his wife a written notice of dismissal and send her away. Jesus' answer appeals to the first creation account where God creates man and woman equally to the divine image (1:27). Here, we have the only reference in the Bible, outside Genesis, to this text in the first creation[17] account (1:1–2:4). All other references to woman's creation build on the second account beginning in 2:4. There, she is formed from the first man and dependent on him. In this account, the man gives names to all the animals and to the woman also (Gen 2:19–23). He calls her "woman" because she has the same flesh and was taken out of "man" (2:23). Then, the text follows, "Therefore a man leaves his father and his mother and clings to his wife, and they become one flesh" (2:24).

However, in Jesus' answer there is a remarkable piece of exegesis.[18] This last verse is in the second creation account but is moved to directly follow the first declaration of creation as male and female equally to the divine image (Gen 1:27). Thus, the personal covenant of man and woman follows from God's creation in making them both according to the divine image, not from the woman's similarity and origin from the man! Therefore, there can be no patriarchal right of a man to dismiss his wife as an unequal subordinate.

There is also a second important difference in Mark. Jesus says to his disciples: "Whoever divorces his wife and marries another commits adultery against her; and if she divorces her husband and marries another, she commits adultery" (10:11–12). Only Mark's version in comparison with Matthew and Luke gives the woman also the possibility of divorcing her husband.

Father and Children

Children were in the lowest household rung of hierarchy, just above slaves. They had no one to whom they could go for defense of their rights. So, it is not surprising that the male disciples exercise their patriarchal "rights" to chase away and rebuke women who were bringing their children to Jesus that he might touch them (with a blessing):

> But when Jesus saw this, he was indignant and said to them,
> "Let the little children come to me; do not stop them; for it is
> to such as these that the kingdom of God belongs. Truly I tell
> you, whoever does not receive the kingdom of God as a little
> child will never enter it." And he took them up in his arms,
> laid his hands on them, and blessed them. (10:14–16)

Jesus completely reverses the position of children from the lowest to the highest rank. This starts in a similar previous passage in 9:33. There, the disciples on a journey had been arguing about which of them was the greatest—meaning the closest to Jesus. The answer is in action and in words:

> He sat down, called the twelve, and said to them, "Whoever
> wants to be first must be last of all and servant of all." Then
> he took a little child and put it among them; and taking it in
> his arms, he said to them, "Whoever welcomes one such child
> in my name welcomes me, and whoever welcomes me wel-
> comes not me but the one who sent me." (9:35–37)

In the above texts, Jesus changes the position of a child from the least, or last, to the greatest. They are models for those who wish to enter the kingdom. In addition, he identifies with them as one who deliberately chooses to be as a child in his service of others. The culmination is his special blessing for them. Jesus gives no one else such a blessing in this Gospel. This action, reminiscent of Jacob's final blessing of his children, hints that they will succeed Jesus in a spiritual way (Gen 48:1—49:28).

The theme of the child, or the least person, prompts Mark to connect other stories or sayings. First, there is the "outsider," someone who was not a disciple, casting out devils in Jesus name; the disciples tried to stop him. Jesus in turn told them not to stop the outsider from doing so (9:38–41). Then, there are those who put a stumbling block, *skandalisē*, or temptation in the way of little ones. They are the worst offenders of all (9:42–48).

Household Possessions

Mark does not have the abundant material on justice and possessions that we will later see in Matthew and Luke. However, he includes in his household instructions questions of sharing possessions, resources, and relationships. This begins with the story of the rich man who wanted Jesus to teach him how to inherit eternal life (10:17–22). Jesus reminded him of the commandments, but he replied that he had kept them since his youth. "Jesus, looking at him, loved him and said, 'You lack one thing; go, sell what you own, and give the money to the poor, and you will have treasure in heaven; then come follow me.' When he heard this, he was shocked and went away grieving, for he had many possessions" (10:21–22).

The above story is not a solitary occasion. Jesus generalizes it for the Gospel audience by saying, "How hard it will be for those who have wealth to enter the kingdom of God" (10:23). As his disciples are taken aback by this statement, Jesus repeats it a second time, "Children, how hard it is to enter the kingdom of God." Then, a third time, "It is easier for a camel to go through the eye of a needle than for someone who is rich to enter the kingdom of God." They were greatly astounded and said to one another, "Then who can be saved?" Jesus looked at them and said, "For mortals it is impossible, but not for God; for God all things are possible." Peter then said to him, "Look, we have left everything and followed you" (10:23–28).

When Peter says, "everything," he refers to Jesus' call by the lake of Galilee. At that time, Peter was part of a profitable fishing corporation with his brother, James, and John, along with hired workers (1:20). To join with Jesus in his missionary journey to preach repentance, "they left their nets and followed him" (1:18).

Jesus' New Family Relationships

Jesus then explains how sharing of wealth and resources can take place. It is motivated by compassion resulting from shared relationships in a new family. He said,

> Truly, I tell you, there is no one who has left house or brothers or sisters or mother or father or children or fields, for my sake and for the sake of the good news, who will not receive a hundredfold now in this age—houses, brothers and sisters, mothers and children, and fields with persecutions—and in the age to come eternal life. (10:28–30)

This is similar to Jesus' earlier response when his own family was concerned that his zeal for preaching kept him so busy he did not have even time to eat (3:20). They sought to restrain him, for people were saying, "He has gone out of his mind" (3:21). Jesus' "mother and brothers" came to a house and summoned him to come out. (Joseph is not mentioned in Mark's Gospel, so "mother and brothers" together represent the patriarchal household authority.) Jesus replied,

> "Who are my mother and my brothers?" And looking at those who sat around him, he said, "Here are my mother and my brothers! Whoever does the will of God is my brother and sister and mother." (3:33–35)

In contrast to the hierarchical household authority ordering him to come out, Jesus makes a deliberate gesture toward his disciples as the new family of equals: "my brother and sister and mother." There is no mention of *father* because there will be no typical household patriarchal head (as in the previous text). Instead, God will be loving Father. Matthew makes this more explicit by writing, "the will of *my Father* in heaven" (12:50).

With the biblical views of sharing possessions and property so that all have sufficient goods, the rich man's unwillingness can be better understood. He could not make that commitment.

Competition to Serve Others Rather Than Rule over Them

At the core of Social Justice and equality is the renunciation of power over other people and situations. The story of James and John is really a continuation and summary of Mark's household instruction. The two brothers came up to Jesus and requested, "Grant us to sit, one at your right hand and one at your left, in your glory." Jesus replied, "You do not know what you are asking" (10:37–38). On the surface, they are asking for positions of power and prestige, along with possessions. Underneath, there seems to be a subtle irony, for later Mark will say that there are two beside Jesus, one on his right and one on his left *on the cross* (15:28).

When the other ten disciples heard about this, they were furious with anger. But Jesus called them together and reminded them that competition for power and control of others was common and typical in the Roman world. However,

> It is not so among you; but whoever wishes to become great among you must be your servant, and whoever wishes to be first among you must be slave of all. For the Son of Man came not to be served but to serve, and to give his life a ransom for many. (10:43–45)

Jesus does not do away with competition but states that it should be for the "lowest" (which are really the highest) places of service of others. Then, Jesus says, "The Son of Man came not to be served but to serve, and to give his life as a ransom for many" (10:45). This final statement about actually giving his own life is not theoretical. It makes the transition to the next section of the

Gospel where he goes ahead to Jerusalem for his ministry of preaching repentance, even though it means risking his life.

The New House of Prayer for All Nations (11:17)

Jesus' cleansing of the Temple is a focal point of the Gospel of Mark. The Jerusalem Temple was the center of Jewish worship at the time of Jesus. It was also the capital seat of Judea. Although Judea was under the Roman governor Pontius Pilate, the Romans left the administration of Jewish law to a council of seventy members under a high priest appointed by Rome.

The Temple itself was a small building where only priests could enter. One half of it was the Holy of Holies, which once contained the sacred Ark of the Covenant in which the stone tablets of the Ten Commandments were kept as a sign of God's presence and power. A heavy veil separated this dark room from the rest of the building. Only once a year on the day of Atonement, *Yom Kippur,* the high priest entered behind the veil to pour the blood of sacrifice to atone for the sins of the people.

The other room contained an altar of incense at which priests entered morning and evening to offer incense and prayer. It had a perpetually burning seven-branch oil stand signifying God's continual presence. There was also a table on which there were always twelve fresh loaves of bread representing the people of Israel. Outside the Temple, the Court of Priests contained the great altar of sacrifice along with bronze lavers for purification. Surrounding this court was the court of Israel for Jewish men, then another court around this for women, and finally another court divided by a low wall, called the court of the Gentiles. Signs on this wall prohibited Gentiles from farther entry under pain of death. Archaeologists have found copies of this inscription. The whole Temple took in an area about 200 yards square.

A modern visitor would have been shocked to enter the Temple area but not someone in ancient times accustomed to animal sacrifices. It was a crowded, noisy, busy area accommodating not only visitors but also hundreds of priests and their assistants to take care of all the many details of sacrifice. There were stalls to keep the numerous bellowing or bleating animals that had to be available for people to buy, if they could not bring their own from distant places. The smell of blood permeated the atmosphere. There were the haggling noise and the clinking of coins of money changers, who were necessary to convert outside coinage to the required coins needed to purchase animals.

These coins were not only necessary for the many required Temple sacrifices and feast days, but also for the many voluntary offerings by people. The main sacrifices were of two kinds: joyful peace offerings for thanksgiving and sacrifices of atonement to obtain forgiveness for sin and avert angry repercussions from the deity. These sacrifices could only be offered at Jerusalem by priests who became so by birth into a designated family of the tribe of Levi. The priests were the necessary mediators to bring favors as well as forgiveness to the people. The priests also administered the Temple area, collecting rents from those who needed space for their work. The Temple rituals not only supported the priests but also were the source of considerable wealth and power.

Mark attaches special importance to the symbolic action of Jesus' entry into and cleansing of the Temple.

> Then they came to Jerusalem. And he entered the temple and began to drive out those who were selling and those who were buying in the temple, and he overturned the tables of the money changers and the seats of those who sold doves; and he would not allow anyone to carry anything through the temple. He was teaching and saying, "Is it not written, '*My house shall be called a house of prayer for all the nations*'? But you have made it a den of robbers." (11:15–17)

Mark's audience already knew that the Temple had been destroyed. They understood Jesus' action as a prophetic sign that he would replace the exclusive Temple animal sacrifices and offerings. His intention was to have "a house of prayer for all the nations." This signified a new inclusive worship that would break down the wall separating Gentiles from Jews and make it a place of worship and forgiveness for the whole world. The text then continues, "And when the chief priest and the scribes heard it, they kept looking for a way to kill him" (11:18). Jesus' act of authority meant that he was taking their place. The Gospel audience would understand that Jesus' death and sacrifice would be the means to replace the Temple sacrifices for forgiveness and access to God.

The Fig Tree and the Temple

Before and after the Temple cleansing, Mark has a literary frame[19] about Jesus' curse of the fig tree in order to further explain the Temple incident and show the power of Jesus' word about the future Temple:

> On the following day, when they came from Bethany, he was hungry. Seeing in the distance a fig tree in leaf, he went to see whether perhaps he would find anything on it. When he came to it, he found nothing but leaves, for it was not the season for figs. He said to it, "May no one ever eat fruit from you again." And his disciples heard it. (11:12–14)

The story is strange to modern ears until understood as the symbolic action of a prophet. The fig tree is the special fruit of this land and represents its leaders. As a prophet, Jesus came to Jerusalem seeking "fruit" from the response of religious leaders to his message of repentance. However, he finds none. Rejection of a prophet's message is rejection of God and results in a barren fruit tree. The incident is just before the cleansing of the Temple and suggests that the Temple will become barren and empty, no longer a vessel for God's action. Instead, Jesus would form a new Temple open to all nations and bearing fruit for everyone.

After the Temple story, the fig tree parable continues:

> In the morning as they passed by, they saw the fig tree withered away to its roots. Then Peter remembered and said to him, "Rabbi, look! The fig tree that you cursed has withered." Jesus answered them, "Have faith in God. Truly I tell you, if you say to this mountain, 'Be taken up and thrown into the sea,' and if you do not doubt in your heart, but believe that what you say will come to pass, it will be done

for you. So I tell you, whatever you ask for in prayer, believe that you have received it, and it will be yours. (11:21–24)

This conclusion first of all illustrates the power of Jesus' word in what happened to the fig tree. It also describes how the impossible task of building such a new Temple could ever be accomplished. Prayer with complete trust in God is an absolute necessity. Jesus will later provide the example of such prayer for his disciples to imitate. The explicit reference to *this mountain* points to the Temple Mountain of Zion, which is the obstacle of the exclusive sacrificial system that must be replaced if there is to be a house of prayer for *all the nations* (11:22).

The verse that follows is closely linked. The Temple sacrifices through the Levitical priesthood were the ordinary way to obtain forgiveness. But in the new dispensation, people will call out directly to God as priests themselves: "Whenever you stand praying, forgive, if you have anything against anyone; so that your Father in heaven may also forgive you your trespasses" (11:25). Here, we have a petition of the Lord's prayer as in Luke and Matthew: Forgive us our debts /sins, as we have forgiven others (Luke 11:4; Matt 6:12). "Your Father in heaven" is parallel to the opening of the Lord's Prayer in Matthew 6:9.

The centrality of the new Temple theme continues in Mark. At Jesus' trial, some stood up and gave false witness against him, saying, "We heard him say, 'I will destroy this temple made with hands, and in three days I will build another, not made with hands'" (14:57–58). The Gospel audience understands that the statement is half true: Jesus did not say he would just destroy the Temple, but that he would create a new Temple not built with hands through his resurrection. Later, while Jesus hangs on the cross, some passersby deride him, saying, "Aha! You who would destroy the temple and build it in three days, save yourself and come down from the cross!" (15:29). They do not know, as the audience does, that Jesus will indeed "come down from the cross" in victory to build this new Temple.

The Final Summary Teaching and Covenant Summary in the Temple Area

The Temple cleansing is part of a whole series of Jesus' final teachings centered in the Temple area. They conclude in 13:1 when Mark writes that Jesus came out of the Temple enclosure and predicted the future destruction of the Temple buildings. Previous to this, Mark brings Jesus' teachings to a close in a triple series linked about the word *scribe* (12:28, 35, 38). First, one of the scribes asks him, "Which commandment is the first of all?" (12:28). Matthew and Luke also have this question, but Mark has the answer in a unique form.

Only Mark has the original solemn form of Deuteronomy 6:4–5, "Hear, O Israel, the LORD is our God, the LORD alone." This oneness seems emphasized because the scribe repeats the same words and adds, "besides him there is no other," from Deuteronomy 4:35, 39; 32:39 and repeated elsewhere in the scriptures. The likely reason for this emphasis is Jesus' statement in the Temple cleansing about a "house of prayer for all the nations" (which would be prayer to one God). Secondly, only Mark has a "double *Shemah*" in the sense of the scribe repeating every word that Jesus had said. Like the other Gospels, love of neighbor is connected to the *Shemah*. This is an ancient midrash linking the *Shemah* with the Leviticus texts regarding love of neighbor in 19:17–19. The linking words are *you shall love* (your neighbor), common to the opening *you shall love* (the Lord your God) of the *Shemah*; also the *heart* in the latter and in the injunction not to hate one's neighbor in the *heart* (Lev 19:17).

The final difference in Mark is the scribe's addition, "This is much more important than all whole burnt offerings and sacrifices"(12:33). This is a fitting conclusion to Jesus' cleansing of the Temple of exclusive animal sacrifices. Worship, praise, and response to God will take place in devotion to one's neighbor "as one's self." This is not just a psychological sense but a biblical view of regarding another as truly "one's self," created to the same divine image (Gen 1:27).

Jesus' reply to the scribe, "You are not far from the kingdom of God" (12:34), tells us how central a part this final summary of the Torah plays in this Gospel.

Prayer and the Decision to Build the House of Prayer for All the Nations

A decision to build a house of prayer for all must begin with Jesus' own prayer and decision. For this purpose, after the Last Supper, he withdrew for prayer to a quiet place called Gethsemane near Jerusalem.

> He took with him Peter and James and John, and began to be distressed and agitated. And he said to them, "I am deeply grieved, even to death; remain here, and keep awake." And going a little farther, he threw himself on the ground and prayed that, if it were possible, the hour might pass from him. He said, "Abba, Father, for you all things are possible; remove this cup from me; yet, not what I want, but what you want." (14:33–36)

When Jesus prayed, "Not what I want, but what you want," he was thinking of his baptismal call to be a prophet preaching the need of repentance in terms of the Social Justice taught by the Hebrew prophets. Repentance meant a decided movement toward equality in land and possessions. Jesus knew he could not omit Jerusalem from the area of his preaching, for the capital city was the center of wealth and power. Yet, he knew that determined opposition there could lead to his death, even that on the cross. "What God wanted" in terms of scripture was a later insight, which the church had after Jesus' death and resurrection, when they felt that Jesus' Spirit was teaching them the meaning of the scriptures.

The Cross and the Completion of the House of Prayer for All the Nations

A sign that Jesus is building this new Temple through divine, not human, hands comes at Jesus' final loud cry on the cross, an indication of confidence and victory: "Then Jesus gave a loud cry and breathed his last" (15:37). This loud cry was Jesus' final call to *Abba* his Father. The immediate effect of it was that "the curtain of the temple was torn in two from top to bottom" (15:38). This rending symbolized the opening of the Holy of Holies so that divine forgiveness would be extended also to the rest of the world. This was "the house of prayer for all the nations" that he had promised at the cleansing of the Temple.

The first indication of this was the conversion of the hardened Roman centurion, "Now when the centurion, who stood facing him, saw that in this way he breathed his last, he said, 'Truly this was God's Son!'" (15:39). This man was a professional, skilled executioner specializing in the most cruel type of execution the world has ever known. Two others were crucified with Jesus, part of the hundreds this man may have supervised. He looked upon each execution as one more victory for Rome, as another salute to the "son of god," a favorite title for Roman emperors. Instead, by way of shocking contrast, the centurion faces a disgraced, humiliated, and powerless criminal and proclaims him instead as son of God.

There is a very likely connection between Jesus' last cry (as to *Abba*) and the emphasis on the *way he breathed his last* that prompted the title "God's Son." In fact, many important ancient Greek manuscripts add that the centurion saw that he (Jesus) "cried out and" breathed his last.

The meaning of the contrast between power and weakness is also brought out by the author in his description of the soldiers' mockery of Jesus:

> And they (the soldiers) clothed him in a purple cloak; and after twisting some thorns into a crown, they put it on him. And they began saluting him, "Hail, King of the Jews!" They struck his head with a reed, spat upon him, and knelt down in homage to him. (15:17–19)

The soldiers were imitating a popular game in which one of them was blindfolded and dressed as the emperor. The others would insult him, slap him, and kneel down in homage. In turn, the victim would try to guess the identity of his tormentor. If that was correct, they had to change places. The title "King of the Jews" was really a title of folly and contrast. Mark's intention is to show that even Roman soldiers would actually later bend their knees in faith and give homage to Jesus as a crucified king.

The whole story of Jesus' death is designed to give the audience confidence that their persecution, and even death, would make possible the conversion of other centurions and thus contribute to Jesus' goal in creating a new "house of prayer for all the nations." This whole process of breaking social and religious barriers would come about through prayer and the dedication of their lives to that purpose.

Women's Leadership Roles in Mark

When the people in Jesus' hometown synagogue describe his family, they do so in typical patriarchal terms. The names of all his brothers are given: James and Joses and Judas and Simon. But regarding his sisters, they only say, "Are not his sisters here with us?" (6:3). However, Mark describes a complete reversal in their roles in the central Gospel events. In fact, the whole Gospel depends on the eyewitness of Mary Magdalene and the other women with her.

All the male disciples of Jesus had previously fled at his arrest (14:50). They were not ready to be arrested and crucified also as followers of a suspected revolutionary. Judas, a trusted apostle, had already betrayed his Master, and Peter had denied under oath that he even knew Jesus at all. In regard to the women, Mark carefully notes that the women were the sole witnesses not only of Jesus' death, but also of the place where he was buried and of the empty tomb. To emphasize this witness, the author keeps repeating the verb *see*. They actually saw him dying on the cross (15:40); they saw where he was laid (15:47); they saw the stone rolled back (16:4); they saw the young man dressed in white garments, who directed them to *see* the place where Jesus had lain (16:5, 6).

The women do not just pop up at the end, but Mark has carefully prepared for them right from the start. Jesus' beginning in Galilee after the arrest of the Baptist is already a shadow of Jesus' death on the *cross.* In *Galilee,* Jesus calls his first disciples Simon and Andrew, James and John with the words "Follow me and I will make you fish for people" (1:17–18). However, the four disciples named never did *follow* Jesus as far as the cross. The three themes—the cross, Galilee, and following—are found in the description of the women at the cross:

> There were also women looking on from a distance; among them were Mary Magdalene, and Mary the mother of James the younger and of Joses, and Salome. These used to follow him and provided for him when he was in Galilee; and there were many other women who had come up with him to Jerusalem. (15:40–41)

Mark is making a link between this account and the first call in Galilee. These women are the only ones who followed Jesus all the way to the cross from Galilee. Thus, they became "fisher women" and made possible the spread of the Gospel to the world.

Another prominent person is the anonymous woman at Bethany, who anointed his head with a precious ointment (14:1–9). She is the first one to really answer the central question of the Gospel about Jesus' true identity: "Who do you say that I am?" (8:29). Peter was able to confess that Jesus was Messiah but refused to make the connection to death and the cross. When Jesus began to teach about the coming suffering of the Son of Man, Peter took him aside and rebuked him. In front of all the disciples, Jesus in turn rebuked Peter and said, "Get behind me Satan! For you are setting your mind not on divine things but on human things" (8:32–33).

The Bethany woman did not make her response with words but by life and actions: Her hands poured ointment on Jesus' head to show he was the anointed one. The ointment represented the total personal gift of all she had. In this way, it was like the gift that Jesus made of his own life. Some of the male disciples complained that the ointment should have been sold and its price given to the poor. They did not understand that a similar response was what Jesus looked for from a disciple, the giving of one's whole life. Jesus defends her action as a personal gift: "She has done what she could; she has anointed my body beforehand for its burial" (14:8).

Then, Jesus made the extraordinary Amen statement: "Truly (Amen) I tell you, wherever the good news is proclaimed in the whole world, what she has done will be told in remembrance of her" (14:9) With these words Jesus announces that her story is to be told all over the world to illustrate what it means to be a true disciple.

There is also a remarkable story of a woman of great daring, trust, and courage who publicly broke every society barrier to approach Jesus for what seemed an impossible cure. She had been suffering from recurrent hemorrhages for more than 12 years. This meant that she was usually afflicted with the heaviest type of uncleanness. It was the type that was "contagious" affecting any person, or even furniture or dishes, she touched. It was impossible for her to marry or have children (Lev 15:19–30). People carefully avoided her wherever she went to avoid contracting the same ritual impurity.

Despite all these barriers, she managed to sneak up behind Jesus in the crowds and touch the hem of his garment. She said to herself, 'If I but touch his clothes I will be made well.' Immediately…she felt in her body that she was healed….Immediately aware that power had gone forth from him, Jesus turned about…and said, 'Who touched my clothes?' The woman could have easily maintained silence. If it were known who it was, everyone would be shocked that she had so deliberately conveyed ritual uncleanness to a great teacher. However, she went to her knees, acknowledged what had happened, and gave public testimony about what had happened before the whole crowd (5:28–33).

Finally, we should recall the foreign woman previously mentioned who challenged Jesus to provide bread in a second multiplication in terms that symbolized a sharing of the one bread with the rest of the world (7:21–30). She is portrayed as the key person in making Jesus "change his mind" in regard to expanding his mission.

Summary

Mark begins with the radical call of the prophets for reform in the path of justice. Jesus and his disciples make this the priority of their preaching and lives. Mark will apply this to breaking down the separating barriers between people. Examples will be the social stigma from sickness, ritual uncleanness, and contacts with the outcasts and marginalized. This last group finally becomes extended to Romans, Greeks, and other Gentiles. The multiplications of the loaves teach a new food language providing for table fellowship and bread for all the world. Teachings on household ethics break down patriarchal domination in regard to marriage, children, and acquisition of wealth. Jesus' cleansing of the Temple symbolizes the effect of his death in creating a new worship that is all-inclusive for all peoples.

6

Matthew: The Gospel of Justice

Introduction

Matthew wrote his Gospel in the late first century, after Mark's Gospel. Mark had previously written during severe Roman persecution, after the destruction of Jerusalem in A.D. 70 during the Jewish War with Rome. For Mark's audience time was short as they awaited Jesus' return even within their own lifetime. Jesus tells them that the best witness is the willingness to suffer and even give one's life if necessary for their beliefs. However, Matthew's Gospel, written some decades afterward, has much less anxiety over persecution. The emphasis is more on Jesus' authoritative words as a guide to daily life. This present focus is due to a different time perspective and the situation of Matthew's audience.

This *time* in Matthew has become extended because they no longer feel that Jesus will return very shortly. This belief emerges in the author's version of some parables. In the parable of the unfaithful slave, this "wicked slave says to himself, 'My master is *delayed*' and he begins to beat his fellow slaves, and eats and drinks with drunkards" (24:48). In the ten bridesmaids' parable, they all went out to meet the bridegroom, but "As the bridegroom was *delayed,* all of them became drowsy and slept" (25:5). In the parable of the Talents, "*After a long time,* the master of those slaves came and settled accounts with them" (25:19). In each case, Jesus advises vigilance and good works. The master will certainly return, but the time is uncertain and catches most people unaware (24:24–44, 50; 25:13).

This emphasis on good works reaches a climax in the great judgment scene in 25:31–46. No one is asked whether they are circumcised or have kept the biblical laws. Nor are there special benefits for Christian charismatics who prophesy, cast out demons, or "do many deeds" (7:22). Instead we have simple examples of reaching out to those in need: food for the hungry, refreshment for the thirsty, visits to the sick or those in prison, hospitality for the homeless and strangers. Why is there such an emphasis on these types of good works?

The Affluent Atmosphere of Matthew's Gospel

The prime reason for a focus on justice[20] and good works is that many of Matthew's audience have settled down in the world and imitated secular values. There were rich households of believers along with an opposite extreme of very poor people. This atmosphere of affluence and its contrasts is reflected in the Gospel itself. Matthew's is sometimes called the "golden Gospel" because of its many descriptions of money, business, and wealth. The author describes many converts as upper-class scribes when Jesus spoke of tax collectors coming to John's Gospel in repentance (21:32). Writing itself was a profession in those days, and the scribe was trained in law, contracts, taxes, real estate, business, government, and diplomacy. They were the religious and secular (both went together) teachers as well. Many held important government positions. In the Gospels, along with the chief priests, they were the leaders of the people. The training and education of a scribe furnished the gateway to success and wealth in the ancient world.

Matthew, as a Gospel writer, was certainly a scribe and perhaps at times a tax collector before his conversion. He may have humorously changed the name of Levi (as in Mark and Luke), the tax collector called by Jesus, to Matthew because it was his profession also (9:9). On the list of apostles, he names himself "Matthew the tax collector" (10:3). Like Levi in the original story, he had many rich friends with whom he shared the good news of his conversion. Only this Gospel has a *scribe* asking Jesus if he can be a follower: "A scribe approached him (Jesus) and said,

'Teacher, I will follow you wherever you go'" (8:19). Jesus had to warn him not to expect the comfort and security that usually went with his profession: "Foxes have holes, and the birds of the air have nests; but the Son of Man has nowhere to lay his head" (8:20). Matthew surely thought of himself in the concluding parable of chapter 13: "Every *scribe* who has been trained for the kingdom of heaven is like the master of a household who brings out of his treasure what is new and what is old" (13:52).

In regard to affluence, Matthew's Gospel is quite distinct from Luke's. For example, Jesus is not born in humble circumstances and visited by poor shepherds. Instead, the Magi visit him in a *house* and share their wealth by bringing expensive gifts of gold, frankincense, and myrrh (2:11). Matching this rich atmosphere is the story of Jesus' burial. A *rich man* provides it. He places Jesus in his own new tomb, which he has designed and built perhaps over many years, for it is *carved out of rock* (27:57–60). A Gospel hero is a woman in a wealthy home who gives all she has saved for an expensive anointing perfume and pours it on Jesus' head. In return, Jesus tells her that the story of what she has done will be told all over the world (26:13). In the Sermon on the Mount, Jesus emphasizes inner detachment from riches more than external divestiture of material goods. He says, "Blessed are the poor *in spirit*" (5:3). However, in Luke's corresponding Sermon, Jesus says, "Blessed are you who are poor" (6:20).

Other Gospel details lend support to calling Matthew the "Golden Gospel." In fact it is the only Gospel that mentions gold. Matthew does this five times, beginning with the regal gift of the Magi. There is a touch of humor in the contrast between Jesus' instructions to the apostles in Mark, Luke, and Matthew. In the first two, they are to take no money or purse or copper coins for their preaching tour (Mark 6:8; Luke 9:3). However, in Matthew, they must not have gold, silver, or copper coins in their belts (10:9). This Gospel actually has more about the different types of money than any other Gospel. Above all, it has the most descriptions of the typical homes of more affluent people. This was the extended patriarchal household that we will now describe.

The Patriarchal Household Under the *Oikodespotēs,* Father and Household Manager

The etymology of the word, from *oikos,* "house," and *despotēs,* "owner, lord, or manager," already has sent its vibrations through the centuries into the dictionary in which a *despot* means a tyrannical ruler. Here, we will refer to the *oikodespotēs* as the "householder" or "household manager."[21] This household was an extended residence consisting of the household master and father, the wife and children, and frequently, relatives, workers, and slaves.

In the Roman world, the translation of *oikodespotēs* was *paterfamilias,* a word that has even lingered in modern dictionaries as "the male head of a household" or "the father of a family." The early Latin version of Matthew carried *paterfamilias* as the usual translation of "householder." Literally, the word meant "father of a family." Wherever Roman authority and power was established in the world, it soon became a familiar word. However, *paterfamilias* was much more than a title. In Roman law, it was a juridic entity for the person who held the *patria potestas* or patriarchal power. This was an exclusive title of family property over wives, children, slaves, and possessions. No other family member could enter into a transaction solely on their own. However, Romans sometimes permitted local regions to keep their own traditional laws.

The Household Manager in Matthew

Matthew mentions the householder seven times (texts below). Because he is familiar with their roles, he supposes that his readers are also. So, we can only obtain limited information on the house manager from these texts. Mark has only one occurrence of the title, significantly when Jesus sends his disciples to find a place to celebrate his last supper (14:12–16). The description is that of a large building with a guest room, "a large room upstairs, furnished and ready"—one that could accommodate the Twelve and other disciples. Luke follows Mark regarding the Last Supper (22:1) and has three other references to the householder in

12:39, 13:25, and 14:21. Interestingly enough, while Mark and Luke describe a room in a large household for the Last Supper, Matthew's Gospel has Jesus take over a house—perhaps as a model for Christian meetings (26:17–19).

Matthew 10:25—"It is enough for the disciple to be like the teacher and the slave like the master. If they have called the master of the house (the *householder*) Beelzebub, how much more will they malign those of his household." Here, the image is that of a large enterprise and many slaves—like that of the devil!

Matthew 13:27 (in the parable of the weeds and the wheat)— "The slaves of the *householder* came and said to him, 'Master, did you not sow good seed in your field? Where then did these weeds come from?'" In this parable, the householder is a large landowner employing slaves to tend his crops and report to him.

Matthew 13:52—"Every scribe who is trained for the kingdom of heaven is like the master of a household (a *householder*) who brings out of his treasure what is new and what is old." Here, we have a large house with a spacious storeroom to provide for many people. The similarity is to a teacher drawing from a storeroom (treasure) old things (the ancient scriptures) and the new (the sayings of Jesus). This image of the scribe is a likely self-description of the author's work in composing the Gospel narrative. There may be a play on the name *Matthew* in the Greek word for "trained or instructed," which is *mathēteutheis*.

Matthew 20:1—"The kingdom of heaven is like a landowner *(householder)* who went out early in the morning to hire laborers to work for him in his vineyard." He even has a manager (verse 8) under him whom he directs to pay the workers at sundown according to biblical law.

Matthew 21:33—"There was a landowner *(householder)* who planted a vineyard, put a fence around it, dug a wine press in it, and built a watchtower. Then he leased it to tenants and went to another country." This time we have an absentee landlord who owns a vineyard and wine press but lets it out to tenants. He is also a slave owner who sends slave after slave to collect his rents, even when they are beaten and badly treated.

Matthew 24:43—"If the owner of the house *(householder)* had known in what part of the night the thief was coming, he would have stayed awake and would not have let his house be broken into."

Matthew 24:45—"Who then is the faithful and wise slave, whom his master has put in charge of his household?" Both of these texts refer to the care and protection that the householder has over those under him. In the second text, there is a household with numerous slaves, and one in charge to watch over it while the master is away. However, when the master's return is delayed, he begins to have parties and beats the slaves under him. This cruel treatment of other slaves was a frequent occurrence.

The Householder and Household Structure in Hellenistic Judaism

The primary tradition of household authority, even in the earlier Greek world, was described by Aristotle.[22] He considered the household as the primary unit of the city or state. Within the household, he defines four areas: 1) husband and wife, 2) father over children, 3) master over slaves, 4) household management, supervision of workers and business. In each of these areas, there is hierarchical control: The husband rules over the wife; the father over the children; the master over the slaves; and the father as manager of the household and business matters.

The Book of Sirach (Ecclesiasticus) was written by a Jerusalem Judean in the second century B.C. The author tries to win admiration for the Hebrew tradition of wisdom and law to encourage readers influenced and tempted by Hellenistic culture and learning. Within his book, we find regulations and advice about the basic Jewish Hellenistic household structure of husbands-wives, father-children, and master-slaves. For example, in regard to wives, the husband should not lightly divorce his spouse but at the same time not continue to entrust himself to her if he cannot love her (7:26). Sirach considers a quiet wife as a virtuous one: "A silent wife is a gift from the Lord, and nothing is so precious as her self-discipline" (26:14). Because of her status under control of the household head, her choices for marriage become limited by her father's will. While children were abused and controlled by physical means, women often suffered more from male verbal abuse and attitudes.

As to children, the author writes, "Do you have children? Discipline them, and make them obedient from their youth. Do you have daughters? Be concerned for their chastity, and do not show yourself too indulgent with them. Give a daughter in marriage and you complete a great task; but give her to a sensible man" (7:23–25). Behind the word *discipline,* there was often the cruel reality of harsh physical punishment. In a later passage, we have the following: "He who loves his son will whip him often so that he may rejoice at the way he turns out" (30:1).

Philo was a Jewish scholar who lived in Alexandria, Egypt, about the time of 30 B.C. to A.D. 40. He represents the best source for Hellenistic Judaism in the period closest to Jesus' lifetime. Philo discusses household structure and duties in two of his books.[23] In his study of the Ten Commandments he includes the whole household under the commandment "Honor your father and mother." For Philo, this involves the relationship of old to young, rulers to subjects, and masters to slaves. The "superior class" consists of parents, elders, benefactors, and masters. The "lower class" includes children, young people, receivers of benefits, subjects, and slaves. In another book, he contrasts the values of the good and wicked. The latter despise "the best things of the world." These include honor to princes, the care of a wife, raising children, a proper relationship with slaves, and house management.

Josephus (from his Roman name, Flavius Josephus) was a Jewish commander in Galilee captured by the Romans early in their war with the Jews around the year 66. After the war, he devoted himself to writing the history of the war and a history of his own people. Toward the end of his life around the year A.D. 100, he wrote a treatise, *Against Apion.* Book Two of this work is a defense of the laws and customs of the Jews in answer to attacks on their character and history by Gentile philosophers and writers. In writing about marriage and children, his concern is to impress his readers with the strictness of Jewish ethics.

In this book, Josephus uses the title *despotēs* when writing about living under the law as under a father or *master* (2.18). While defending Jewish laws of marriage, he presents a picture of well-regulated subordination of wives under their husbands (2.25). He emphasizes wives' obedience and states that husbands have a God-given authority over them. He supports this by a quotation from scripture, "A woman is inferior to her husband in all things." However, this is nowhere to be found in the Hebrew scriptures. Regarding children, he writes that they are brought up in learning and practice of the laws. Parents are to be honored in the first place after God. Ungrateful sons are liable to a death penalty. Young men should respect elders because "God is the eldest of all beings" (2.28).

Household Instructions in the New Testament

In the later New Testament writings, we have adaptations of the typical household instructions found in non-Christian sources. In Colossians, a letter attributed to Paul but unlike his earlier genuine writings, these are brief and hardly distinguishable from non-Christian parallels, except for mention of "in the Lord."

> Wives, be subject to your husbands, as is fitting in the Lord. Husbands, love your wives and never treat them harshly. Children, obey your parents in everything, for this is your acceptable duty in the Lord. Fathers, do not provoke your children, or they may lose heart. Slaves, obey your earthly masters in everything, not only while being watched and in order to please them, but wholeheartedly, fearing the Lord. (3:18–22)

The letter to the Ephesians expands and further Christianizes the instructions in Colossians. The picture is that of a Christian household hierarchy (6:1–5). The First Letter of Peter encourages a tightly controlled household structure. In regard to slaves, the author tells them to accept their beatings patiently. Thus, he brings in a new motivation based on the value of suffering unjustly and imitating Christ who suffered unjustly on the cross. In regard to wives, this letter has a long section encouraging wives to "accept the authority" of their husbands (3:1–6). Women are advised to dress simply and modestly in imitation of Sarah, who called her husband "lord" like other women through history who have accepted the authority of their husbands. Only two lines are addressed to husbands: "Husbands, in the same way, show consideration for your wives in your life together, paying honor to the woman as the weaker sex" (3:7). This description of women as "the weaker sex" has come down for 2,000 years and even has an unfortunate place in modern dictionaries.

The strongest descriptions of a rigid patriarchal household are found in the letters to Timothy and Titus. They open with a description of proper order in the liturgy. The author instructs that men should pray aloud, lifting up their holy hands (1 Tim 2:8). Women, however are to "learn silence with full submission." They are to dress plainly and with modesty so as not to attract attention. They are never to exercise authority over men or assume the role of teachers (2:8–12). Regarding children, the bishop should be a man who knows how to rule well over his own household, "keeping his children submissive and respectful in every way—for if someone does not know how to manage his own household, how can he take care of God's church?" (3:5). The same should be true of deacons (3:12).

In regard to slaves,

> Let all who are under the yoke of slavery regard their masters as worthy of all honor, so that the name of God and the teaching may not be blasphemed. Those who have believing masters must not be disrespectful to them on the ground that they are members of the church; rather they must serve them all the more, since those who benefit by their service are believers and beloved. (6:1–2)

(It would seem that being a Christian slave requires even harder work than being a non-Christian slave!)

Looking back over all the descriptions of the *oikodespotēs* and his powers over women, children, and slaves, it is easy to see why the *despotēs* part of his name acquired such a bad press over the centuries. In modern languages, *despot* means "someone who exerts harsh control over others." We can also perceive that the title of father or master was one that connoted power and rigid control more than endearment, equality, and intimacy.

Matthew's Gospel Program of Social Justice

For purposes of clarity, we will follow this outline: Introduction: Heavenly Father vs. Earthly "Fathers." 1) The Opening Call of the Baptist and Jesus to Prophetic Justice. 2) Instructions for Subverting the Affluent Patriarchal Household and Changing It to a House of Justice. 3) The Temptations of Jesus and Those of the Matthaean Community. 4)The Sermon on the Mount and Justice. 5) Jesus' Identification with Others and the Roots of the Golden Rule.

Introduction: Heavenly Father vs. Earthly "Fathers"

Here, we have the first principle of Matthew's "upside-down" theology. In Jesus' new family, no one should assume the typical patriarchal household manager/paterfamilias title and honor. Jesus' heavenly Father becomes the community's own Father. They are baptized into him, and his son Jesus, sharing his Spirit (28:19). Jesus describes the role of his and their heavenly Father some 44 times in Matthew. These far surpass anything a human father/head of household would do.

Some examples are the following: He is the supreme model of imitation in the Sermon on the Mount (5:45–48); he rewards those who pray and fast secretly (6:1, 4); the "Our Father" is Jesus' own example of prayer (6:9), covering spiritual and material needs; he is the model for forgiveness, which depends on our forgiveness of one another (6:15, 18); he watches over and protects animals and all nature (6:26; 10:29). He is kinder than all human parents (7:11); following his will is more important than miracles and charismatic gifts (7:21–22). He reveals himself especially to children and little ones (11:25). He reveals Peter's future role in the church (16:17). He waits in heaven to reward those who confess him on Earth (16:27). The angels at his side watch over and care for every human individual. His greatest concern is that no little one shall ever perish (18:14). He has prepared a future kingdom for those who serve the hungry, poor, and needy (25:36 and following). Jesus confidently prays to him in Gethsemane and in his darkest moments.

However, followers must often make the choice of leaving even father or mother. The sons of Zebedee, James and John, leave their father when Jesus calls them by the lake of Galilee (4:22). A disciple who asks to first wait until his father's death is told to let the dead bury the dead (8:21–22). Jesus tells his disciples that anyone who loves father or mother more than him is not worthy of him (10:35–37). However, Jesus promises that anyone who leaves houses or brothers or sisters or father or mother or children or fields will receive a hundredfold and will inherit eternal life (19:29).

Heavenly Father vs. the Roman Emperor/Father

Antioch in Syria has been suggested by scholars as the place of origin of Matthew's Gospel. As one of the largest cities of the Roman Empire, it was a gateway to the East for trade and commerce. Roman power was everywhere evident with a governor in residence and around 15,000 Roman soldiers under his command. A prize title of the Roman emperor was that of *Pater Patriae,* Father of His Country. This title was awarded to Caesar Augustus by the Senate in 2 B.C. and later to most of his successors. As the Roman Empire extended, the emperors considered themselves gods like father Jupiter and fathers of the Roman world.[24] This is also a reason why Matthew emphasizes so much the one heavenly Father as not only kind and good but also as all-powerful.

However, Matthew's Gospel of justice aims to subvert the patriarchal household by a new pattern for a family of Jesus based on justice and characterized by equality and service. The new authority within will be God as heavenly Father, not despotic human authority. Jesus declares, "Call no one your father on earth, for you have one Father—the one in heaven" (23:9).

1) The Opening Call of Jesus and the Baptist to Prophetic Justice

There is a basic literary *inclusio*[25] about justice at the very beginning of Jesus' ministry and at a climax following the Temple cleansing and the chief priests' challenge to his authority. In answer to the Baptist's protest, Jesus' first Gospel words are, "It is fitting to fulfill all righteousness (justice, *dikaiosynē*)" (3:15). In 21:32, Jesus declares that the Baptist came "in the way of righteousness (justice)." In other words, Jesus fulfills the justice path started by the Baptist. To highlight this, only Matthew has Jesus begin his ministry with the identical first words of John: "Repent, for the kingdom of heaven has come near" (3:2). In this way, the theme of justice becomes a framework for the whole Gospel.

Yet, behind the Baptist's proclamation is the authority of God's voice speaking to the prophet Isaiah. This voice introduces John (3:3). Isaiah is the favorite prophet of Matthew who quotes him six times in addition to indirect references. He is also the great Hebrew prophet of justice. The same Greek noun *justice* occurs more than 50 times in his book, more than in all the other prophets put together. Matthew starts his Gospel stating that the Baptist fulfills Isaiah who wrote God's words, "The voice of one crying in the wilderness: 'Prepare the way of the Lord'" (3:3). This "way of the Lord" is a "way of justice" in Isaiah 40:14. These are the identical words of Jesus in describing the work of the Baptist (21:32).

As we noted in Mark, Isaiah's first five chapters contain the basics of the Baptist's preaching (return to justice, washing, forgiveness). Isaiah proclaims the opening of the way of the Lord stating that Zion was once the city of justice (1:21), but now, she has become a harlot. "Wash yourselves; make yourselves clean" (1:16). "Seek justice...defend the orphan, plead for the widow" (1:17). If this happens, even though their sins are as red as scarlet they will become white as snow (1:18). Once this happens, Jerusalem will again become a city of justice (1:26). The prime cause for this injustice is inequality. Resources and land have become concentrated in the hands of a few people: God expected his beloved vineyard to produce *justice* (5:7), but instead, a terrible cry arose from those who lost their land and livelihood through debts and mortgages: Woe to "you who join house to house, who add field to field," taking it from a neighbor (5:8).

While not directly quoted by Matthew, there are writings from other major prophets supporting Isaiah's earlier teaching on Social Justice. These may be seen in chapter 2 on the prophets and Social Justice.

Messianic Fulfillment of the Way of Justice

Matthew gives special attention to Jesus' fulfillment of the Baptist and Isaiah's way of justice. The Baptist in prison had sent his disciples to ask Jesus if he was the one who is to come (11:2–19). In his reply, Jesus quotes part of Isa 61:1–3, "The spirit of the Lord GOD is upon me, because the LORD has anointed me; he has sent me to bring good news to the oppressed,…to proclaim liberty to the captives,…to proclaim the year of the LORD'S favor,…to comfort all who mourn." When part of a scripture section is read, the audience is meant to keep in mind the whole passage. The verb *anointed, echrisen,* links with the Baptist's question about whether Jesus is the Messiah, which means "anointed one." The text in Isaiah is about good news for the landless poor exiles on their return to Israel. In writing in this way, the author uses Jubilee year terminology that announced the release of debts and an acceptable year of the Lord (Lev 25:1–55).

2) Subverting the Affluent Patriarchal Household; Changing It to a House of Justice

In chapters 19 and 20, Matthew presents Jesus as overturning the traditional roles of patriarchal domination in a) husband and wife, b) father and children, c) master and slaves, d) business for unlimited profit. The evangelist makes a clear transition after his community discourse by a literary ending, "When Jesus had finished saying these things" (19:1). He has previously used similar phrases at the end of the Sermon on the Mount (7:28) and the Parables Discourse (13:53). Then, he describes Jesus' revolutionary attack on the basic *oikodespotēs/paterfamilias* power structure and motifs.

a) Husband and Wife (19:1–12)

See the discussion on this passage in chapter 4 as well as the discussion of women's leadership in texts that are in both Matthew and Mark.

b) Father and Children (19:13–15)

Here, we witness a conflict scene as women bring their little children to Jesus for him to lay his hands on them and pray (19:13–15). Again, there is a similar passage in Mark 10:13–16, which we discussed in the last chapter. In other parts of Matthew, more than in Mark, Jesus demonstrates that children have the highest place in his family and community. This is especially true in the discipleship discourse in chapter 18. This chapter could even be called the "children's discourse." Jesus first asks, "Who is the greatest in the kingdom of heaven?" (18:1). Then, he answers by placing a child in their midst and making a solemn Amen statement:

> Truly (Amen) I tell you, unless you change and become as children, you will never enter the kingdom of heaven. Whoever becomes humble like this child is the greatest in the kingdom of heaven. Whoever welcomes one such child in my name welcomes me. (18:3–5)

Jesus' favorite name for a child was a *mikros,* a little one. The worst sin is to scandalize one of these *little ones* (18:6). They are so precious that only Matthew's Gospel has Jesus' statement about guardian angels: "Take care that you do not despise one of these *little ones;* for I tell you in heaven their angels continually see the face of my Father in heaven (18:11). Jesus welcomes every disciple as a child, not because children are perfect but because they fail so often, yet continue to rise again. They fall dozens of times a day as they struggle to walk; they make ludicrous mistakes as they learn to talk; their runaway emotions cause them to say and do things they soon regret.

In Jesus' statements about children we have an essential part of Matthew's reversal theology. The "least" is the greatest and the so-called greatest must become like the least. The rest of the Gospel continues with examples of this new place for children. Only Matthew's Gospel emphasizes that children must have an equal share of nourishment in both multiplications of the loaves (14:21; 15:38). In prayer, Jesus thanks his Father who has hidden his secrets from the wise and intelligent and revealed them to infants (11:25). When Jesus makes his final entry into Jerusalem, the children in the Temple cry out, "Hosanna to the Son of David" (21:15). The chief priests and custodians of the Temple became angry and said to Jesus, "Do you hear what they are saying?" Jesus answers by quoting Psalm 8, which speaks of children's wonder at God's great deeds: "Have you never read, 'Out of the mouths of infants and nursing babies you have prepared praise for yourself?'" (21:16).

c) The Acquisition of Wealth and the Conduct of Business

The goal of the typical house manager was to become literally "a wealthy man." Along with this and often more important were the prestige and honor this brought him in the community. The next story concerns a typical rich man. He asks Jesus, "What good deed must I do to have eternal life?" (19:16). In comparison to Mark, Matthew has a practical bent already to the question in the literal words, "What *good* (work) must I do?" Jesus answers that he should keep the commandments. Only in Matthew does the youth answer, "Which ones?" This prepares for the answer in Matthew, in which Jesus adds the commandment, "Also, you shall love your neighbor as yourself." The young man replies, "I have kept all these; what do I still lack?" (19:16–20).

Jesus answers, "If you wish to be perfect, go sell your possessions and give to the poor, and you will have treasure in heaven; then come, follow me" (19:21). Jesus' answer shows that the young man has not really kept the command to love his neighbor as himself, for this would have led to equality and *sharing* of possessions. Jesus' answer is a challenge to a new direction in life instead of the goal of acquiring more wealth and possessions. His new goal is to create literally a *commonwealth* by sharing with the poor. This is simply too much for the young man. "When the

146

young man heard this word, he went away grieving, for he had many possessions" (19:22).

To confirm this hard sounding teaching, Jesus addresses his disciples with a solemn Amen statement: "Truly I tell you, it is hard for a rich person to enter the kingdom of heaven." To make it even more forceful, he says, "It is easier for a camel to enter through the eye of a needle than for someone who is rich to enter the kingdom of God." The disciples are astounded at this teaching and ask if anyone at all could possibly be saved given this requirement. Looking directly at them, Jesus replies, "For mortals it is impossible, but with God all things are possible" (19:23–26).

This comment leads to an illustration of the above "possible-impossible" reversal. Peter replies to Jesus, "Look, we have left everything and followed you. What then shall we have?" (19:27). Jesus answers, "Everyone who has left houses or brothers or sisters or father or mother or children or fields for my sake, will receive a *hundredfold,* and will inherit eternal life" (19:29). The word *hundredfold* means "a miraculous reward from God completely beyond human hopes," as in the parable of the seed (13:23). Mark's Gospel spelled this out by distinguishing between present and future: "There is no one who has left house or brothers or sisters or mother or father or children or fields, for my sake and for the sake of the good news, who will not receive a hundredfold now in this age—houses, brothers and sisters, mothers and children, and fields with persecutions—and in the age to come eternal life" (10:29–30).

Thus, Mark's version brings out what is implicit in Matthew—those who make the choice of leaving possessions and household for the Gospel will find new supporting relationships in Jesus' family of brothers and sisters along with a new sharing of material resources. We note that the disciple may find a new family in mothers (as older women) along with brothers and sisters of equal age but no mention of finding a new father. This is because the new father is God as heavenly Father. The Christian family will have no new father in the sense of a controlling master or household manager. Nor will the great father be Jupiter, father of Rome, or the Roman emperors with their title of *Pater Patriae*.

So, Matthew will conclude with his favorite reversal theme: "Many who are first will be last and the last will be first."

The Workers in the Vineyard parable (20:1–16)[26] follows to illustrate how to overturn householder business values: "The kingdom of heaven is like a man, a householder." At a critical time for his vineyard and grape harvest, he must hire a large number of dayworkers to complete the required work in a short time. He is not sure how many men will be needed, so he prudently begins hiring early in the morning with a minimum team, so he can later hire more if needed. After agreeing with them for the usual sufficient wage of a denarius a day, he sent them into his vineyard. As the day progresses, he discovers he needs more workers and goes out to hire them at nine o'clock, noon, and even at five. Those, at this last hour, have only an hour to work before sunset and darkness. The owner made no contract with the later workers but only promised, "I will pay you whatever right (just, *dikaion*)" (20:4).

At sunset, according to biblical law, the landowner instructed his manager to pay the workers, beginning with those who came at five. This gave the earlier workers the opportunity to observe the process and react to it. Also it prepared for the concluding statement and meaning of the parable.

> When those hired about five o'clock came, each of them received the usual daily wage. Now when the first came, they thought they would receive more; but each of them also received the usual daily wage. And when they received it, they grumbled against the landowner, saying, "These last have worked only one hour, and you have made them *equal* to us, who have borne the burden of the day and the scorching heat." (20:9–12)

The household manager replied to one of them in a pleasant manner, "Friend, I am doing you no wrong; did you not agree with me for the usual daily wage?...I choose to give this last the same as I give to you....Are you envious because I am generous?" (literally, "Is your eye evil because I am good?") (20:13–15).

Most interpretation has emphasized the householder's generosity, but if this were true, he should have given more to those who worked so hard for many more hours. Instead, the central matter is that the landowner wants "to do what is *right*" (20:4). This means that regardless of the fact that some workers labored only an hour, they still need a full daily wage to feed, clothe, and care for their families. The complaint, "You have made them *equal* to us," actually expresses what the owner is trying to do—promote true equality in his temporary household family of workers. But, in doing so, at added expense, he is subverting the typical household goal of acquiring more wealth—which would entail cutting costs, especially the salaries of poor workers.

We can see why Matthew repeats his favorite expression as his upside-down theology: "So the last will be first and the first will be last" (20:16).

3) The Temptations of Jesus and Those of the Matthaean Community

Jesus began his ministry with 40 days and 40 nights of prayer and fasting (4:1–2). Only Matthew adds "forty nights" to underline the intensity of Jesus' prayer. This also made it similar to Moses' prayer: He neither ate nor drank during the time he received the covenant and Ten Commandments from God (Exod 34:28). Fasting and prayer gave Jesus the strength to resist the temptations of the devil.

The devil's temptations are also those that face the Gospel audience as they listen to its reading. The first is, "If you are the Son of God, command these stones to become loaves of bread" (Matt 4:3). This insidious temptation is for Jesus to use his special powers to provide bread (and all this signifies in the way of possessions) only for himself. In contrast, the Lord's Prayer petition "Give *us* this day our daily bread" is a community prayer for self-sufficiency based on unlimited trust. Jesus replies to the devil, "One does not live by bread alone, but by every word that comes from the mouth of God" (4:4). These words are a quotation of Deuteronomy 8:3. In chapter 1, we explained that these words refer to the "word" or command of God (Exod 16:16) that must be followed in regard to the bread that God will send to them in the wilderness. God's words of instruction are to gather all the bread each day in such a way that it is equally shared by all despite how much each person was able to gather.

The second temptation, a corollary of the first, is the invitation to seek honor, fame, esteem, and recognition by spectacular deeds. The devil takes Jesus to the pinnacle of the Temple and says, "If you are the Son of God, throw yourself down" (4:6). This amounted to trusting that a stunning display of angels would parachute him gently to the ground amid wide acclaim. Jesus answers sharply, "Do not put the Lord your God to the test" (4:7). This temptation also faces the Sermon audience. Avoidance of display is very important in Matthew. The very opposite of personal honor, respect, and acknowledgment is the theme of the concluding Beatitudes of the Sermon on the Mount: "Blessed are those who are persecuted for righteousness' sake....Blessed are you when people revile you and persecute you and utter all kinds of evil against you falsely on my account" (5:10–11).

The third and last temptation deals with power and control, summing up every possible test by the powers of evil. The devil brings Jesus to the top of a high mountain and offers him the whole Earth if Jesus adores him (in the sense of complete allegiance). Jesus replies forcibly, "Away with you, Satan! for it is written, 'Worship the Lord your God and serve him only'" (4:10). Jesus' reply is a complete avowal of dedication to the Father and his plans.

The audience knows that this dedication will lead him to the cross. There, the devil's last temptation of Christ will echo the words of the first: "If you are the Son of God..." (4:6; 27:40). But, after his triumphant death and resurrection, Jesus will bring his disciples to a mountain, share his authority with them, and give them a mandate to go to the whole earth (28:18–19). As the audience prays, "Deliver us from the evil one" (6:13), they are confident they can go with the presence of Jesus on this mission as the Gospel concludes, "I am with you always, to the end of the age" (28:20).

4) *Justice in the Sermon on the Mount*

Justice is the central theme of the Sermon on the Mount. This is Matthew's introductory summary of Jesus' teachings. The overall pattern began with Jesus' first words at his baptism about the necessity of fulfilling all justice (3:15). The literary frame ended with his declaration after the cleansing of the Temple that the Baptist began the "way of justice" (21:32). These first two references to justice will be completed in the Sermon on the Mount to make a total of seven.[27]

The Introductory Eight Beatitudes and Justice

The Beatitudes (5:3–11) introduce the Sermon on the Mount with the words "Blessed are the poor in spirit, for theirs is the kingdom of heaven." This echoes Jesus' fulfillment of Isaiah 61:1, with its good news for the poor and oppressed returned exiles in their hopes for justice in recovering their land. The second is, "Blessed are they who mourn, for they will be comforted." This goes back to the next verse in Isaiah speaking of God's desire "to comfort all who mourn" (for the loss of their land). The third is, "Blessed are the meek, for they will inherit the earth." The same words are in Psalm 37:11 but are part of the introduction to Isaiah 61 in the words "All your people shall be righteous and inherit the earth forever" (60:21). Thus, the first three Beatitudes center about the land of Earth.

The next Beatitude is, "Blessed are those who hunger and thirst for *justice* for they will be filled." Here, we have the third mention of justice; the fourth Beatitude really summarizes the preceding three about the poor, the land, and possessions. The poor often became poor by losing their lands to rich lenders who foreclosed lands indebted because of the urgent needs of the poor. Matthew focuses on the inner essential attitude of longing and hunger for justice. Those who hunger and thirst will be filled (by God) because the prophets taught that to know God was to know justice. We have seen that Jeremiah addressed the king of Judah in these words:

> Are you a king because you compete in cedar? Did your
> father eat and drink and do justice and righteousness? Then it
> was well with him. He judged the cause of the poor and
> needy; then it was well. Is not this to know me? says the
> LORD. (Jer 22:15–16)

The fifth Beatitude is, "Blessed are the merciful, for they will
receive mercy." The justice and mercy of God go together in the
Hebrew Bible, so Jesus in Matthew unites them also. When Jesus'
hungry disciples are criticized for plucking grain to eat on the Sabbath, he quotes Hosea 6:6, "I desire mercy and not sacrifice"
(12:7). He quotes the same text again when the Pharisees criticize
his eating with tax collectors and sinners (5:13).

The seventh Beatitude reads, "Blessed are the peacemakers,
for they will be called children of God." Those who work for
peace promote the right relationships that characterize justice.
Justice has two arms: equal sharing of possessions and right relationships. The eighth and last Beatitude echoes the first with its
repetition of the kingdom of heaven: "Blessed are those who are
persecuted for righteousness' *(justice's)* sake, for theirs is the kingdom of heaven." This fourth mention of justice is then applied to
those who even lose their good name and reputation in their quest
for what is right: "Blessed are you when people vilify you and persecute you and utter all kinds of evil against you falsely on my
account. Rejoice and be glad, for your reward is great in heaven."

The Beatitudes begin and end on the theme of the kingdom
of heaven. This phrase is found some 44 times in Matthew. Often
it refers to the future kingdom at the end of the world when Christ
returns. The Beatitudes do end with the idea of a future reward:
"Your reward is great in heaven." However, the Sermon on the
Mount is always concerned with the present actions of believers
on Earth who make that future possible.

The Covenant Justice Theme in the Sermon on the Mount

Jesus introduces the Sermon on the Mount with his intention
to fulfill the law and the prophets. He declares, "Do not think that I
have come to abolish the *law or the prophets;* I have not come to

abolish but to fulfill" (5:17–19). This opening leads to a conclusion at the end of the Sermon on the Mount teaching section (7:12) with the same words: "In everything do to others as you would have them do to you; for this is the *law and the prophets*." Here, we note the principle of equality and justice that will dominate the Sermon on the Mount. This equality is so important that only Matthew will repeat that conclusion two other times in his Gospel. He alone adds "You shall love your neighbor as yourself" to the commandments given to the rich young man (19:19). Another occasion is when Jesus was asked what was the greatest commandment of the law. He replies that the greatest is to love God with one's whole heart and soul. Then, he adds, "A second is like it: 'You shall love your neighbor as yourself.' On these two commandments hang all the *law and the prophets*" (22:36–39).

After this law and prophet opener, Jesus specifies it in the area of justice: "I tell you, unless your righteousness *(justice)* exceeds that of the scribes and Pharisees, you will never enter the kingdom of heaven" (5:20). This is the third mention of justice in the Sermon on the Mount and the fifth in the Gospel. It introduces a series of six antitheses of Jesus' own justice as compared to the Law. Each begins with the phrase "You have heard it said…but I say to you." The first is regarding the commandment "You shall not murder." Jesus goes to the roots of the problem: the inner attitude to others as brothers or sisters, mentioned four times. This sets the underlying motif of justice in right relationships to others as to their own family members.

The fifth antithesis (5:27–32) concerns relationships to a woman or wife. It repeats the divorce instruction we have seen in 19:1–9 but adds an interior emphasis on respect—that to look at a woman with lust shows that adultery has already been committed in the heart. This reinforces the breakdown of patriarchal domination over women. The last antithesis (5:43–48) deals with a great contrast to the father-child household-subjection pattern. In place of this contrast, there is imitation of God, the highest idea of Jewish piety. Jesus says, "Be children of your Father in heaven; for he makes his sun rise on the evil and on the good and sends rain on the righteous and on the unrighteous" (5:45). Disciples are called to imitate a Father who distributes his gifts justly and equally to all his children, regardless of their merit and conduct.

The Lord's Prayer and the Quest for Justice

The Lord's Prayer is centrally situated in the Sermon on the Mount between the frame of the sixth and seventh justice keys. The first is, "Beware of practicing your piety *(justice)* before others on order to be seen by them" (6:1). The final and seventh is, "But strive first for the kingdom of God and its righteousness *(his justice)*" (6:33). Within this enclosure, almost half the verses are proper to Matthew. Because they are adjacent to the Lord's Prayer and its themes, they resemble a commentary on the meaning of the Lord's Prayer.

The Lord's Prayer has its own special introduction: "When you are praying, do not heap up empty phrases as the Gentiles, for they think that they will be heard because of their many words. Do not be like them, for your Father knows what you need before you ask him" (6:7–8). This resembles the opening of the prophet Isaiah. There, God insists that multiplying words in prayer is useless without a sincere search for justice for the oppressed, widows, and orphans (Isa 1:15). The Lord's Prayer introductory warning with its contrast to the Gentiles and God's preknowledge of needs also reappears at the end of the justice enclosure: Jesus says, "It is the Gentiles who strive for all these things; and indeed your heavenly Father knows that you need all these things" (6:32). The Lord's Prayer petitions are prayers in action, not information to God about personal needs he knows about already.

The Lord's Prayer Petitions and Justice

Jesus begins by saying, "Pray then in this way" (6:9). The Lord's Prayer is not a formula but a way of prayer that is Jesus' very own and a gift to his disciples. At the same time, it is an authoritative statement. At the beginning of the Sermon on the Mount, Jesus sat down on the mountaintop, like Moses, to teach (5:1). At the end, the crowd was astonished at his words, for he spoke with *authority* (7:29). This authority came from his own inner sources in contrast to that of other teachers, *the scribes.* The early church, in the *Didachē* 8:3, considered the use of the Lord's prayer as arising from a command of Jesus. Matthew looks upon this prayer as Jesus' own prayer. He shows this by taking the exact Greek words, *Father, Your will be done,* and (pray) *that you may not enter into temptation* and making them the repeated prayer of Jesus in Gethsemane (26:39, 41, 42, 44).

Our Father in Heaven

The simple word *our* along with the eight other plural pronouns *(we, us, our)* in the prayer tell us that it is community, not individual, centered. Only here in the four Gospels do we have the title "*our* Father." This family centeredness is also shown by the use of *brother/sister* more than in any other Gospel. Matthew also has Jesus refer to God as "your Father" or "your heavenly Father" 33 times, more than the other three Gospels combined. Twelve of these are in the Sermon on the Mount. They are an invitation to share in Jesus' unique, intimate relationship with God as his Father. Matthew gives special attention to this, citing Jesus' reference to God as "my Father" 13 times, more than Mark and Luke together. We find the most moving example of this in Jesus' prayer at Gethsemane where he calls on his Father again and again in three periods of prayer (26:36–46).

For the Gospel audience, the title assures confidence and certainty. They are children of a Father of unlimited power as well as love. They can trust that if human parents can be so good, "how much more will your Father in heaven give good things to those who ask him" (7:11)! Matthew insists that the community should have no earthly "father" in the sense of a patriarchal master of the household to whom everyone owes obedience. Nor can this title be given to the Roman emperor if he wishes to be honored as the great father, *Pater Patriae.* The title of God as heavenly Father opposes the honorific, power titles of "father." Jesus will later state, "Call no one your father on earth, for you have one Father—the one in heaven" (23:9).

Only Matthew has the word *perfect*—"Be perfect, therefore, as your heavenly Father is perfect" (5:48). The evangelist has the word in only one other place, when Jesus says to the rich young man, "If you wish to be perfect, go sell your possessions,…and you will have treasure in heaven" (19:21). In that text, *perfect* is used in regard to the distribution of possessions. The expression "treasure in heaven" is also found in Matthew's little commentary on the Lord's Prayer, "Store up for yourselves treasures in heaven" (6:20). The community of Qumran near the Dead Sea also called themselves the community of the *perfect,* especially in view of their communal sharing of possessions. They also linked this with their messianic hopes.

Hallowed Be Your Name

There is only one reference to the *name* of the Father in Matthew, but a most significant one in the Gospel conclusion: Jesus commissions his disciples to go and baptize in the *name* of the Father and the Son and the Holy Spirit. As joint children of God with Jesus the Son, believers carry the name and honor of the Father in their actions. This name must be hallowed (literally, *sanctified*) in the sense of being honored and not polluted.

Hallow, or *sanctify,* is almost the same as *glorify.* Jesus compares his disciples to an illuminated house shedding its light upon others so they can witness their good works and give *glory* to their Father in heaven (5:15–16). This explains the triple warning surrounding the Lord's Prayer concerning secrecy—not acting, praying, or fasting in order to be seen and praised by others (6:2–6; 6–18). It also hints that the Lord's Prayer is a private gift given to disciples that is not to be exposed to the outside world in which it might not be respected. While material success is usually number one in the modern world, the recognition of others, honor, and esteem were the most desirable goals in Matthew's time. To renounce them was simply heroic, so the last Beatitudes honor those who are persecuted for justice's sake, slandered, or lose their reputation.

The address *Our Father* has an even broader scope in view of the Gospel's outreach to all the world. The Gospel concludes with

Jesus entrusting his apostles with a mission to all peoples: "Go therefore and make disciples of all nations" (28:19). Then, he says they are to baptize them in the name of the *Father.* This means that the Jewish-born apostles will have the same Father as Gentiles—peoples from every land on Earth—and be able to pray *Our Father* together with them. The introduction to the Sermon on the Mount reflected this universal outreach. The Jewish disciples of Jesus are called to be "the salt of the earth" and the "light of the world." When this happens, people will "see your good works and give glory to your Father in heaven" (5:16). This effect will show up at the last judgment scene when "all the nations are gathered together before the Son of Man" as witnesses.

Your Kingdom Come

In the Sermon on the Mount, *kingdom* is found seven times, almost always in terms of justice manifested through good actions toward others. The first is in the opening Beatitude, "Blessed are the poor in spirit, for theirs is the kingdom of heaven" (5:3). This is a deliberate first choice because Jesus' mission as Messiah, as articulated in his answer to the Baptist, is to bring good news to the poor (11:5). In our discussion of wealth in the extended household, we have seen that the poor will be blessed when they receive an equal share of limited resources.

The second text is, "Blessed are those who are persecuted for righteousness' (justice's) sake, for theirs is the kingdom of heaven" (5:10). This is closely linked to the first because of Jesus' prophetic mission to the poor. This made it necessary for him to go to Jerusalem, like other prophets. There, he would risk his life by confronting the powerful and rich government leaders who controlled the Temple, land, and property. Disciples must be ready to make similarly difficult decisions. The third and fourth kingdom texts (5:19) describe teachers who must also be *doers* if they are to have a part in the kingdom. The fifth Beatitude explicitly links kingdom and justice: "Unless your righteousness (justice) exceeds that of the scribes and Pharisees, you will never enter the kingdom of heaven"

(5:20). This introduces a detailed explanation of justice in terms of Jesus' new view on the commandments in antithesis to Moses.

The sixth text is closely linked to the Lord's Prayer as a closing literary statement on charity, fasting, and possessions: "Strive first for the *kingdom* of God and his righteousness *(justice)*" (6:33). The seventh and final text joins practical good works, the will of the Father, and the kingdom: "Not everyone who says to me 'Lord, Lord' will enter the kingdom of heaven but only the one who does the will of my Father in heaven" (7:21).

The Sermon on the Mount completes the interpretation of this petition by warnings against creating "earthly kingdoms" of power and wealth. The first is that of storing permanent treasures in heaven, not corruptible ones on Earth (6:19–20). Jesus goes to the root of the problem by describing the pursuit of wealth as an addiction: "No one can serve two masters; for a slave will either hate the one and love the other....You cannot serve God and mammon" 16:24. *Mammon,* an Aramaic word for "possessions," often has a bad sense in common usage. Luke refers to "unjust mammon" (16:9, 11). Placed in contrast to God's worship, pursuit of wealth is false worship as to a god. Matthew then has Jesus spell out what this false worship means in terms of excessive worry about food, drink, clothing, and even the length of life itself (6:25–34).

Your Will Be Done

This petition is parallel to and almost the same as that of the kingdom. Luke omits it in his version of the Lord's Prayer (11:2–4). Yet, Matthew considers it important and has it word for word as Jesus' repeated prayer in Gethsemane (26:28, 30). The words affirm his willingness to remain in Jerusalem even though it would lead to his death. Those who repeat this prayer *with him* (26:38, 40) experience its power and fellowship for he said, "Everyone who does the will of my Father in heaven is my brother and sister and mother" (12:50). The Sermon on the Mount insists on this *doing,* using the verb 20 times. The Sermon concludes with the image of a house built on solid rock, those who hear and do, in contrast to a flimsy house of sand, those who hear but not *do* (7:26).

Give Us This Day Our Daily Bread

Once again we have the plural to include everyone, men women, and children. Matthew confirms this by adding "besides women and children" to the number of the 5,000 *men* in 14:21 (cf. 15:36) who received the distribution of loaves from Jesus' miracle. The meaning of *bread* is a central concern of Matthew. Two chapters of the Gospel, 14 and 15, are given over to the two multiplications of loaves and connected episodes. The word *bread* itself is found 21 times in his Gospel. The special bread of Jesus is very much on the evangelist's mind. He describes Jesus' Last Supper distribution in the words very similar to those in the miraculous multiplication loaves of bread (14:19; 26:26).

However, there are signs that this petition has added meaning when understood in the background of one of the greatest miracles in Hebrew history. This was God's provision of manna to Israel in the desert of Sinai. God said to Moses, "I am going to rain bread from heaven for you, and each day the people shall go out and gather enough for that day. In that way I will test them, whether they will follow my instruction or not" (Exod 16:4). This testing and instruction are a central issue in the story. When the "bread" appeared in the morning, God commanded them to gather as much as each person needed, an omer to a person. Some people gathered more (the younger and stronger); others gathered less (the elderly and infirm). However, when the bread was distributed at the end of the day, each person had as much as they needed. The story of this "miracle of distribution" was told over and over through the centuries, sometimes as the greatest miracle of all. St. Paul was very familiar with it and pointed to it as an example for his ecumenical collection. He stated twice that there should be *equality* in the distribution of God's gifts (2 Cor 8:14–15).

However, in the Exodus story, some people failed the test of following God's instructions (16:4). Moses had told them not to hoard bread by keeping some for the next day (16:19). But some people mistrusted and kept bread overnight; in the morning it was foul and wormy. The Lord then said to Moses, "How long will you refuse to keep my commandments and instructions?" (16:28). The story contains two lessons that appear carried over into the Lord's Prayer: that God wishes to provide what is needed—bread for each day, not storage for the future—and that God's gift of bread (which can have a broad range of meaning) is meant to be shared equally by all. In saying this, we are not eliminating the eucharistic sense but underlining a present, often neglected, meaning. The word *daily, epiousion,* has caused difficulty to translators because of the rarity of its occurrence outside the Bible. Today, scholars lean toward the meaning of "daily," or "necessary," bread.

And Forgive Us Our Debts as We Also Have Forgiven Our Debtors

The translation "have forgiven" corresponds to the usage of the Greek perfect tense, *aphēkamen.* Luke has the present tense, "forgive us our sins, for we ourselves forgive everyone indebted to us" (11:4). The use of the words *debts* and *debtors* raises questions because *debts* is only used in regard to business matters both in Greek and Aramaic. Luke has *sins* instead of *debts* toward God but *debts* in regard to people. This lends support to the theory that it includes financial transactions. The second century Christian document, the *Didachē,* also has the wording, "Forgive us our debts as we forgive our debtors" (using the present Greek tense instead of the perfect in Matthew).

There are good reasons to maintain that Matthew intends this forgiveness of debts to include actual financial remission. The Gospel author knows the Torah very well, and has quoted Jesus saying that "not one letter, not one stroke of a letter will pass away from the law until all is accomplished" (5:18). Not only that, the author also models his own Gospel on the Book of Deuteronomy.[28] Above all, Deuteronomy 15:1–11 on the seventh year remission of debts contains the most lofty contribution to the elimination of poverty in the entire Hebrew Bible. Matthew could not have sidestepped this in any way. He wrote that Jesus warned against legal stratagems that prevent, for example, justice and support for one's parents (15:1–9). We have already pointed out in Mark the attempts that were made to circumvent Deuteronomy 15 in the practice of *prosbol*. These would surely have been condemned by Jesus in the same way. Likewise, Jesus could not have said that he fulfilled the law and prophets (5:17) or that his disciples' justice "should exceed that of the scribes and Pharisees" (5:20) while ignoring Deuteronomy 15. We have seen in chapter 4 that the Qumran community was very careful to observe this law.

Instead, Matthew has taken the text of Deuteronomy 15 and made it a permanent matter instead of one that occurred every seven years. Later, Matthew has Jesus tell Peter that there are no bounds to forgiveness of offenses. Peter thought he was generous by asking, "As many as seven times?" Jesus replies, "Not seven times, but I tell you seventy-seven (or seventy times seven) times" (18:21–22). This extension of Deuteronomy 15 is supported by Matthew's use of the same terminology as the Greek Old Testament translation of the Deuteronomy text. The Greek verb, *forgive, aphes,* is the same as that used in the Greek version of Deuteronomy 15:2. Likewise, the words *debts* and *debtors* in the Lord's Prayer derive from the same verb *opheilō* in Deuteronomy 15:2. In fact, the only places in the Bible in which those two verbs occur together is in the corresponding texts of Matthew and Deuteronomy. In addition, both Deuteronomy 15:7–8 and Matthew 5:42 encourage believers to make loans freely, despite the fact that they may not be repaid: "Give to everyone who begs from you, and do not refuse (literally, turn aside) anyone who wants to borrow from you" (Matt 5:42). Here again, both Deuteronomy and Matthew use the same Greek roots for *turn aside* and *borrow.*

Later in the Gospel, Matthew has Jesus' parable of the unforgiving slave (18:23–35) which brings out the strong connection between sin and debt forgiveness. In the parable, a king has a slave who owes him 10,000 talents. This is a hyperbolic sum so large it could not be repaid in many lifetimes. Yet, the king, after the slave's plea for mercy, forgave him all the debt. This symbolizes God's unlimited pardon and forgiveness. However, the slave goes out and meets a companion who owed him 100 denarii. This was a considerable sum, but nothing in comparison to the debt that was just forgiven him. In anger, he throttled the debtor and demanded immediate repayment. His companion fell on his knees and asked for mercy in the same words previously addressed to the king: "Have patience with me, and I will repay you." In contrast to the king, the slave refused and had his fellow slave thrown into prison until the debt was paid.

The king heard about this, called the slave, and said to him, "Should you not have mercy on your fellow slave, as I had mercy on you?" Then, in anger, the king had the slave receive the same punishment the latter had planned for his companion. In summary, Jesus then says, "So my heavenly Father will also do to every one of you if you do not forgive your brother from your heart." The parable conclusion shows that sin can be the failure to forgive a debt. Debts and sin go together, not only in regard to human slavery but also the economic slavery of other human beings. Control of others through debts and mortgages was an essential part of the patriarchal system of control. It was the great sin of the Greco-Roman world of which the extended household was the primary unit of a vast ruling hierarchy. In this parable, Matthew uses the same Greek debt terminology as in the Lord's Prayer (6:12), "Forgive us our debts."

And Lead Us Not into Temptation, but Deliver Us from Evil (or the Evil One)

The Greek noun for *temptation* is only found elsewhere in Matthew during Jesus' agony in the garden. In that setting, it provides an understanding of this verse. Jesus asks his disciples to join him as he prays to his Father for strength to go ahead. But, after an hour of prayer, he wakes Peter and the sleeping disciples and tells them, "Pray that you may not come into the time of trial." Then, he gives the reason, "The spirit indeed is willing but the flesh is weak" (26:41). The "flesh" is weak human nature despite the good intentions of the "willing spirit." This is especially true of situations that demand great risk, even of one's life. Jesus addressed Peter as an example. Later, he would deny three times that he even knew Jesus (26:69–75).

The petition illustrates the teaching of the Sermon on the Mount. The power and attraction of evil, especially of money and wealth, is so great that it amounts to a false god, or Satan in opposition to God. So, Jesus calls for a definite choice: "No one can serve two masters....you cannot serve God and mammon" (wealth) (6:24). Service of God, as in the first commandment, must be all-absorbing. This first commandment is the source of the central repeated prayer of Israel, called the *Shemah,* after its first two words, "Hear (O Israel)." Then, it continues, "You shall love the Lord your God with all your heart and with all your soul and with all your mind" (22:37; Deut 6:4–5).

To maintain this complete dedication, Jesus emphasizes intensive prayer. He uses an unusual triple image that is repeated twice. In Greek, the verb is the present imperative used for continued action: "Keep on asking and it will be given you (by God); keep on searching and you will find; keep on knocking and the door will be opened to you." Then, Jesus repeats this in another form to emphasize its certainty: "For everyone who asks receives, and everyone who searches finds, and for every one who knocks, a door will be opened" (7:7–8).

Matthew's Commentary on the Lord's Prayer

The Lord's Prayer is in its own special enclosure formed by the mention of *justice* at the beginning (6:1), where the text reads literally, "do your justice," and at the end (6:33) with the text "Strive for the kingdom of God and his righteousness (justice)." Within the enclosure, we find much material only in Matthew that is assembled in what resembles a little commentary on the Lord's Prayer. The first collection is about works of charity:

> So whenever you give alms, do not sound a trumpet before you, as the hypocrites do in the synagogues and in the streets, so that they may be praised by others. Truly I tell you, they have received their reward. But when you give alms, do not let your left hand know what your right hand is doing, so that

your alms may be done in secret; and your Father who sees in secret will reward you. (6:2–4)

The instruction on prayer that follows (6:5–6) uses the same or similar wording on secrecy, types of rewards, and a Father who sees in secret. This attitude is so important that it is repeated a third time with regard to fasting (6:17). The exact words, "Your Father who sees in secret," occurs three times, with the word *secret* found an unusual six times. These words are used to focus on the importance of the petition, "Hallowed be your name," and counter the human tendency to hallow or glorify one's own name through "good publicity." In regard to charity, the secrecy injunction highlights the true nature of sharing. Only God can really know whether it is true justice.

Immediately following the Lord's Prayer, there is a short commentary, "For if you forgive others their trespasses (sins, offenses), your heavenly Father will also forgive you; but if you do not forgive others, neither will your Father forgive your trespasses" (6:14). This interpretation provides a wider meaning to "Forgive us our debts" that is not limited to monetary matters. It is also parallel to the parable ending in 18:35, "So my heavenly Father will also do to every one of you, if you do not forgive your brother or sister from your heart."

The instruction on fasting (6:16–18) recalls that it should be a *hunger and thirst for justice* as in the fourth Beatitude (5:6). As such it is linked to the prophetic teaching on true fasting and justice in Isaiah 58:1–12. There, the fast that God chooses is one that looses the bonds of injustice and makes it possible to share bread with the hungry, take care of the homeless poor, and clothe the naked. This Isaian description of ministry to the hungry, naked, and homeless is similar to that of the *just* in Matthew's last judgment scene (25:37).

Following the fasting instruction, the little commentary moves to another area of threefold evil through the goal of constantly increasing wealth: 1) "Do not store up for yourselves treasures on earth, where moth and rust consume and where thieves break in and steal, but store up for yourselves treasures in heaven" (6:19–20). Here, the *evil* is symbolized by the rotting and rusting of earthly goods. Later on in the Gospel, treasures in heaven will be the reward of the rich young man if he shares his possessions with the poor (19:21). 2) The evil intention: "For where your treasure is, there your heart will also be" (6:21). This is reinforced by the simile of the eye as intention that makes the whole body either full of light or darkness. Literally, this reads in Greek, "If your eye is evil, *poneros,* your whole body will be in darkness" (6:22). The same Greek word for evil is found in the Lord's Prayer petition, "Deliver us from evil."

Matthew then goes to the root of the problem with Jesus' statement about the pursuit of wealth as an addiction: "No one can serve two masters; for a slave will either hate the one and love the other....You cannot serve God and mammon" (6:24). Luke refers to unjust mammon (16:9,11). The power of that statement has made it linger 2,000 years so that the word *mammon* still finds a place in an English dictionary.

The above three instructions on treasures, a sound eye, and serving two masters are connected to the petition about delivery from temptation and evil. The use of the same word, *evil, poneros,* we already saw as one link. The mammon as evil is another. In addition, the parable of the sower regards riches as a *snare* that chokes the seed of the word so that it yields nothing (13:22).

The next teaching on *worry* also has special ties to the Lord's Prayer. The introduction to the Lord's Prayer stated that the disciples should not be like the *Gentiles* in prayer for "your Father knows what you need before you ask him" (6:8). The end of the "worry" section closes with a warning that the Gentiles strive for all these things, but "Your heavenly Father knows that you need all these things" (6:32). The petition "Give us this day our daily bread" is the main subject of this commentary. Jesus says, "Do not worry about your life, what you will *eat* (and *what you will drink* in some mss.) or about your body, what you shall wear. Is not life more than food, and the body more than the clothing?" (6:25).

Life itself is a gift from God, the source of life. We already noted that the bread petition appears inspired by God's gift of manna to Israel in the desert in Exodus 16. Here, the teaching goes further. God stressed that the bread was to be gathered *each day*, without worry for tomorrow. Those who disobeyed and hoarded for *tomorrow* found it already spoiled and rotten. Living for *today* is the theme of this instruction instead of overconcern for the future: "If God so clothes the grass of the field, which is alive *today* and *tomorrow* is thrown in the oven, will he not much more clothe you—you of little faith?" (6:30). So, the teaching is summarized in the last line, "Do not worry about *tomorrow*, for tomorrow will bring worries of its own. Today's trouble is enough for today" (6:34). The repetitions of *today* and *tomorrow* belong to the techniques of oral preaching in order to impress a truth and make it easier to memorize.

5) *Just Relationships to Others and to God (7:1–12)*

"Do not judge that you may not be judged....Why do you see the speck in your neighbor's eye but do not notice the log in your own eye?" (7:1–3). The tendency after listening to the Sermon on the Mount is to focus on someone else that Jesus surely had in mind. This is avoidance of self-judgment and responsibility, which means that God must do it for us in ways that we would like to avoid. Likewise, it is not regarding a neighbor as an equal but taking on a superior attitude, as if that of God. The true attitude should be that of a humble child, continually asking God for our needs, above all for forgiveness. Along with this, the child should have complete confidence in the heavenly Father as greater than any human parent. Even with their human limitations, parents would hardly refuse any good gift to their children (7:11).

The Sermon on the Mount's Surprising and Simple Teaching Summary

Jesus started off the Sermon with the challenge that he had come to fulfill the law and the prophets (5:17). Surely an advanced degree would be necessary to know all that the law and prophets required and then heroic efforts would be needed to fulfill these demands. Instead Jesus declares, "In everything do to others as you would have them do to you; for this is the *law and the prophets*" (7:12). With these words, Jesus concludes the teaching section of the Sermon on the Mount.

This matter of equality is so important for Matthew that he repeats it in two other places in his Gospel. He alone adds the commandment "You shall love your neighbor as yourself" to the commandments given to the rich young man (19:19). Also, on being asked which is the greatest commandment of the law, Jesus replies that the first and greatest is to love God with one's whole heart and soul. Then, he says, "A second is like it: 'You shall love your neighbor as yourself.' On these two commandments hang all the law and the prophets" (22:39–40). This triple affirmation of the Golden Rule tells the audience that it is a central key to understanding other important themes in Matthew that flow from it.

6) *Jesus' Identification with Others as the Root of the Golden Rule*

Servant of the Lord Identification in the Healing Miracles

After the cure of Peter's mother-in-law, Matthew adds a summary of Jesus' healing ministry followed by a scriptural reference to Isaiah's Servant of the Lord that we discussed in chapter 2:

> That evening they brought to him many who were possessed with demons; and he cast out the spirits with a word, and cured all who were sick. This was to fulfill what had been spoken through the prophet Isaiah, "He took our infirmities and bore our diseases." (8:16–17)

From Isaiah 53:4, the above text in this context describes Jesus as the Servant of the Lord who compassionately identifies with his people and takes upon himself their burdens. This will be confirmed and amplified in a later summary. In Matthew's Sabbath stories, Jesus is motivated by compassion. In the first of these, the disciples were hungry and plucking heads of grain as they walked through the fields. The Pharisees complain to Jesus, "Look, your disciples are doing what is not lawful to do on the sabbath" (12:2). Jesus replies by recalling how King David gave precedence to mercy in allowing his soldiers to even eat the holy special loaves of presence within the Temple (1 Sam 21:1–6). Then, Jesus said, "I tell you, something greater than the temple is here. But if you had known what this means, 'I desire mercy and not sacrifice,' you would not have condemned the guiltless" (12:6–7; Hos 6:6).

In the second story, Jesus heals a man on the Sabbath, justifying himself by noting that compassion prompts people to help a trapped sheep on the Sabbath and saying, "How much more valuable is a human being than a sheep?" (12:12). Jesus again quotes the prophet Hosea speaking in the name of God, "I desire steadfast love and not sacrifice" (Hos 6:6). After this Matthew notes, "The Pharisees went out and conspired against him, how to destroy him" (12:14). The fact that Jesus is risking his life by making mercy a priority over every law prompts a second reference to the Servant of the Lord.

> When Jesus became aware of this, he departed. Many crowds followed him, and he cured all of them, and he ordered them not to make him known. This was to fulfill what had been spoken through the prophet Isaiah: "Here is my servant, whom I have chosen, my beloved, with whom my soul is well pleased. I will put my Spirit upon him, and he will proclaim justice to the Gentiles. He will not wrangle or cry aloud, nor will anyone hear his voice in the streets. He will not break a bruised reed or quench a smoldering wick until he brings justice to victory. And in his name the Gentiles will hope." (12:15–21; Isaiah 42:1–4)

Mercy to the Outcast and Marginalized

Matthew continues his theme of merciful identification in other areas. Both Mark and Luke relate the story of Jesus' call of the unpopular tax collector Levi (2:14 and 5:29–32). Matthew has obviously the same story but with his own name inserted: "As Jesus was walking along, he saw a man called *Matthew* sitting at the tax booth; and he said to him, 'Follow me.' And he got up and followed him" (9:9). Is this the author's way of identifying with the tax collector and inviting the Gospel audience to do so also? When Jesus then had dinner with tax collectors and sinners, the Pharisees objected, because these people were obviously unclean due to their occupation or contact with Gentiles. Jesus replies (as in Mark and Luke), "Those who are well have no need of a physician but those who are sick" (9:12). However, only Matthew adds the text from Hosea 6:6, after Jesus says, "Go out and learn what this means: 'I desire mercy and not sacrifice'" (9:13).

The theme of welcome for the marginalized reaches a high point during Jesus' symbolic cleansing of the Temple. At that time, "The blind and the lame came to him in the temple, and he cured them" (21:14). These were people considered unclean because of handicaps mentioned specifically in Leviticus 21:16–21. Jesus' action shows that the "house of prayer" (Matthew does not have "all the nations" as in Mark) will be a place where the marginalized and outcasts will be welcomed.

Jesus' Final Teaching on Identification in the Judgment Scene

Jesus' final teachings before the events leading to his passion and death are found in Matthew's chapters 24 and 25. Central to these is a final judgment scene in which all the nations are gathered together before Jesus, the Son of Man. He separates the people into two parts, the sheep on his right and the goats on his left. Then, he says to those on his right hand:

> Then the king will say to those at his right hand, "Come, you that are blessed by my Father, inherit the kingdom prepared for you from the foundation of the world; for I was hungry and you gave me food, I was thirsty and you gave me something to drink, I was a stranger and you welcomed me, I was naked and you gave me clothing, I was sick and you took care of me, I was in prison and you visited me." (25:34–36)

The just are surprised that the judgment seems already accomplished and ask, "When was it that we saw you hungry and gave you food, or thirsty and gave you something to drink?" (25:37), repeating all that Jesus has said to them. This repetition seems unnecessary to modern ears, but it is Matthew's way in oral teaching to show how important something is by presenting again and again. In all, there will be four repetitions as those on the left side hear the same words of Jesus in a negative sense and reply in like manner. The king responds to each group by a solemn "Amen" statement, first to the just, "Truly (Amen) I tell you, just as you did it to one of the least of these who are members of my family (literally, "my brothers"), you did it to me" (25:40). Then, to those on the left hand, "Truly (Amen) I tell you, as long as you did not do it to one of the least of these, you did not do it to me" (25:45).

The scene above is really a final practical summary of Jesus' triple presentation of love of neighbor (5:12; 19:19; 22:38–39) as the fulfillment of the law and the prophets. In the last of these, 22:38–39, love of neighbor is connected with love of God in the *Shemah*. This is because identification with Jesus in love of neighbor is really imitation and love of God. All through the Gospel of Matthew, from Jesus' baptism onward, Matthew presents Jesus as Son of God, seven times in all. Jesus' mission of Social Justice through his preaching of repentance, his care for the sick and outcasts, the poor, hungry, homeless, strangers, and prisoners is the model for the audience to identify with in fulfilling the law and the prophets.

The Gospel closes with what resembles a graduation day ceremony. Jesus brings his disciples to a high mountain platform. There, he shares with them his own authority and the teachings presented throughout the Gospel, especially the Sermon on the Mount. Now the disciples can continue what Jesus has not yet been able to do by going out to all the nations of the world:

> And Jesus came and said to them, "All authority in heaven and on earth has been given to me. Go therefore and make disciples of all nations, baptizing them in the name of the Father and of the Son and of the Holy Spirit, and teaching them to obey everything that I have commanded you. And remember, I am with you always, to the end of the age." (28:18–21)

Summary

Matthew directs his Gospel to a largely affluent audience. He adds to Mark a challenging program of justice based on Jesus' words. The seven-fold repeated keyword is *dikaiosynē,* "justice." In the Sermon on the Mount, Jesus announces he will fulfill the law and prophets and present a more perfect *justice* than that of the scribes and Pharisees. His new covenant will interpret the Ten Commandments in terms of family relationships. The Lord's Prayer will go to the root of social injustice in the forgiveness of debts, based on the model of Deuteronomy 15. Unique to Matthew is a triple repetition and affirmation of love of one's neighbor as fulfilling the law and prophets. To make this a reality, his Gospel stresses Jesus' identification with others as a model. The last judgment scene presents the overall motivation of compassion for others in need and identification with them as the basis for justice.

7

Luke: Theology and Praxis of a Perpetual Jubilee

Luke's Introduction and Purpose

Only Luke has a two-volume work, his Gospel and the Acts of the Apostles. He explains his general purpose in his Gospel introduction:

> Since many have undertaken to set down an orderly account of the events that have been fulfilled among us, just as they were handed on to us by those who from the beginning were eyewitnesses and servants of the word, I too decided, after investigating everything carefully from the very first, to write an orderly account for you, most excellent Theophilus, so that you may know the truth concerning the things about which you have been instructed. (1:1)

The "many" previous writers in his first verse include Mark and at least another document containing material common to Matthew and Luke that is not in Mark. This is often called Q from the German word *Quelle,* "source." It is also likely that Luke knew at least parts of Matthew. If so, that would place the time of composition after Matthew, toward the end of the first century. There are no definite indications to tell us where it was written.

Luke writes that his purpose is to write an orderly account of the events "fulfilled among us." This refers to the promises of God found in the scriptures. The Gospel ending also refers to this fulfillment of scriptures as Jesus says, "These are my words that I spoke to you while I was still with you—that everything written about me in the law of Moses, the prophets, and the psalms must be fulfilled" (24:44). Luke then states that these things have been handed down to him by *eyewitnesses and servants* of the Lord. Luke himself has never seen the earthly Jesus.

There will be many references to scripture in Luke. Among the most important are those that refer to Jesus' mission to preach repentance characterized by justice.

Luke's Gospel and Prophetic Justice

If one word were to sum up a dominant concern of Luke, it would be *metanoia,* meaning "repentance"—literally, a change of mind or heart. The beginning and end of Luke's two volumes focus on this word. John the Baptist first appears at the Jordan River, "proclaiming a baptism of *repentance* for the forgiveness of sin" (13:3). Among Jesus' last words is the directive that "*repentance* and forgiveness of sins is to be proclaimed in his name to all nations, beginning from Jerusalem" (24:47). In the beginning of the Acts of the Apostles, Peter addresses the crowds with the words "*Repent* and be baptized every one of you in the name of Jesus Christ so that your sins may be forgiven" (2:38). When on trial before King Agrippa, Paul states that his mission has been to preach to the Gentiles that they should *repent* and turn to God and do deeds consistent with *repentance* (26:20). All in all, Acts mentions this word eleven times.

While all the Gospels center on forgiveness, Luke emphasizes more than the others that repentance as real change must accompany forgiveness. That is why Jesus' last words proclaim forgiveness *and repentance.* In the story of the tax collector's call, Matthew and Mark end with Jesus' statement "I have come to call not the righteous but sinners" (Matt 9:13; Mark 2:17). However, Luke's version adds, "to repentance" (5:32). In Matthew's Gospel, Peter asks Jesus, "Lord, if another member of the church sins against me, how often should I forgive? As many as seven times?" Jesus answered him, "Not seven times, but I tell you seventy-seven times" (18:21–22).

In a similar passage in Luke, Jesus says, "If another disciple sins, you must rebuke the offender, and if there is *repentance,* you must forgive. And if the same person sins against you seven times and says, 'I *repent,*' you must forgive" (17:3–4). The repentance of even one sinner is the occasion for community joy in heaven and on Earth more than for 99 righteous people who do not need it (15:1–7). In all, the verb or noun for *repentance* is found 14 times in the Gospel of Luke, more than in all the other Gospels combined.

John the Baptist's Ministry of Justice

While the Gospels consider the Baptist as a prophet, only Luke writes specifically that the *word of God* came to John in the wilderness (3:2). Isaiah, the great prophet of justice, introduces him. Luke has a passion for specifics. It is not enough for him to write that John preached a baptism of repentance. He also describes what this will mean in practice for various people.

> The crowds asked him, "What then should we do?" In reply he said to them, "Whoever has two coats must share with anyone who has none; and whoever has food must do likewise." Even tax collectors came to be baptized, and they asked him, "Teacher, what should we do?" He said to them, "Collect no more than the amount prescribed for you." Soldiers also asked him, "And we, what should we do?" He said to them, "Do not extort money from anyone by threats or false accusation, and be satisfied with your wages." (3:10–14)

These were substantial demands. Food and clothing were to be shared equally. This goes along with the radical message of the prophets. Tax collectors made much more than their salary through extra charges. Roman soldiers used their power to gain many advantages their minimal allowance could not provide them.

A Model Conversion for Luke's Audience

As an example for the Gospel audience, Luke describes the conversion of Zacchaeus, a rich chief tax collector. This occurs at a key juncture just before the end of Jesus' journey to Jerusalem (19:1–10). Zacchaeus was "short in stature" in more ways than one and climbed up a tree to see Jesus as he passed by on the road to Jericho. Jesus must surely have laughed when he saw him up the tree and called, "Zacchaeus, hurry and come down; for I must stay at your house today." Zacchaeus was overjoyed by these words and hurried down to welcome Jesus into his home. Many other people, however, were not happy at all. They recalled how often Zacchaeus had defrauded them on their tax bills. Surely the Master could have made a better choice of a house in which to stay and enjoy hospitality. They said, "He has gone to be the guest of one who is a sinner."

Zacchaeus heard the murmuring and quickly responded. He stood up and said to the Lord, "Look, half of my possessions, Lord, I will give to the poor; and if I have defrauded anyone of anything, I will pay them back four times as much" (19:8). This restitution of fraud was beyond the requirements of biblical law, which called for full restitution plus one fifth (Lev 6:1–7). However, the equal sharing of half of his possessions with the poor was an effort to fulfill prophetic justice, which was not satisfied with generous gifts but moved toward equality.

Generous giving out of abundance does not satisfy the requirements of justice. Luke has Jesus make a comparison between rich people who gave from abundance and a poor widow who could only contribute two small copper coins: "Truly…this poor widow has put in more than all of them; for all of them have contributed out of their abundance, but she out of her poverty has put in all she had to live on" (21:1–4).

The Acts of the Apostles provides examples of people in the Jerusalem church who voluntarily chose to have much less so others could have a sufficient amount: "All who believed were together and held all things in common; they would sell their possessions and distribute the proceeds to all, as any had need" (2:44–45). Also, "There was not a needy person among them, for as many as owned lands or houses sold them and brought the proceeds of what was sold. They laid it at the apostles' feet, and it was distributed to each as any had need" (4:34–35). Singled out by name is an early believer named Barnabas: "He sold a field that belonged to him, then brought the money and laid it at the apostles' feet" (4:37).

For Luke, giving up abundance for others to have enough will be repaid in God's kingdom. He alone records Jesus' saying, "Do not be afraid, little flock, for it is your Father's good pleasure to give you the kingdom. Sell your possessions, and give alms. Make purses for yourselves that do not wear out, an unfailing treasure in heaven, where no thief enters and no moth destroys. For where your treasure is, there your heart will be also" (12:32–34). In explaining the high cost of discipleship, Jesus said to his disciples, "None of you can become my disciple if you do not give up all your possessions" (14:33).

Jesus' Inaugural Sermon and Jubilee Platform

After his temptation, Jesus begins his ministry in Galilee and comes to Nazareth, where he was brought up. On the Sabbath, he goes to the synagogue, where he is asked to speak. Luke takes advantage of this occasion to summarize Jesus' mission and teaching. This is Jesus' first sermon, and the Gospel audience is present in spirit listening with great attention: "The eyes of all in the synagogue were fixed on him" (4:20).

> He stood up to read, and the scroll of Isaiah the prophet was given to him. He unrolled the scroll and found the place where it was written: "The Spirit of the Lord is upon me, because he has anointed me to bring good news to the poor. He has sent me to proclaim release to the captives and recovery of sight to the blind, to let the oppressed go free, to proclaim the year of the Lord's favor." And he rolled up the scroll, gave it back to the attendant, and sat down....Then he began to say to them, "Today this scripture has been fulfilled in your hearing." (4:16–21; Isa 61:1–2)

Jesus said the scripture was fulfilled, because the words described one whom God anointed, *echrisen,* and because he took upon himself the role described. Originally Isaiah proclaimed the good news of Israel's freedom from captivity and the return of the land to homeless, poor exiles returning from captivity. However, Jesus saw that this was not yet realized and made this his mission. The terms used by Isaiah seem influenced by the Jubilee texts in Leviticus 25. This was the great *year* of God's favor. The word for *release, aphesis,* of the captives is the same word used to describe the Jubilee: a year of *aphesis* (Lev 25:13).

This inaugural address of Jesus sheds light on the whole Gospel with its focus on compassion and forgiveness. This forgiveness includes not only personal offenses but also the great financial sin of the heavy burdens of debt laid upon the poor which cause them to lose their land. Further on, we will see how this influences Luke's version of the Lord's Prayer with its petition, "Forgive us our sins, for we ourselves forgive everyone indebted to us" (11:4). This Jubilee spirit makes the Sermon on the Plain reference to debt more understandable. Only Luke has, "Lend, expecting nothing in return" (6:35).

Luke's Sermon on the Plain, Justice with Overflowing Mercy

Luke has a series of four blessings and four woes to set the tone for the Sermon on the Plain. The first two blessings are, "Blessed are you who are poor, for yours is the kingdom of God. Blessed are you who are hungry now, for you will be filled" (6:20–21). The two corresponding woes are, "Woe to you who are rich, for you have received your consolation. Woe to you who are full now, for you will be hungry" (6:24–25). By proclaiming blessings or happiness on the poor and hungry, Jesus does not mean that deprivation is by any means desirable. Nowhere in the Bible is there such a message. In his first sermon at Nazareth, Jesus announced that he had come to bring good news to the poor (4:18). This was in effect a proclamation of a perpetual Jubilee in which debts would be forgiven and lands returned to the poor. Mary sang in her *Magnificat* that God "has filled the hungry with good things." The fulfillment was not done by dropping food and money from the skies but by prompting people to return to the justice of the prophets, which required equality in sharing the resources and good things of the Earth. Zacchaeus was an example

of this, for he was a rich tax collector who gave half of his possessions to the poor (19:1–10).

In contrast, the woes on the rich seem an extreme contrast,
but they reflect prophetic justice perfectly with the black-and-white
views we previously discussed in Isaiah. There is no in-between
"gray area" or compromise. Justice must move toward equality.
This is because the abundance of some, when there are limited
resources, is as inherently evil as robbing the poor. Luke will illustrate this contrast in the story of the rich man and Lazarus:

> There was a rich man who was dressed in purple and fine
> linen and who feasted sumptuously every day. And at his gate
> lay a poor man named Lazarus, covered with sores, who
> longed to satisfy his hunger with what fell from the rich man's
> table; even the dogs would come and lick his sores. The poor
> man died and was carried away by the angels to be with
> Abraham. The rich man also died and was buried. In Hades,
> where he was being tormented, he looked up and saw Abra-
> ham far away with Lazarus by his side. (16:19–23)

The story continues with the rich man's appeal for the mercy
he had failed to give Lazarus. However, Abraham tells him that
reversal is no longer possible. The rich man then begs that Lazarus
be sent to warn his five brothers about the terrible future awaiting
them also. Abraham replies, "They have Moses and the prophets;
they should listen to them." The rich man replies, "No, father
Abraham; but if someone goes to them from the dead, they will
repent." So a second time Abraham replies, "If they do not listen
to Moses and the prophets, neither will they be convinced even if
someone rises from the dead" (16:29–31). In this story, Luke has
twice mentioned Moses and the prophets. This is a double reference to the theme of prophetic justice in Luke. The overabundance
of some when others are in need is evil in itself for which there are
serious consequences that cannot be reversed.

Luke even goes beyond strict justice to a deeper imitation of
God as a Father. In Matthew, Jesus had called on his disciples to
be perfect like his heavenly Father who sends his gifts equally on
the good and bad, just and unjust (5:45). In the Lucan parallel
passage, Jesus says, "Love your enemies, do good, and lend,

178

expecting nothing in return. Your reward will be great, and you will be children of the Most High; for he is kind to the ungrateful and the wicked. Be merciful, just as your Father is *merciful*" (6:35–36).

The Greek word for *merciful, oiktirmōn,* is not found elsewhere in the New Testament except in James 5:11. In the Greek translation of the Hebrew Bible it is found prominently in Exodus 34:6. This is the awesome moment when God "passes by" Moses and reveals his name to him: "The Lord, the Lord, a God merciful *(oiktirmōn)* and gracious, slow to anger, and abounding in steadfast love and faithfulness." The Greek word translates the Hebrew *rahum,* from *rehem,* meaning "womb." Therefore, it is a word conveying deep feeling, that of womb love for a child. In the Exodus text, it is the first and highest attribute of God corresponding to the deepest love within a human being, that of a mother's womb love.

Matthew has gone as far as justice will go in imitating God's equal distribution of his gifts. Luke has gone further. Matthew can write, "Love your enemies and pray for those who persecute you (5:44). But Luke adds good actions and words also: "Do good to those who hate you, bless those who persecute you, pray for those who abuse you" (6:27–28). Matthew can generously write that we should not refuse those who would borrow money (5:42). Luke will add that this should be done even if no return can be hoped for: "Do good and lend, expecting nothing in return. Your reward will be great, and you will be children of the most high for he is kind to the ungrateful and wicked" (6:35).

The Lord's Prayer in Luke and Social Justice

The Introduction to the Lord's Prayer

Luke carefully prepares an introduction to the Lord's Prayer (10:25–42) and then follows it with a commentary and completion (11:5–26). As a preparation we find a *lawyer* asking Jesus, "Teacher, what must I do to inherit eternal life?" (10:25). Jesus turns the question back to him, asking what the biblical law directed. The lawyer repeated familiar words of the central daily prayer of the Jewish people beginning with the words "Hear O Israel," and continuing, "You shall love the LORD your God with all your heart and with all your soul, and with all your might" (Deut 6:4–5). Then, the lawyer added a text from another location, "But you shall love your neighbor as yourself" (Lev 19:18).

Jesus praised the lawyer's answer, saying, "You have given the right answer; do this and you will live." But wanting to justify himself, he asked Jesus, "And who is my neighbor?" Jesus then replied through the parable of the Good Samaritan (10:28–37). The lawyer was really separating the first part about God from the second part about one's neighbor. The first part is really a repeated prayer, and the second part is the action flowing from it. However, Jesus' parable places both together as a prayer-in-action. In contrast to a priest and Levite who passed by, a Samaritan, regarded as a foreigner, was "moved with pity" and responded with every means possible to a stranger beaten and lying nearly dead by the road. At the end of the parable, Jesus asked the lawyer which of the three proved to be a neighbor. The lawyer replied, "The one who showed him mercy." Jesus then says to him (and the Gospel audience), "Go and do likewise." The story is also a prayer-in-action because Luke has cited Jesus' words in the Sermon on the Plain: "Be merciful as your Father is merciful." In acting with this supreme quality of God, a person has already achieved the communion of prayer.

The next story about Martha and Mary works from the opposite direction (10:38–41). When Jesus visits their home, Martha is busy practicing the great biblical virtue of hospitality, rushing feverishly to provide for Jesus and his large hungry group of disciples. Her sister Mary, however, is totally taken up with listening to Jesus, sitting at his feet in the attitude of a disciple. Of course, this troubled Martha, who was left alone with all the work. She asks Jesus for a command: "Tell her then to help me." Jesus answers in these famous lines: "Martha, Martha, you are worried and distracted by many things; there is need of only one thing. Mary has chosen the better part, which will not be taken away from her" (10:40–42). ("One thing" in Luke does not have an exclusive meaning.) In this story, prayer comes first as united to action. Mary is *listening*. In the Sermon on the Plain, listening and doing come together. Jesus says, "I will show you what someone is like who comes to me, hears my words, and acts on them" (6:46).

The two stories, the Good Samaritan along with Martha and Mary, prepare the way for the Lord's Prayer which is made up of action-petitions. In 11:1, the disciples, like Mary, have listened to Jesus (biblical prayer was usually out loud) and want to learn to pray and act as he does.

The model of John the Baptist provides the immediate introduction to the Lord's Prayer: "As he (Jesus) was praying in a certain place, and after he had finished, one of his disciples said to him, 'Lord, teach us to pray, as John taught his disciples'" (11:1). The atmosphere is a private, secret one as in Matthew's Gospel. Jesus has been praying by himself and the disciples want to learn how he prays. So, when Jesus instructs them, he is sharing the secret of his own way of communion with God. This gives it the nature of a special gift or grace.

The reference to the Baptist is apropos for he combined his ministry of preaching with prayers and taught others to do likewise. Luke provides brief indications of the Baptist's practices. Even before his birth, the angel Gabriel told his father Zechariah, "He must never drink wine or strong drink; even before his birth he will be filled with the Holy Spirit" (1:15).

Prohibition of wine was part of the Nazarite vow described at length in chapter 6 of Numbers. In addition, those men or women were not to cut their hair during the time of their vow as a sign of their dedication to God. At the end of the period, during a solemn ceremony, they cut off their hair and offered it to God along with animal sacrifices. This vow was for a limited amount of time, but for the Baptist it was lifelong. This is why artists through the centuries have portrayed John the Baptist with unusually long hair. In addition, Nazarites were obliged to keep continual ritual cleanness, not even breaking this for the sake of a funeral of father, mother, brother, or sister (Num 6:1–21). The fact that the Baptist only ate "locusts and wild honey" (Matt 3:4) may be an indication that he limited himself to "clean" foods, because Leviticus names locusts among the clean foods (11:22).

On one occasion, Luke relates an objection some opponents raised about Jesus' disciples: "John's disciples, like the disciples of the Pharisees, frequently fast and pray, but your disciples eat and drink" (5:33; 18:12). Fasting often accompanied periods of intense prayer because it absorbed all the bodily energies and directed them to God. All of the above descriptions point to an austere image of the Baptist and a strict ascetic life. Some people regarded him as an extremist: Jesus said, "John the Baptist has come eating no bread and drinking no wine, and you say, 'He has a demon'; the Son of Man has come eating and drinking, and you say, 'Look, a glutton and a drunkard, a friend of tax collectors and sinners!'" (7:33–34).

In answer to objections, Jesus replied, "You cannot make wedding guests fast while the bridegroom is with them" (5:34). This was the joyful seven-day wedding celebration when such fasting and ascetical practices were put aside. Jesus' approach to prayer was simple and joyful. His prayer was connected primarily with his mission and the decisive actions that needed to be made. That is why the Lord's Prayer petitions are simple and direct. They are the prayers of Jesus himself. As in Matthew, several are found within Jesus' prayer in Gethsemane (22:39–46).

The Petitions in Luke

> He (Jesus) said to them, "When you pray, say,
> Father,
> hallowed be your name.
> Your kingdom come.
> Give us each day our daily bread.
> And forgive us our sins,
> for we ourselves forgive
> everyone indebted to us.
> And do not bring us to the
> time of trial." (11:2–4)

The Petitions Especially Related to Justice

Father

Matthew has "our Father" in view of the audience community. Luke has only "Father" to better reflect Jesus' own prayer. On the Mount of Olives, he will open his prayer to the Father in the same way, "Father, if you are willing, remove this cup from me; yet, not my will but yours be done" (22:42). Significantly the very first words of Jesus recorded in Luke are about his Father. At the age of 12, after he was lost and found in the Temple visit, his mother said to him, "Child, why have you treated us like this? Behold, your father and I have been searching for you in great anxiety" (2:48). Jesus replied, "Why were you searching for me? Did you not know that (literally) I must be about the things of my Father?" These words are both a comparison as well as contrast to an earthly parent. The beginning and end of the Gospel come together, as Jesus' last words on the cross are addressed to his Father when he prays, "Father, into your hands I commend my spirit" (23:46). Thus, he completed to the end his loving concern for "the things of his Father."

The same parallel between God and a loving, searching parent is found in Luke's parable of the Prodigal Son (15:11–32). A better title might be the "Prodigal Father"! Eleven times the name "father" occurs in this parable. First, he gives in to the outrageous request of a younger son for his share of the inheritance while he is still alive (12–13). Then, his son foolishly spends all this hard-earned money in loose living. He finally becomes reduced to the lowest extreme possible to a Jew, a job feeding pigs. There, in destitution, the boy remembers his *father's* house where there is bread in abundance and resolves to return to his *father*. Far from forgetting his son, his *father* had been watching for him every day and was so moved with compassion that he ran to meet him, embraced him, and kissed him. The young man began his prepared speech, "*Father*, I have sinned against heaven and before you; I am no longer worthy to be called your son" (15:21). But his father instead prepares a great party with music, dancing, and choice food.

In the Sermon on the Plain, Luke singles out the unique quality of the Father's mercy as one that God's children should strive to imitate: "Be merciful as your Father is merciful" (6:36). On the cross, Jesus' final concern is to extend this mercy to those most desperately in need. He prays, "Father, forgive them; for they do not know what they are doing" (23:34). His final words to a crucified criminal are an answer to that prayer as he tells him, "Truly I tell you, today you will be with me in Paradise" (Luke 23:43).

Your Kingdom Come

Once again the words are the same as in Matthew (6:10). However, Luke's audience would understand them in the sense they assume in his Gospel and the Acts of the Apostles. This sense is in reference to Jesus' death as inaugurating the kingdom of God.

Just before his death, Jesus assured the repentant criminal at his side, "Truly I tell you, today you will be with me in Paradise (23:43). This means that Jesus is about to enter his kingdom and can promise to immediately distribute its rewards to others. This connection of Jesus' death to the kingdom is confirmed in the Acts of the Apostles by Peter's explanation of the effects of Jesus' death. Peter describes Jesus as enthroned in the kingdom after his death and distributing the gift of the Spirit: "This Jesus God raised up, and of that we are all witnesses. Being therefore exalted at the right hand of God, and having received from the Father the promise of the Holy Spirit, he has poured out this that you both see and hear" (2:32–33).

Luke wants to prepare his audience to receive the full impact of Jesus' death as inauguration of the kingdom. So, he presents Jesus as the way and model for the *here and now* aspect of the kingdom. He can do this in anticipation because Jesus makes the decision to face death early in his Gospel. This decision is definitively made by his victory over the initial temptations of the devil. Especially this is true of the last temptation, that of exposing his life to death by leaping from the Temple pinnacle and then saving himself. Luke then notes, "When the devil had finished every test, he departed from him until an opportune time" (4:13).

In view of this kingdom's *nowness,* Luke omits the proclamations of Jesus and the Baptist in Matthew 3:1; 4:7 and Mark 1:15 that the kingdom of God is near. Instead, Jesus declares, "I must proclaim the good news of the kingdom" (Luke 4:43). In Luke's Sermon on the Plain, the Beatitudes are much more present oriented: "Blessed are you who are poor, for yours is the kingdom of God. Blessed are you who are hungry *now,* for you will be filled. Blessed are you who weep *now,* for you will laugh (6:20–21). In the same vein, Jesus sends out the 12 to preach the kingdom of God and to heal (9:1).

This kingdom is not merely reserved for the future; Jesus already entrusts it to his disciples: "Do not be afraid, little flock, for it is your Father's good pleasure to give you the kingdom" (12:32). Heroic measures to equalize the goods of this world are not "eschatological ethics" of an awaited future. Jesus can add to that statement, "Sell your possessions, and give alms. Make purses for yourselves that do not wear out, an unfailing treasure in heaven" (12:33).

Other passages also reflect the present activity of the kingdom in Jesus' ministry. When the Pharisees ask Jesus point blank when the kingdom of God is to come, he answers, "The kingdom of God is among you" (17:21). Thus, Jesus' presence is a sign of the kingdom's activity. Jesus declares to Zacchaeus, the notorious chief collector of Jericho, "I must stay at your house *today.*" After Zacchaeus welcomes Jesus and sincerely repents, Jesus tells him, "*Today,* salvation has come to this house" (19:7–9). This *now* of the kingdom does not mean that the future is eliminated. On the contrary, it makes the future a reality. So neglecting the poor man Lazarus at the gate means that the rich man will not be able to eat with him in God's future banquet with Abraham and the just (16:19–31).

The petition "Your kingdom come" is Jesus' own prayer. As a model for the audience, Luke presents Jesus' public life as a "work and pray" journey where Jesus prays for help and guidance before important acts or decisions regarding the kingdom. His ministry began when he was praying after his baptism (3:21). As a result, the Holy Spirit descended upon him and a voice from heaven proclaimed he was God's beloved Son. For guidance and energy about his mission as God's Son, he fasted and prayed 40 days in the wilderness (4:1–13). Before beginning his first preaching tour, he rose at daybreak and went to pray in a deserted area (4:42).

To prepare for the key decision of choosing his 12 apostles, he went to a mountain and prayed all night (6:12). Before Peter's first confession of faith, he retired to pray alone with his disciples (9:18). His transfiguration took place as he was praying on top of a mountain (9:28). The teaching of the Lord's Prayer itself came after a period of prayer (11:1). At the Last Supper, he prayed that Peter would repent even though he knew that Peter would fail (22:31–32). He obtained the strength to risk his life in Jerusalem after a long agonizing prayer on the Mount of Olives (22:39–44). Even on the cross, the conversion of one of the crucified criminals came about as the result of Jesus' prayer (23:34, 42–43). The Gospel of Luke ends with Jesus rising into heaven giving the Gospel audience a special blessing (24:50).

Give Us Each Day Our Daily Bread

Matthew's version has, "Give us this day our daily bread" (6:11). "Give" is a present continuous tense, "keep on giving," in Luke. He also has "each day" *(kath'ēmeran),* instead of Matthew's "this day." This is significantly closer to the story of the manna in the desert (Exod 16), which we cited as an influence on Matthew. God instructed the people to go out and gather a day's portion *each day,* and then shared it equally among all. Like St. Paul's model of equality (2 Cor 8:14–15), Luke will use the same sharing motif of bread or food each day, using the identical expression, *each day,* as in the manna story and in the Lord's Prayer. In Jerusalem, Luke describes the distribution *each day* to provide help for poor widows. The theme of bread each day also occurs in Luke's description of early believers *each day* spending time together in the Temple and breaking bread at home (Acts 2:46).

In the gathering of manna, everyone did their part, some more, some less, but it was divided equally among all according to their need. Luke relates that early believers "would sell their possessions and goods and distribute the proceeds to all, as any had need" (Acts 2:45). In a second summary of this lifestyle, he writes that "there was not a needy person among them," thus fulfilling the idea expressed in Deuteronomy 15:4, 7, 11. "As many as owned lands or houses sold them and brought the proceeds of what was sold...and it was distributed according to each as any had need (Acts 4:34–35). The slogan "from each one according to ability, to each one according to need" has been attributed to Karl Marx, but it really goes back to the gathering and "miraculous" sharing of manna in the Exodus story.

And Forgive Us Our Sins, For We Ourselves Forgive Everyone Indebted to Us

First, we note the differences with the corresponding petition in Matthew: "And forgive us our debts, as we also have forgiven our debtors" (6:12). In regard to God, Luke has the more generic and understandable "sins," *hamartias,* instead of "debts." In reference to other people, Luke is more specific in writing literally "every person owing us." The verb tense is also the present instead of the Greek perfect in Matthew. This makes it a more continual process. In Luke's Sermon on the Plain, there is another reference to what amounts to forgiving a debt even in advance with Jesus' saying "Lend, expecting nothing in return" (6:35). Matthew and Luke provide the same message in this petition, "a perpetual Jubilee" to provide relief for the poor laden by debts. Here, we will not repeat the arguments previously given for the meaning in Matthew but only sketch what Luke's Gospel has added.

The Practical Conclusion of Luke's Inaugural Nazareth Sermon

At Nazareth, Jesus had read the scriptures of Isaiah with their Jubileelike language beginning with the words "The Spirit of the Lord is upon me, because he has anointed me to bring good news to the poor" (4:18). We have previously pointed out that the following words, *release* to the captives and the *year* of favor, are like the Jubilee *Year* of release, *aphesis* (Lev 25:10), for the captives. Luke uses the same verb, *release,* in this petition in reference to debts. Thus, the Lord's Prayer has the practical conclusion to put in effect Jesus' promise when he said at Nazareth that he was fulfilling the scriptures. Without this active responsive the Lord's Prayer becomes a wishful ideal.

Luke's version seems to distinguish between sins against God and sins of evil lending, whereas Matthew has used the same terminology for both. This can be better understood if we see the relationship between the day of atonement and the Jubilee. The Bible describes the fiftieth year Jubilee as an actual continuation of the *Yom Kippur,* day of atonement:

> You shall count off seven weeks of years, seven times seven years, so that the period of seven weeks of years gives forty-nine years. Then you shall have the trumpet sounded loud; on the tenth day of the seventh month—on the day of atonement—you shall have the trumpet sounded throughout all your land. And you shall hallow the fiftieth year and you shall proclaim liberty *(aphesis)* throughout the land to all its inhabitants. (Lev 25:8–10)

The Jubilee Year thus begins and ends on the day of atonement. This day is more directed to sins against God, whereas the Jubilee Year extends this to sins and debts of people. In the same way, Luke's version has the first part asking for forgiveness of sins against God; the second part extends this in regard to the debts of others.

Debts in Luke's Gospel and the Lord's Prayer

Like Matthew, Luke has the Golden Rule as a model for action: "Do to others as you would have them do to you" (6:31). As an example of this, Jesus says, "If you lend to those from whom you hope to receive, what credit is that to you? Even sinners lend to sinners, to receive as much again. But love your enemies, do good and lend, expecting nothing in return. Your reward will be great and you will be children of the Most High; for he is kind to the ungrateful and the wicked. Be merciful, just as your Father is merciful" (6:34–36). This double mention of *lending* illustrates its central importance.

A first reaction to the above statement might be to dismiss it as "impossible ethics"; however, the instructions surrounding the sabbatical year prove a practical example. The description of this year starts as follows: "Every seventh year you shall grant a remission of debts (make a release, *aphesis,* the root word in the Lord's Prayer). And this is the manner of the remission (release): every creditor shall remit *(aphēseis)* the claim that is held against *(opheilei,* as in the Lord's Prayer) a neighbor" (Deut 15:1). However, there is a warning near the end: "Be careful that you do not entertain a mean thought, thinking, 'The seventh year, the year of remission, is near,' and therefore view your needy neighbor with hostility and give nothing; your neighbor might cry to the LORD against you, and you would incur guilt" (15:9). The connection to the Lord's Prayer both in the language of Deuteronomy and in regard to lending when there is little hope of return is significant.

A second connection between debts and sin is found only in the story of the Penitent Woman (7:36–50). Simon the Pharisee is shocked by the lavish display of affection that a woman of the city demonstrated by bathing Jesus' feet with her tears and drying them with her hair, along with kissing and anointing them. In response, Jesus gave this illustration: "A certain creditor had two debtors; one owed five hundred denarii, and the other fifty. When they could not pay, he canceled the debts for both of them (the verb is *echarisato,* from the root *charis,* "favor" or "grace"). Now which of them will love him more?" Simon answered, "I suppose the one for whom he canceled the greater debt." Jesus concluded by saying, "Therefore I tell you, her sins, which were many, have been forgiven; hence she has shown great love. But the one to whom little is forgiven, loves little" (7:41–48). Several points are significant. A debt forgiveness is placed on parallel with a sin forgiveness. Also the same verb, *aphi⁻emi,* "release," or "forgive," is used for forgiveness of sin and the forgiveness of a debt. In both cases, they are the result of love. This parallels Luke's Lord's Prayer petition.

And Lead Us Not into Temptation

This is exactly the same as in Matthew but without the next part, "But deliver us from evil (or the evil one)." A number of ancient texts have this second part also in Luke, but it may have been influenced by Matthew. Whether or not it originally belonged to Luke is of little import because Luke writes of "the evil one," the devil, as the instigator of temptation, as in the story of Jesus' temptation after his baptism (4:1–13).

Luke himself informs his readers that he attaches a special meaning to this petition. At the beginning and end of Jesus' prayer on the Mount of Olives, he tells his disciples (and audience), "pray that you may not come into the time of trial" (22:39, 46). Luke's version of this prayer describes a resumption of Jesus' struggle with Satan after Jesus' initial victory during his initial period of forty days of prayer and fasting (4:1–3). After the last temptation, Luke relates, "When the devil had finished every test, he departed from him (Jesus) until an opportune time" (4:13). In Luke's version of Jesus' prayer, he omits the expressions of Jesus' fear and hesitation found in Mark and Matthew. Instead, it is the disciples who are "sleeping because of grief" (22:45). This grief is in contrast to Jesus' confident struggle. That is why he twice warns them to pray lest they enter into temptation. Their own strength could not win a victory over the dark forces assembled against Jesus. Jesus referred to these forces as such when he was arrested and said, "This is your hour and the power of darkness" (22:53).

The Cosmic Struggle with the Powers of Darkness

Luke presents Christians with a model of combat against the forces of darkness[30] so they can learn how Jesus was victorious and follow his example. This path starts with the devil's first temptation. Luke introduces this with a genealogy of Jesus that goes back not to Abraham as in Matthew, but to Adam who is called "the son of God" (3:38). This hints that Adam's struggle with the serpent in the Garden of Eden is parallel to that of Jesus and can be understood better in contrast. The designation of

Adam as Son of God links with the devil's first two temptations beginning with the words "If you are the Son of God" (4:3, 9). In the Garden, the devil in the New Testament view, "the ancient serpent" (Rev 20:2), tempted Adam to eat a forbidden food, just as the devil tempted Jesus to eat a "miracle" bread that he was not to eat according to God's plans. In the Garden, Satan suggested to Adam and Eve that they could avoid death by following his plans about eating the forbidden fruit. In parallel, in the third temptation of Jesus, the devil tempts him to jump off the Temple pinnacle and escape death by falsely trusting God will save him.

Returning now to the Mount of Olives, the parallel conflict theme of Adam and Satan can be better understood in the following description: "Then an angel from heaven appeared to him and gave him strength. In his anguish, he prayed more earnestly, and his sweat became like great drops of blood falling down on the ground" (22:43–44, according to some prominent Greek texts). The angel's appearance fits the image of a struggle with the devil, also an angelic being. According to tradition in Revelation 12:7, the good angels fought against Satan and his cohorts, finally ejecting them from heaven. On Earth, they assist human beings in a similar struggle. "In agony he prayed more earnestly." The English word, *agony,* does not correspond fully with the Greek *agōnia,* which means "a sharp conflict." The words *sweat* and *earth* remind us again of the Garden of Eden parallels. There, God told Adam, "By the sweat of your face you shall eat bread until you return to the ground, for out of it you were taken" (Gen 3:19). All these Adam-Jesus parallels and contrasts would invite the Gospel audience to face their own temptations and struggles with new confidence because they had a leader and model in a new Adam to bring them to victory.

This combat theme against the forces of evil is also found scattered through the Gospel. In the mission of the 12, Luke more than Matthew and Mark places special emphasis on the power over demons: "Jesus...gave them power and authority over *all* demons" (9:1). When the seventy other apostles return, they exclaim, "Lord, in your name even the demons submit to us!" Jesus replied, "I watched Satan fall from heaven like a flash of lightning. See, I have given you authority to tread on snakes and scorpions and over all the power of the enemy; and nothing will hurt you" (10:17–19). After healing a crippled woman, Jesus says, "Ought not this woman, a daughter of Abraham whom Satan bound for eighteen long years, be set free from this bondage on the sabbath day?" (13:16).

Luke's "Gospel of Women"

To open this chapter, we noted Luke's Gospel purpose to fulfill the scriptures. A central text of the prophet Joel concerned the spirit at the last times. The author has Peter quote this at the first Pentecost:

> In the last days it will be, God declares, that I will pour out my Spirit upon all flesh, and your sons and your daughters shall prophesy, and your young men shall see visions, and your old men shall dream dreams. Even upon my slaves, both men and women, in those days I will pour out my Spirit; and they shall prophesy. (Acts 2:17–18 from Joel 2:28–29)

Peter proclaims that the great outpouring of the Spirit on Pentecost has fulfilled God's plans in scripture. It is universal because it breaks down the great divisions in society, whether age, social standing, race, or gender. Luke's first volume shows how Jesus has prepared the way for this. In regard to gender, Luke is very anxious to present this for his audience, for he has seen it come true in his own missionary experience. This has earned for his Gospel the title of "The Gospel of Women."[31]

Women's Leadership in the Acts of the Apostles

First, let us look at Luke's second volume. There, we find the names of women who played key roles in the early church. In Jerusalem, there was a central meeting place at the house of a certain Mary, mother of Mark (Acts 12:12). After Peter had miraculously escaped from prison, he went to that home in which Christians had gathered to pray for him. This may also have been the house where the first Pentecost experience took place. Luke takes special note of that home's upper room where the 12, Mary the Mother of Jesus, Acts and a group of women gathered in prayer (Acts 1:14).

The initiative of women made possible the rapid missionary thrust of the early church. A great step forward was the entry of the Gospel into Europe. Paul's entry into Europe was through the city of Philippi in Greece. His activity promptly brought him into conflict with public authorities anxious to preserve the religious status quo. They stripped him, beat him with rods, and threw him into prison (Acts 16:22–23). Paul had to appeal to his Roman citizenship and leave the city quickly.

However, a Christian community began because of the efforts of a lady named Lydia. She was an independent business woman, head of a household and dealer in purple cloth. She had invited Paul to stay at her house and make it the center of the Christian community. The church at Philippi was the most loyal and fervent church founded by Paul. They followed him with their gifts and letters wherever he went. This gave him more time to give to the needs of the apostolate (Phil 4:10–20).

At Corinth, a Christian couple named Priscilla and Aquila received Paul into their home, which became an important church center (Acts 18:1–4). Luke names Priscilla first, so she was probably more active than her husband. Paul also wanted to establish the faith in Ephesus, the capital of the Roman province of Asia, and one of the largest cities of the empire. The fervent couple decided to accompany him there. Actually, they seem to have started the community as Paul soon went off on a journey to Jerusalem. Luke also tells us how they instructed Apollos, a noted Jewish preacher and disciple of John the Baptist (18:24–28).

Luke also mentions other groups of women who were remarkable for their special gifts. At Joppa, the Apostle Peter visited a community of widows on the occasion of the death of Tabitha, one of their members. They dedicated themselves to helping the poor, because they showed Peter tunics and cloaks that Tabitha had made while she was with them (9:39). Women also had special charismatic gifts. On his final journey to Jerusalem, Paul visited the home of Philip the evangelist in Caesarea. Acts mentions that he had four unmarried daughters with the gift of prophecy (21:9).

The Prominence of Women's Stories in Luke's Gospel

This outstanding work of women in the early church along with concern for the fulfillment of prophecies prompted Luke to insert many more women's stories in the Gospels. The following are examples found nowhere in Mark and Matthew: The extraordinary role of Mary as the model for believers is found in Elizabeth's words "Blessed is she who has believed" (1:45). Elizabeth, mother of the Baptist, is also a model of faith. Despite her husband's wavering, she believed that even in their old age they would have a son who would prepare the way for the Messiah (1:1–25; 57–66). Even at the age of 84, a prophetess called Anna came into the Temple when the child Jesus was presented there. She spoke about the child to all those who were awaiting the Messiah (2:36–38).

Luke alone mentions (along with Mary Magdalene) Joanna and Susanna who accompanied Jesus on his journeys and provided for him and his companions out of their own means (8:2–3). Jesus visits a home of two women, Martha and Mary, to emphasize that women not only provide hospitality but also are even more prominent as disciples (10:38–42). Luke inserts the story of a penitent woman as a model for conversion, forgiveness, and love (7:36–50).

There are also many parables and other illustrations about women. Luke has the parable of the woman's lost coin-ornament to illustrate loss, search, finding, and joyful community reconciliation (15:8–10). The persistent widow and the unjust judge illustrate prayer and perseverance (18:1–8). The cure of the woman on the Sabbath is told with detail and humor to illustrate the new meaning of the Sabbath (13:10–17).

The "Gospel of Women" at First Disappoints Them

We have seen that Matthew and Mark featured God's great surprise regarding women's key roles. Jesus had called his first disciples by the Lake of Galilee and invited them to follow him and thus become fishers of people. However, all 12 men deserted him at his arrest; the only ones to follow to the cross were Mary Magdalene and other women who became the key witnesses of Jesus' death, burial, and empty tomb. We also noted that these Gospels led up to this surprise ending through a cycle of women's stories.

However, if we look carefully at Luke, we find that the above connection between the beginning call at Galilee and the cross has largely disappeared. Only in Luke 5:1–11 we find a miraculous draught of fish. It appears that Luke is already anticipating Jesus' resurrection, for this story is the same as a post-resurrection apparition in John 21:1–14. In Luke, Jesus does not say, "Follow me and I will make you fishers of people." Instead, after the catch of fish, he says to *Peter,* "From now on you will be catching people" (5:10).

This is already a prediction and assumption that Peter will lead the later apostolate. Jesus speaks directly to Peter, not to the group including Andrew, James, and John as in Matthew and Mark. Their names are only added by Luke as part of the scene. At the end, Luke writes about all of them: "When they had brought their nets to shore, they left everything and followed him" (5:11). Luke's emphasis on Peter will continue through the Gospel and result in diminishing the role of women at the end.

The next significant difference in Luke is the enhancement of the image of Peter and the 12 by omitting their desertion of Jesus at the time of his arrest. Even Jesus' prediction after the Last Supper that all will abandon him is omitted. In Luke, Jesus predicts that Peter will deny him but his conversion and return are "guaranteed" with the words at the Last Supper, "Simon, Simon, listen! Satan has demanded to sift all of you like wheat, but I have prayed for you that your own faith may not fail; and you, when you have turned back, strengthen your brothers" (22:31–32).

This will affect the portrait only of Mary Magdalene and the women at the cross that we saw in Matthew and Mark. In those Gospels, the women are mentioned by name three times: at the cross, at the burial, and at the empty tomb. Instead, Luke has these women as part of a larger group at the cross and does not even mention their names: "But all his acquaintances, including the women who had followed him from Galilee, stood at a distance, watching these things" (23:49).

Luke makes the above change because he has omitted the fact that all the male disciples fled at Jesus' arrest, as in Matthew and Mark. Neither does Luke have Jesus, as in the first two Gospels, predict that all the male disciples would abandon him. Luke does this to strengthen the credibility of Peter and the 12 at the culminating episode of the Gospel in which they receive Jesus' final commission (24:34–49). In doing this, he will place the women in a secondary position, lest the burden of witness rest primarily on them.

This "downsizing" of the women's roles continues at the scene of the empty tomb. The anonymous women at Jesus' death and burial (23:55–56) return on Easter Sunday morning to anoint Jesus' body. However, they receive no commission to announce Jesus' resurrection to others as in Matthew and Mark. The women did, however, return from the tomb and "told this to the eleven and all the rest" (24:9). At this point, the author introduces their names for the first time: "Now it was Mary Magdalene, Joanna, Mary the mother of James, and the other women with them who told this to the apostles" (10). Yet, we notice that Luke has weakened the place of Mary Magdalene by making her part of a much larger delegation of women.

Luke then downplays this message of the women by writing that Peter and the 11 did not accept their testimony: "But these words seemed to them an idle tale, and they did not believe them" (24:11). The evangelist carefully builds a strong case on direct apparitions of the risen Jesus to the male disciples; Jesus does not appear to the women. First, Jesus appears to the disciples on the way to Emmaus (24:31); then he appears to Simon Peter alone (34); finally, he appears to the assembled disciples (36) and gives them their final commission. As for the women, their part is again discounted. The two disciples take off on a trip to Emmaus despite the women's stories:

Moreover, some women of our group astounded us. They were at the tomb early this morning, and when they did not find his body there, they came back and told us that they had indeed seen a vision of angels who said that he was alive. Some of those who were with us went to the tomb and found it just as the women had said; but they did not see him. (24:22–24)

In fairness to Luke, we need to stress that he has no intention of down-staging the women just because they are women. We have seen his efforts earlier in the Gospel to feature women's stories and earn the title of a "Gospel of Women." The author places women in a secondary place at the climactic end of the Gospel because he needs to offset some teachings about the reality of Jesus and his bread that are a threat to the early church.

Right from the beginning of the Gospel we can note this defensive stance: Luke writes to Theophilus so that he may know "the truth" concerning the things about which he has been instructed (1:3). This is a hint that there are some things that Theophilus finds doubtful or uncertain. Luke also tells us in his second volume about fears of false teachings in Paul's last address to the presbyters of Ephesus:

I know that after I have gone, savage wolves will come in among you, not sparing the flock. Some even from your own group will come distorting the truth in order to entice the disciples to follow them. (Acts 20:29–30)

In the above text, there is emphasis on the *truth,* just as in Luke's Gospel introduction. Luke does not furnish a list of the errors he has in mind, but one important one appears at a crucial point near the end of the Gospel. When Jesus first appears to the assembled disciples, there are considerable doubts about the reality of his bodily presence. Jesus has to dispel these by asking them to touch him. When they persist in disbelief, Jesus asks for something to eat to show he is real:

They were startled and terrified, and thought that they were seeing a ghost. He said to them, "Why are you frightened, and why do doubts arise in your hearts? Look at my hands

and my feet; see that it is I myself. Touch me and see; for a
ghost does not have flesh and bones as you see that I have."
And when he had said this, he showed them his hands and his
feet. While in their joy they were disbelieving and still won-
dering, he said to them, "Have you anything here to eat?"
They gave him a piece of broiled fish and he took it and ate it
in their presence. (24:37–43)

The reality of Jesus' presence is essentially connected to the
breaking of the bread when the disciples on the way to Emmaus
first recognized Jesus: "Then their eyes were opened and they recognized him, and he vanished from their sight" (24:31). When these
disciples tell the story to the others, they repeat the connection with
the bread and "told what had happened to them on the road, and
how he had been made known to them in the breaking of the
bread" (24:35). Then, while they are talking about this bread manifestation, Jesus appears and addresses the whole group (36).

The above reality of Jesus' appearance after his death is a
focal point of the Gospel. Luke wants to stress the role of Peter
and the 11 as carrying authentic tradition about the meaning and
reality of Jesus' presence as connected with this bread. Right from
the beginning of the Gospel, Luke stresses the unique call of Peter.
In the miracle of the loaves, the 12 have more of a part than in the
other Gospels. Peter's confession of faith follows immediately
after the multiplication of loaves as if connected with it (9:18–20).
At the Last Supper, the place of Peter and the 12 is even more
prominent than in Matthew and Mark. It is *Peter and John* who
make preparations for the Passover meal and Jesus promises they
will preside over this meal in the kingdom of God (22:30).

This connection between Jesus' bread and the 12 continues
in the Acts of the Apostles. To establish their position, Luke gives
all their names again at the beginning of this second volume
(1:13). The place of the 12 in regard to community meals receives
special emphasis: The early Christians' unity is around "the apostles' teaching and fellowship and the breaking of bread" (2:42).
They direct the daily meal and distribution of food for the widows
and the poor (6:1).

We can see then why Luke wants Peter and the 12 to be central in the witness of Jesus' resurrection and his appearance to them in the breaking of the bread. Consequently, the women must take a subordinate role to this central matter. However, Luke does have a special role for them in another area that is essential to the beginnings of the church.

The Special Role of Women as the First to Remember Jesus' Words

Right from the beginning of his Gospel, Luke gives special attention to the *remembering* role of women. In his Gospel, Mary the mother of Jesus carefully observes and ponders over the meaning of words and events. Concerning the shepherds' words at Bethlehem, "Mary treasured all these words and pondered them in her heart" (2:19). Also, after the child Jesus was found in the Temple, the Gospel notes, "His mother treasured all these things in her heart" (2:51).

This *remembering* is extremely important to Luke especially in respect to the women at the empty tomb. The angel said to them, "*Remember* how he told you, when he was still in Galilee, that the Son of Man must be handed over" (24:6). Then, Luke writes that the women *remembered* his words, and returning from the tomb, they told this to the 11 and to all the apostles (24:8). *Thus, the women along with Mary, the mother of Jesus, have an extraordinary role as being the first to remember.* This "remembering" makes possible the beginning of the church.

One New World Embracing Diversities of Nation, Race, or Culture

Returning to Luke's purpose of seeing the prophecies fulfilled, he knew well how the Spirit had spoken about such a world to the ancient prophets of Israel. Luke as a missionary had seen this taking place as he journeyed from place to place as an apostle. Although he had never seen Jesus in the flesh, he experienced the presence of the Spirit of the risen Jesus. For Luke, there was only one Jesus, whether in Nazareth or in the early church. In writing about Jesus of Nazareth, he described him as already having in mind an apostolate to the Gentiles and others after his death. Luke knew that the present gives birth to the future, and therefore in a sense, the future has already happened.

The Birth of Jesus Heralds a New World

"In those days a decree went out from Emperor Augustus that all the world should be registered" (2:1). Of course, Augustus wanted to strengthen and expand his control over the Roman world through taxes and military conscription, and no one could resist the power of Roman legions to accomplish that purpose. Luke in contrast writes with a sense of humor. The very power of the emperor makes it possible for Mary and Joseph to journey to Bethlehem to register. There, in fulfillment of scriptures, Mary gives birth to a child so great that a choir of angels descends from heaven to declare that this child will be the source of "peace on earth." This contrasts with the *Pax Romana* enforced by the power and violence of the invincible Roman military.

Again the theme of *peace* for the whole Earth is proclaimed 40 days afterward when Jesus' parents bring him to Jerusalem to present him to the Lord in the Temple. An elderly man named Simeon was confident he would not die until he had seen the Lord's Messiah. Now, he takes the child Jesus in his arms and praises God that he can die in peace because he has seen God's salvation *for all peoples,* "a light of revelation to the Gentiles and for glory to your people Israel" (2:32).

John the Baptist Meets Soldiers by the Jordan

Luke prepares for this by again mentioning the Roman emperor; this time it is the "fifteenth year of the reign of the Emperor Tiberius" (3:1). Luke provides a worldwide dimension to John's baptism by writing that the word of God came to John in the desert according to the prophet Isaiah. In quoting him, he adds a verse not mentioned by Matthew or Mark, "All flesh shall see the salvation of God" (3:6; Isa 40:5). At the Jordan River, soldiers approached the Baptist. They could have been Roman soldiers or those of Herod or the Temple police. Regardless, all were instruments of Rome. They asked John, "And we, what should we do?" John replied, "Do not extort money from anyone by threats or false accusation, and be satisfied with your wages" (3:14).

The Family Tree of Jesus Is Traced Back to Adam, Son of God (3:23–38): The Theme of Paradise Reopened

In Matthew, this genealogy goes back to Abraham, Father of the Jewish people. Luke's concerns, however, go out to the whole human race. Adam and Eve were tempted by the devil, as described in late Jewish literature; e.g., "Through the devil's envy death entered the world, and those who belong to his company experience it" (Wis 2:24). Following the genealogy in Luke, we find the temptations of Jesus, which are thus connected with the temptation of the first parents in the Garden of Eden—in which they suffered defeat. The work of Jesus will be to reverse this loss and turn it into victory. We have outlined this struggle in the Lord's Prayer petition, "Lead us not into temptation" (page 190–92). There, we noted the whole theme of the cosmic struggle against the powers of darkness in Luke's Gospel.

Here, we will describe the moment of victory on the cross. One of the men crucified with Jesus acknowledges his deserved punishment but declares that Jesus has done nothing wrong. Then, he turns to Jesus and says, "Jesus, remember me when you come into your kingdom." Jesus replies, "Truly I tell you, today you will be with me in Paradise" (23:42–43). *Paradise* comes from the Greek, *paradeisos,* which in turn translates the Hebrew, *eden,* meaning "pleasure." In Genesis, "The LORD God planted a garden in Eden, in the east" (2:8).

Now, the climactic meaning of this scene can be understood. Luke calls this crucified man a "criminal" *(kakourgos),* literally an evildoer. By itself, the text tells us that even a person in the most desperate circumstances after a life of evil can hope for forgiveness and entry into "paradise." However, the theme of Jesus' cosmic struggle against darkness introduced by his genealogy from Adam and Eve brings us to a much wider meaning. The "criminal" stands for a defeated human race excluded from Paradise. Jesus wins a victory over the powers of evil and opens up a new future for the whole human race without the exception of any single person.

Gentiles Who Love Jews

Both Matthew and Luke carry the story of a Roman centurion whose servant Jesus cures from a distance. However, Luke has added some very significant details. In his story, the centurion sends Jewish elders to appeal to Jesus. They tell him, "He is worthy of having you do this for him, for *he loves our people,* and it is he who built our synagogue for us" (7:4–5). Luke recounts the story in this way because it reflects his knowledge of similar people in the early church. In the Acts of the Apostles he writes about a certain centurion called Cornelius. He describes him in this fashion: "He was a devout man who feared God with all his household; he gave alms generously to the people and prayed constantly to God" (10:2).

Following this story, Luke describes the first community of both Jewish and Gentile believers at Antioch in Syria, one of the largest cities in the Roman Empire. He notes that "It was at Antioch that the disciples were first called 'Christians'" (Acts 11:26). The small community was anxious to show their bonds with and practical concern for Jewish believers in Judea who were suffering during a famine that took place in the time of Emperor Claudius. Luke writes, "The disciples determined that according to their ability, each would send relief to the believers (brothers) living in Judea; this they did, sending it to the elders by Barnabas and Saul (Paul)" (Acts 11:29).

Paul the Apostle learned much from this model he had seen in Antioch. His missionary approach usually began in a synagogue preaching to Jews. This attracted some Gentiles present who were already influenced by Jewish beliefs and ethics. These in turn brought in other Gentiles. It was only when this last group responded best to his teaching that he turned his attention primarily to them but never neglecting his own Jewish people. For Luke, *one world* means "a world in which Gentiles and Jews are together with mutual respect and love," like the centurions in the above stories.

Crossing Ethnic Barriers

In the opening chapter of Acts, the risen Jesus explains how the good news will spread to the world: "You will receive power when the Holy Spirit has come upon you; and you will be my witnesses in Jerusalem, in all Judea and Samaria, and to the ends of the earth" (1:8). Samaria was the first halfway step to the world. To this day, there still exists a Samaritan community in Israel. Its origin goes back partly to the Assyrian conquest of the northern tribes of Israel in the eighth century B.C. Many Jews were carried away into exile while others remained in the land and often intermarried with settlers who had been brought in by the Assyrians.

When the Jews in the southern kingdom later came back from the Babylonian exile, they refused to accept everyone who had intermarried with Gentiles unless they parted from their families. Many refused to do so and were regarded as outsiders and not really Jews. This created a great rift between the two groups. The returned Jews also prohibited the Samaritans from helping to rebuild their Temple, which further increased hostility. This hostility prompted the Samaritans to build their own Temple on top of nearby Mount Gerazim. In practice, the Samaritans were regarded as unclean (as was the woman in John 4:9) and sometimes further apart from Jews than Gentiles.

Luke's Gospel presents Jesus as healing that rift with the Samaritans. He rebukes James and John who want to call down lightning upon the Samaritans when they were unwilling to offer hospitality as the disciples journey to Jerusalem (9:51–56). Jesus tells the parable of the Good Samaritan as an example of what it really means to love one's neighbor (10:29–37). Later, he cures ten lepers, one of whom was a Samaritan. Only this man returned to thank Jesus, who then asked, "Were not ten made clean? But the other nine, where are they? Was none of them found to return and give praise to God except this foreigner?" (17:17–18).

The Gospel stories reflect a great turning point in the early church when Philip the evangelist was the first person to bring the good news outside the confines of Judaism. When he preached in Samaria, the people believed his message about Jesus as Messiah and "There was great joy in that city" (Acts 8:8). As a result, many were baptized. This matter was of such surprising importance that the Jerusalem community sent Peter and John to Samaria to confirm what had happened. The two apostles laid hands on the newly baptized, who received and shared the same Holy Spirit that had come down on the Jerusalem community.

The same Philip extended his mission to reach an Ethiopian eunuch who was returning to his home from Jerusalem (8:26–40). The term *Ethiopian* was not a strictly territorial one in the Bible and was sometimes used to designate peoples of darker color. His previous religious situation cannot be certainly defined. He was returning from worship in Jerusalem. However, he was a eunuch, and therefore excluded from the Temple according to Deuteronomy 23:1 and Josephus (*Antiquities* 4:290). But Isaiah 56:3–5 proclaimed a day when eunuchs would no longer be excluded. When Philip baptized him, it may be an indication of the fulfillment of Isaiah's prophecy.

Luke extends his interest in ethnic diversity in his account of an important meeting of prophets and teachers in Antioch, the first city in which we noted there was a community of both Jews and Gentiles (Acts 11:22–26). At this meeting there was a man called Lucius from the Roman province of Cyrene in Africa. Also, there was Simeon, called *Niger,* which is the word in Latin for *black*. In the Gospel, Luke noted that a certain Simon of Cyrene helped Jesus carry the cross (23:26). He may not have been the same person as the Simeon in Acts, but the special mention of an African in connection with the cross is significant.

The Spirit as the New Source of Oneness Despite Diversity

In the Gospel and Acts of the Apostles, the agent of renewal and communion is the Spirit, mentioned 93 times in all, 27 in the

Gospel and 66 in Acts. The first great manifestation is on Pentecost. When the Spirit fell on the community gathered in a home, there was a crowd outside composed of "every nation under heaven living in Jerusalem" (2:5). Luke enumerates 15 or more examples of these areas. They all heard the sound of the Spirit like a rush of the wind.

> And at this sound the crowd gathered and was bewildered, because each one heard them speaking in the native language of each. Amazed and astonished, they asked, "Are not all these who are speaking Galileans? And how is it that we hear, each of us, in our own native language?" (2:6–8)

The cause of this language phenomenon is the Spirit, for Luke had just written about the Spirit filling the house in which the disciples were gathered and stated, "All of them were filled with the Holy Spirit and began to speak in other languages, as the Spirit gave them ability" (2:4). The language they spoke concerned praises of God, for the people said, "In our own languages we hear them speaking about God's great deeds of power" (2:11). From this, we surmise that their new gift of oneness in tongue was a "spirit language" that enabled them to praise God together despite wide differences of places of origin. The opening introduction that "they were all gathered together in one place" (2:1) draws attention to the community's oneness despite diversity. Luke writes later that the believers were "one heart and soul" (4:32). They were so much so that they even shared their possessions.

This was the first of several "Pentecosts" in the Acts of the Apostles. It is really a Jewish Pentecost and experience of the Spirit. Other Pentecosts occur at times of crises or the opening of the Gospel to new places. After the apostles were imprisoned by the Jewish authorities, the community prayed for their freedom. After the apostles were liberated, the community prayed together and repeated the same Pentecost phenomenon: "When they had prayed, the place in which they were gathered together was shaken; and they were all filled with the Holy Spirit and spoke the word of God with boldness" (4:31).

The next Pentecost is the Holy Spirit descending upon Jew and Gentile together as a sign of oneness after Peter preached the good news to a group of Jewish disciples along with Cornelius the centurion and his friends:

> While Peter was still speaking, the Holy Spirit fell upon all who heard the word. The circumcised believers who had come with Peter were astounded that the gift of the Holy Spirit had been poured out even on the Gentiles, for they heard them speaking in tongues and extolling God. (10:44–46)

A third Pentecost occurs after Paul comes to Ephesus and meets a group of disciples of John the Baptist. We find in Acts, chapters 18–19, that some of them knew only the baptism of John and had not become disciples of Jesus. Paul taught them about Jesus and baptized them "in the name of the Lord Jesus." "Then he laid hands on them and the Holy Spirit came upon them, and they spoke in tongues and prophesied" (19:6). The laying on of hands, as Peter and John did at Samaria (8:17), brings out the nature of the Spirit as an inner bond of oneness despite diversity.

A help toward understanding Luke's portrayal of Pentecost may come from looking at the scriptures that seem to have inspired his description. There is an ancient myth that the human race at one time spoke a common language and could all understand one another. This inspired the story of the Tower of Babel beginning with the words, "Now the whole earth had one language and the same words" (Gen 11:1). So, people were proud of themselves and started to build a high tower to reach the sky to celebrate their unity and human achievements. But God saw what they were doing and said,

> Look, they are one people, and they have all one language; and this is only the beginning of what they will do; nothing that they propose to do will now be impossible for them. Come, let us go down now and confuse their language so that they will not understand one another's speech. (Gen 11:6–7)

Luke's Pentecost is really a reversal of the Tower of Babel. God punished humanity trying to build a monument to themselves and their unity. He confused their languages to make this impossible through human striving. Instead, Pentecost makes possible a new oneness of the human race by the gift of the Spirit despite every possible obstacle raised by walls of differences. The Spirit makes it possible for each person to hear one another speaking the praise of God in a commonly understood language.

Summary

More than in any other Gospel, Luke emphasizes the *metanoia* as the root of justice. *Equal sharing* is a practical aspect as he opens the Gospel with the Baptist's social teaching and closes before the passion with the example of Zacchaeus. Luke's stories portray the sharp injustice of the rich in contrast with the poor. His Sermon on the Plain focuses on compassion, like God's own, that must accompany justice. Concern for bread for the hungry must be *each day* as in the Lord's Prayer and the daily distribution in Acts 6. Only in Luke do we find *one* commandment that includes love of both God and neighbor. The Good Samaritan parable exemplifies this. Luke's combat theme stresses the power of the forces of darkness and the need of prayer to overcome them. His emphasis on women earns his writing the title of a "Gospel of Women."

8

John: Ideal Models
for New Relationships

The Gospel of John was written later than the other three, around the beginning of the second century A.D. The writer was familiar with Matthew, Mark, and Luke and did not merely repeat what they have already written.[32] In fact, he has much material not in the other Gospels at all. Even the material that he uses in common with the other Gospels is raised to a new level when it concerns the person of Jesus as Word of God and eternal Son of the Father. The Gospel begins with this proclamation: "In the beginning was the Word and the Word was with God, and the Word was God." This eternal Word, however, became one of us: "The Word became flesh and lived among us." At the same time, the descent of the Word means the ascent of believers. "To all who received him, who believed in his name, he gave the power to become children of God" (1:12). As children of God, like Jesus, they can reach new levels of relationships.

John's Gospel, Social Justice, and New Relationships

Social Justice has two sides: sharing relationships and sharing resources. In the biblical perspective, the two must go together and promote equality. This fourth Gospel, written after the others, presumes them and tries not to repeat. There is nothing here about riches, possessions, moral imperatives, and ethical directions. It is enough for Jesus to state his legacy in the Last Supper: "Just as I have loved you, you also should love one another. By this every-one will know that you are my disciples" (13:35). This type of relationship necessarily includes sharing of possessions moving toward equality. An illustration of Jesus' legacy of oneness is in the area of women's leadership.

Women, Leadership, and Equality

A Samaritan Woman Opens the Way to a World Apostolate

When Jesus said, "As I have loved you," it was not a fuzzy, warm ideal but a practical directive. Although he was a teacher, he wanted equality as person to person. So, he stated, "I do not call you servants any longer, because the servant does not know what the master is doing. But I have called you friends, because I have made known to you everything that I have heard from my Father" (15:14–15). Jesus is not a friend in the loose sense of the word, but one with such a genuine love that he can say, "No one has greater love than this, to lay down one's life for one's friends" (15:13). As a sign of this love, his disciples formed a new family in which they could use the terms *brother* and *sister* in the familiar sense usually reserved for the intimacy of the home.

The author was well aware that during his time, toward the beginning of the second century, the word *sister* did not convey the same idea of equality as *brother* did. A hint in this regard is found in the story of the Samaritan woman. When the disciples came back from purchasing food, they found Jesus talking with her by a well. The text reads, "They were astonished that he was speaking with a woman, but no one said, 'What do you want?' or, 'Why are you speaking with her?'" (4:27). It is interesting that this statement was written some 60 or 70 years after the events. The author is telling another generation that Jesus' intention is to break the pat-terns of separation that were prevalent in the early church.

John's Gospel tries to bring out women's equality by describing them as exercising some of the same leadership roles that male disciples held in the other Gospels. For example, in the first three Gospels, Jesus chooses his first disciples, Peter,

Andrew, James, and John by the lake of Galilee. They leave their fishing nets and follow him. Later, he sends them out to preach (Mark 1:20).

However, in John, the first apostle is the Samaritan woman (4:1–54). Jesus meets her at a well and asks her for a drink while his disciples have gone off to the town to buy some food. In doing so, he breaks the ritual barriers that made such a contact strictly forbidden. Jesus' conversation with her gradually moves to deeper levels. She opens her personal life to Jesus by admitting that she has had five husbands and is now living with another man. Jesus responds also on a deep level and discloses who he really is.

She told him, "I know that Messiah is coming (who is called Christ)." Jesus replied, "I am he, the one who is speaking to you" (4:26). *Thus, the first person in the Gospels to whom Jesus reveals the secret of his identity is this woman.*

At this point, the disciples arrived on the scene. Then, the woman left her water jar (like Peter left his nets!) and went back to the city. There, she reversed social customs and spoke to the men usually gathered at the gates of the city. She told them, "Come and see a man who told me everything I have ever done! He cannot be the Messiah, can he?" (4:29). They listened to her word and left the city to go to Jesus.

The episode then emphasizes the success of the woman's mission:

> Many Samaritans from that city believed in him because of the woman's testimony, "He told me everything I have ever done." So when the Samaritans came to him, they asked him to *stay* with them; and he *stayed* there two days. And many more believed because of his word. (4:39–41)

The italicized words *stay* and *stayed* show that the initial purpose of the Gospel is being fulfilled— that the Word became flesh in order to dwell or stay with people (1:14). This outreach to ethnically half-Jewish Samaritans, who were considered as religious outcasts by the Jews, marks Jesus' first step in bringing the Gospel to the non-Jewish world.

Martha, the First to Proclaim Jesus as Son of God

In Matthew 16:16, Peter makes the first great profession of faith with the words "You are the Messiah, the Son of the living God." In John, instead of in Peter, Martha does the same with the words to Jesus "Yes, Lord, I believe that you are the Messiah, the Son of God, the one who is to come into the world" (11:27). She says this in response to Jesus' challenge as to whether her brother Lazarus would rise again. However, the statements of Peter and Martha are on different levels. That of Peter concerns the messianic and teaching role of Jesus. Martha's confession is a personal one in Jesus as the Word of God giving life to others, even the dead: "Those who believe in me, even though they die, will live, and everyone who lives and believes in me will never die" (11:25–26). The Gospel prologue states, "In him was life" (1:3). Those who are united to Jesus will have *eternal life*. This is a key theme in this Gospel that is repeated seventeen times.

Mary of Bethany, the First to Appreciate Jesus' Coming Death

Mary wants to express her loving gratitude for what Jesus has in mind. She chooses to do this in a way that mirrors Jesus' own actions. In coming to Judea, the capital area, in order to save Lazarus her brother, Jesus has risked his life. When he announced his intention to do so, his alarmed disciples responded, "Rabbi, the Jews were just now trying to stone you, and are you going there again?" (11:8). Jesus' trip to Judea was inspired by a love that went as far as death. This was not only for Lazarus but also for those whom he represents—every believer.

As a result, Martha felt that her own gift must be like that of Jesus as an act of love: "Mary took a pound of costly perfume made of pure nard, anointed Jesus' feet, and wiped them with her hair. The house was filled with the fragrance of the perfume." The word *nard* belongs to love language and is only found in the great love song of the Bible, the Song of Songs. In fact, her whole action is in terms of that book. There, we find a banquet, an anointing, and the special significance of the hair.[33] When Mary let down her hair to dry Jesus' feet, it was an extraordinary demonstration of tenderness and affection.

However, the male disciples became very angry, and Judas was their spokesman, "Why was this perfume not sold for three hundred denarii and the money given to the poor?" (12:5). He was thinking that a large donation for the poor would be a better way to respond to what Jesus had done. The 300 denarii represented a year or more of wages and symbolized the total giving of herself. The author then notes the effect of Mary's action: The odor of the anointed body of Jesus fills the house, which symbolizes the Christian community. Jesus then stated that this woman really appreciated he was willing to die to save Lazarus and others. He said, "Leave her alone. She bought it so that she might keep it for the day of my burial. You always have the poor with you, but you do not always have me" (12:7–8).

Martha and Mary Risk Subversive Action as a Model for Leaders

For Jesus, a prime leadership quality was the willingness to risk even one's life for others: "The good shepherd lays down his life for the sheep" (10:11). After the resurrection of Lazarus, "The chief priests and the Pharisees had given orders that anyone who knew where Jesus was should let them know" (11:57). Government leaders at that time were really Roman puppets who were obliged to report to Pilate, the governor, anyone who had pretensions of being a king or Messiah. Judas, 1 of the 12, as an obedient "good citizen" (with other possible motives also) went to the ruling priests and informed them where and how they could arrest Jesus. Judas later brought a detachment of soldiers with police from the chief priests and Pharisees to arrest Jesus (18:1–3).

However, in subversive contrast, Martha and Mary of Bethany prepared a special testimonial dinner in Jesus' honor, even if they had to defy Roman authority to do so. The Gospel carefully notes the effects of their courage. Their action is contagious and leads others to risk following Jesus. A large crowd came to Bethany and was among those who accompanied Jesus on his Palm Sunday procession into Jerusalem (12:9–11, 17–18). "The

Pharisees said to one another, 'You see, you can do nothing. Look, the world has gone after him'" (12:19). The Gospel author is telling his audience that the courageous example of Martha and Mary reaches even to the world when they risk their lives as Jesus did. This is true for all time, but it was especially true at the time of the Gospel's writing when many believers faced Roman persecution. The action of these women risking imprisonment and death because of their faith was an important example. It would also have special meaning for those like Judas who were tempted (perhaps for rewards) to denounce others to Roman authority.

Mary Magdalene, Apostle of Apostles, the First to See the Risen Jesus

The resurrection stories in John's Gospel feature the special place of Mary Magdalene (20:1–18). She is the first one to find the empty tomb and notify Peter and the Beloved Disciple about it. She even runs in the early morning to find them. Then, she goes back to the tomb to search for Jesus' body. While weeping for her loss, she sees two angels sitting in the tomb. They say to her, "Woman, why are you weeping?" She answers (afraid there may have been a grave robbery), "They have taken away my Lord, and I do not know where they have laid him." At this point, "When she had said this, she turned around and saw Jesus standing there, but she did not know it was Jesus." Jesus said to her, "Woman, why are you weeping? Whom are you looking for?" Mary at first thought he was the gardener and asked where he had taken Jesus' body. Then, Jesus said, "Mary," and "she turned and said to him in Hebrew, 'Rabbouni' (which means Teacher)."

Mary Magdalene is the very first person to see the risen Jesus. He in turn gives her the extraordinary mission to go and announce his resurrection to the others. So, she merits the title of "apostle of apostles" and also "beloved disciple" like Martha, Mary, and Lazarus (11:5). In this Gospel, Mary Magdalene is not an intermediary to the 12 but a disciple and apostle in her own right.

Community Oneness in Diversity
Modeled on Jesus' Own Unity with the Father

In his final priestly prayer, Jesus prays for all those who will believe in him through the word of his disciples: "I ask…that they may all be one. As you, Father, are in me, and I am in you, may they also be one in us that the world may believe that you sent me" (17:21). For greater emphasis this is repeated in regard to the Father's glory. Jesus has also shared this glory with his disciples so "they may be one, as we are one. I in them and you in me, so that they may become completely one, so that the world may know that you have sent me and have loved them even as you have loved me" (17:22–23). In the parable of the Good Shepherd, Jesus declares, "I have other sheep that do not belong to this fold. I must bring them also, and they will listen to my voice. So there will be one flock and one shepherd" (10:16). After Caiphas the high priest unwittingly prophesies that Jesus will die for the nation, the evangelist adds, "not for the nation only but to gather into one the dispersed children of God" (11:52).

In this theme of oneness under one Father, the above verse is an important key in the words "to gather into one the dispersed children of God." The words echo the story of the Tower of Babel in Genesis 10:32–11:9. It begins with the scattering of Noah's sons in the world after the great flood. At that time, "the whole earth had literally one tongue and one speech" (11:1). However, they gathered together to build a monument to themselves before scattering over the Earth. To prevent this, God confused their languages so they would not understand one another. So, the place was called Babel, or "confusion," and from there, "the Lord scattered them abroad over the face of the earth" (11:9).

The high priest thus prophesied Jesus' mission to bring together as one God's children scattered over the whole world. Because Noah's children included Gentiles as well as Jews, these words pointed to a Gentile mission as well. The three great languages, Hebrew, Latin, and Greek together on the cross inscription also symbolize the new unity of the world's language through the one Christ and his seamless robe, which was in woven in *one* piece but not cut and divided (19:20, 23).

Other Johannine texts also point to this new world oneness. The prologue opens with God's universal creative activity through the Word: "He was in the world, and the world came into being through him" (1:10). This creative activity is the action of a loving Father for "God so loved the world that he gave his only Son, so that everyone who believes in him may not perish but may have eternal life" (3:16). The connection to Jesus' death is brought out at the close of the "Book of Signs" in chapter 12. Some Greeks during the Passover came to Philip (a Greek name) and asked to see Jesus (12:20). These were Greek-speaking Jews who had come to Jerusalem from other places for worship. However, no more is said about them. They trigger Jesus' pronouncement that the hour is coming for the whole world to come to him through his loving sacrifice on the cross.

Following this, we find the "little Gethsemane" in John as Jesus prays to his *Abba*: "Now my soul is troubled. And what should I say—'Father, save me from this hour'? No, it is for this reason that I have come to this hour. Father, glorify your name" (12:27–28). Jesus heard his Father's voice in answer, while the people thought it was thunder or that an angel had spoken to him. Jesus then declares to the people (and Gospel audience): "Now is the judgment of this world; now the ruler of this world will be driven out. And I, when I am lifted up from the earth, will draw all people to myself" (12:31–32). The evangelist then explains, "He said this to indicate the kind of death he was to die."

Oneness and the Samaritan Apostolate

Keeping the rift between Jesus and the Samaritans in mind, we can add some significant points to what we have already written about Jesus' encounter with the Samaritan woman. In asking her for a drink at the well, Jesus was breaking the taboo against sharing food and drink with someone who was ritually "unclean." Consequently, the woman asks, "How is it that you, a Jew, ask a drink of me, a woman of Samaria?" (4:7). The Gospel author then explains, "Jews do not share things with Samaritans." But Jesus wishes to share more than her vessel of well water. He desires to share his own gift of living water that brings everlasting life if she only asks for it.

However, there are some obstacles. The Jews worship at Jerusalem, but Samaritans are barred from going there and have their own place of worship. So, the woman declares, "Our ancestors worshiped on this mountain, but you say that the place where people must worship is in Jerusalem" (4:20). Jesus answers that this wall of division is now broken. Jew and Samaritan can be one again. "Woman, believe me, the hour is coming when you will worship the Father neither on this mountain nor in Jerusalem." He then adds, "True worshipers will worship the Father in spirit and truth, for the Father seeks such to worship him" (4:21–23). This double mention of "Father" proclaims the source of true oneness. Then, the woman tells Jesus of her belief in the Messiah: "When he comes (to bring this oneness), he will proclaim all things to us." Jesus then reveals himself to her as this promised one by saying, "I am he, the one who is speaking to you" (4:25–26).

After this, the disciples returned from shopping for food. Then, the woman left her vessel at the well and went to tell the townspeople the great news not only about the change in her own life but also about the hopes of her people. The Samaritans listened to her message, came out to see Jesus, and asked him to stay with them. The evangelist notes, "And many *more* believed because of his word. They said to the woman, 'It is no longer because of what you said that we believe, for we have heard ourselves, and we know that this is truly the Savior of the world'" (4:41–42). The Gospel audience will remember that they have just heard that God so loved the *world* as to send his Son that those who believe may receive eternal life (3:16). Now, this is fulfilled in the water of *eternal life* promised to the Samaritan woman and her people (4:14). The *world* is especially mentioned because the welcoming belief of the Samaritans becomes the gateway for the Gospel to move to the whole world. The Acts of the Apostles notes this also in the great surprise when Philip went to Samaria and the people believed in the good news with great joy (8:4–25).

Toward Oneness in Believing Despite Diversity

An essential element in this oneness will be the final confession of Thomas at the conclusion of the Gospel, "My Lord and My God" (20:28). None of the other Gospels has such an explicit declaration of Jesus' divinity or anything like Jesus' previous statement, "The Father and I are one" (10:30). The fourth Gospel author writes at a later period toward the beginning of the second century and describes the culmination of a long development of understanding about Jesus' person. It was especially important to emphasize this to Christians facing persecution by a Roman emperor who proclaimed himself as a god and even allowed his image to appear on all his coins crowned with a halo. What hope would Christians have unless they believed that Jesus is God incarnate from the first moment of creation? However, the author knows that some of his Gospel audience have not yet reached this highest level of faith content.[34] In his Gospel, he accepts where they are although he attempts to draw them together as one.

Disciples of the Baptist

The first group of these "different" believers were disciples of John the Baptist. Some remained as such and never knew Jesus as a risen, exalted Son of God. We know this because the Acts of the Apostles tells us how Paul and his companions met such disciples. One of these was a renowned Jewish preacher called Apollos: "He had been instructed in the Way of the Lord; and he spoke with burning enthusiasm and taught accurately the things concerning Jesus, though he knew only the baptism of John" (18:25). There was also a group of 12 disciples of the Baptist that Paul met in Ephesus. They had received John's baptism but had not gone further. Paul instructed them, baptized them, and laid his hands upon them. The Holy Spirit came upon them, just as at the first Pentecost, and "they spoke in tongues and prophesied" (19:1–7).

To honor the Baptist and draw his disciples into oneness with his community, the author, unlike in the other three Gospels, describes the first disciples, Peter, Andrew, Philip, and Nathaniel, as being followers of the Baptist before they met Jesus. The Baptist introduced them to Jesus when he came to the Jordan: "The next day he saw Jesus coming toward him and declared, 'Here is the Lamb of God who takes away the sin of the world'" (1:29). With these words, he pronounced a central theme of the Gospel to be completed by Jesus on the cross. This is when the beloved disciple sees him as the Passover Lamb according to the scriptures (19:32–37). John's Gospel also points out that Jesus continued the baptismal ministry of John (3:25–26; 4:1). However, the Baptist humbly stepped aside when his disciples told him that Jesus had been baptizing also and that more people were going to him. He said to them,

> You yourselves are my witnesses that I said, "I am not the Messiah but I have been sent ahead of him." He who has the bride is the bridegroom. The friend of the bridegroom, who stands and hears him, rejoices greatly at the bridegroom's voice. For this reason my joy has been fulfilled. He must increase, but I must decrease. (3:28–30)

Conservative Jewish Christians

These were Jews who believed that Jesus was Messiah and Son of God but not specifically that he was Lord and God, as in Thomas's confession of faith. They kept faithfully all the customs of the law and frequented the synagogue. They believed that Jesus brought Judaism to completion without making any radical changes. Some were "closet believers," who kept their belief in Jesus as a secret. In John's Gospel, Nicodemus represents them: "Now there was a Pharisee named Nicodemus, a leader of the Jews" (3:1).

Nicodemus came to Jesus at night and said to him, "Rabbi, we know that you are a teacher who has come from God; for no one can do these signs that you do apart from the presence of God" (3:2). Jesus welcomes him and does not condemn him. However, he does teach him that a radical change is necessary to enter the kingdom of God: "No one can enter the kingdom of God without being born of water and Spirit" (3:5). Later, Nicodemus has the courage to come out in the open and defend Jesus when the chief priests and Pharisees sent soldiers to arrest him (7:50–51). This left him open to suspicion that he was a follower of Jesus for they tell him, "Surely you are not also from Galilee, are you? Search and you will see that no prophet is to arise in Galilee" (7:52). Finally, Nicodemus took the greatest risk of all by assisting in the burial of Jesus. This was along with another former "closet believer," Joseph of Arimathea. He is described as "a disciple of Jesus, though a secret one because of his fear of the Jews" (19:38–39).

Peter and "Apostolic Christians"

These were Jewish Christians, who followed the example and teachings of Peter and those who came after him. They still kept to the practices of Judaism and had not reached the high Christology of John's Gospel as shown in the Prologue in which Jesus is the eternal Word of God in accord with the final confession of Thomas, "My Lord and My God." However, they did meet apart for the breaking of bread and to listen to the teachings of the apostles (Acts 2:42). This is brought out indirectly in chapter 6 of John in the discourse on the bread of life. At its end, the Gospel relates that many departed from Jesus and did not accept his teachings on the Eucharist. Jesus asked the 12, "Do you also wish to go away?" Peter responded, "Lord, to whom can we go? You have the words of eternal life. We have come to believe and know that you are the Holy One of God" (6:67–69).

The fourth Gospel presents the Holy Spirit, the Paraclete, as the *inner successor* and guide of the community (chapters 14–16). However, the author is anxious to preserve oneness with Peter's group and show that he, as "the rock," is the successor of Jesus in regard to the apostolate. This is emphasized in chapter 21, which appears to be an appendage to the Gospel either by the author or someone else close to him.

In this last chapter, Peter calls the others to a fishing expedition. They labor all night without catching anything. Toward dawn, in a visionary appearance, Peter sees Jesus who tells him to cast his net on the right side of the ship. He did so and enclosed so large a multitude of fish that they could not haul it in. Then, the beloved disciple recognized Jesus, and Peter jumped into the water to come to him. Later, the other disciples dragged in the net and counted 153 large fish. The writer notes, "Though there were so many, the net was not torn" (21:11).

The whole vision illustrates the apostolic ministry headed by Peter and its success. The net remains one and unbroken. Despite the great variety of people/fish brought in, the community retains its oneness. This teaches that oneness does not destroy diversity but, rather, recognition of diversity makes it possible. A parody of oneness is so-called unity characterized by uniformity, which is only maintained by power.

Following this, Jesus affirms Peter's unique role as a nourishing shepherd of the flock. Three times, Jesus asks him, "Simon, son of John, do you love me more than these?" (21:15). This is a very touching reminder of Peter's triple denial of Jesus despite the fact that he had boasted he would even lay down his life for the Master (13:36–38; 18,15–18, 25–27). Each time Jesus repeated the question, "Do you love me?" Peter answered "Yes, Lord, you know that I love you," and finally, "You know everything, you know that I love you." In turn, Jesus replied three times, "Feed my sheep." Finally, Jesus tells him that he will actually lay down his life and prove that he is a good shepherd (10:11).

One Father, Equal Children, and the Breakdown of Hierarchies

In the Gospels of Matthew, Mark, and Luke, there are distinct levels among the followers of Jesus. *Peter,* meaning "rock," is the new Greek name given to Simon by Jesus. He has a special place as the first-named follower of Jesus. Later, Matthew cites Jesus' special words to him, "I tell you that you are Peter, and on this rock I will build my church" (16:18). In all, Jesus chooses 12 apostles, and these Gospels give all their names. In Matthew, Peter is called "first" among these. Jesus then gives them special powers to proclaim his message and to cast out demons (Mark 3:14–15). They went out as Jesus commanded: "So they went out and proclaimed that all should

220

repent. They cast out many demons, and anointed with oil many who were sick and cured them" (Mark 6:13). The exorcisms went together with the healings.

Among the 12, there is an "in-group," besides Peter, composed of his brother Andrew, with James and John, who were originally fishing partners with Peter. This group has a privileged association with Jesus. Only Peter, James, and John are allowed to be with Jesus when he raises up the daughter of Jairus, the synagogue leader (Mark 5:37). The same group accompanies Jesus to the mountain and witnesses his transfiguration in glory. There, Peter is their spokesman who asks if they can build three dwellings for Jesus, Moses, and Elijah (Mark 9:2–8).

Peter is also the one who speaks for the 12 on other occasions (e.g., regarding riches [10:28] and the fig tree [11:21]). All four hear Jesus' prophecy of the destruction of the Temple and the last times (13:2). Because of their close connection to Jesus, James and John ask for special places in the coming kingdom of God (10:35–40). Only Peter, James, and John accompany Jesus as he goes to pray at night in the Garden of Gethsemane (14:33). There, Jesus speaks to Peter to warn him to stay awake and pray. The Gospel ends with the young man clothed in white at the tomb telling the women to bring the news of the resurrection to *Peter* (16:7).

These special ranks among Jesus' disciples are either absent or considerably softened in the fourth Gospel. The evangelist is concerned to present a picture of oneness and equality that transcends levels among Jesus' disciples. To begin with, John's Gospel does not refer to a group called apostles. Jesus sends all his disciples without distinction: "As the Father has sent me, so I send you" (John 20:21). This Gospel acknowledges Peter's special place as a founding rock, but Peter does not have a great confession of faith as in Matthew's Gospel. James and John who aspired to special positions in the other Gospels are not even named, except generically in 21:2 (an appendix added by the author or someone else) as "the sons of Zebedee." In this same appendix, Jesus does tell Peter to "feed his lambs" (21:15–17). This indicates a special role in the eucharistic teaching in this Gospel, as we will see below.

Jesus only addresses the 12 on one occasion, at the close of the bread discourse in chapter 6. When many disciples turned away because of Jesus' difficult teaching, Jesus asked the 12, "Do you also wish to go away?" Peter replies as their spokesman, "Lord, to whom can we go? You have the words of eternal life. We have come to believe that you are the Holy One of God" (6:67–69). Jesus answered, "Did I not choose you, the twelve? Yet one of you is a devil" (6:70). This of course is Judas, who is named as one of the 12.

In this text, Jesus refers to the 12 as especially chosen by him. But the Gospel does not record any special mission or powers given them. The only other person named as among the 12 was Thomas who was not present at Easter Sunday evening when Jesus appeared to his disciples. On the following Sunday, he returned and made the great confession of faith, "My Lord and my God!" (20:28).

When Jesus does transfer powers, it is to the whole group of disciples without distinction. After the washing of feet at the Last Supper, he tells them all, "If I, your Lord and Teacher, have washed your feet, you also ought to wash one another's feet. For I have set you an example, that you also should do as I have done to you" (13:14–15). Jesus' greatest power is that of the forgiveness of sins. On the Sunday night of his resurrection he appears to all his disciples, breathes upon them, and declares, "Receive the Holy Spirit. If you forgive the sins of any, they are forgiven them; if you retain the sins of any, they are retained" (20:22–23).

So-Called Love of God and Social Justice

The dominant theme in John's Gospel is that of love, with the word used 30 times. There are no practical ethics connected with it as in the other Gospels, although the qualities of this love are carefully taught. An example of this is laying down one's life for a friend, as Jesus did. However, there were some Christians who considered this love predominantly as an inner feeling that came from mystical union or identification with the risen divine Christ. In doing so, they largely discounted the earthly human reality of Jesus

222

and his practical commandments. The modern name given to them is that of "gnostics," coming from the Greek word *gnosis,* meaning "knowledge." Above all, they appreciated an inner enlightenment or experience that made them experience the "love of God." The Gospel of John was their favorite because it mentioned love so often and emphasized the divinity of Christ and union with him. They believed that everything else flowed from this.

The first letter of John was written to counteract these gnostic-oriented Christians,[35] sometimes referred to as "docetic," meaning that Jesus only "appeared" to be really human. The author may have been the same as that of the Gospel; however, the differences of language and theology make it likely that he was someone else writing in John's name. The letter was attached to the Gospel to make sure that the Gospel was correctly understood. In fact, we know of no ancient manuscript of John that did not have the letter attached to it. Church authorities may have considered this necessary in order to have John's Gospel on the official canon of the New Testament.

The Opening Message and Theme of the Letter

> We declare to you what was from the beginning, what we have heard, what we have seen with our eyes, what we have looked at and touched with our hands, concerning the word of life—this life was revealed, and we have seen it and testify to it, and declare to you the eternal life that was with the Father and was revealed to us—we declare to you what we have seen and heard so that you also may have fellowship with us; and truly our fellowship is with the Father and with his Son Jesus Christ. (1:1–3)

We note immediately the external similarity to the Gospel prologue of John, "In the beginning was the Word." The Gospel emphasizes the preexistent Word of God and goes on to describe the work of the Word in creation and its final incarnation in Jesus. However, the letter starts differently from what was heard, seen, and touched by disciples on Earth. They in turn (verse 3) relay this to others so they may have fellowship with "us" his disciples. This fellowship is "with the Father and with his Son Jesus Christ." The words *Jesus* and *Christ* emphasize his human reality. This is indirectly saying that there is no direct experience of the risen Jesus except through fellowship with his first disciples among whom is the author.

The Beliefs of These "Radical" Christians

These can only be found as filtered through the eyes of the author, and there may be some exaggerations. There is no question that these Christians were at one time members of the community. The author writes, "They went out from us, but they did not belong to us; for if they belonged to us, they would have remained with us" (2:19). Because they trusted in an inner divine enlightenment, the author starts by writing,

> This is the message we have heard from him and proclaim to you, that God is light and in him there is no darkness at all. If we say that we have fellowship with him while we are walking in darkness, we lie and do not do what is true; but if we walk in the light as he himself is in the light, we have fellowship with one another, and the blood of Jesus his Son cleanses us from all sin. (1:5–7)

Again the author states that the message of God comes from himself and others and not through direct experience. "If we say" is a way to refer to the opponents' beliefs. They claim to have direct fellowship with the Light through experience. However, the author counters by saying that this cannot be true if "we are walking" in darkness. "Walking" was an ancient way to speak of one's actions and deeds, which will be a principal argument of the letter. These actions and deeds accompany "fellowship with one another." This fellowship also involves trust in the mediation of Jesus' blood to forgive sins. This contrasts with an inner experience and identification with the divinity that would make them "sinless."

Counteracting Inner Experience
with Jesus' Command to Love Others

The inner knowing experience of *gnosis* contrasts with Jesus' commandments:

> Whoever says, "I have come to *know* him," but does not obey his *commandments,* is a liar, and in such a person the truth does not exist; but whoever obeys his word, truly in this person the *love of God* has reached perfection. (2:4–5)

The commandment(s) of Jesus will often be referred to in this letter. This is the only way to discern whether there exists real *love of God*. The author is referring to Jesus' specific commands to love others, especially that in the Last Supper:

> I give you a new commandment, that you love one another. Just as I have loved you, you also should love one another. By this everyone will know that you are my disciples, if you have love for one another. (John 13:34–35)

Then, the writer indicates strongly that the two opposites of so-called enlightenment and hating a neighbor cannot coexist: "Whoever says, 'I am in the light' while hating a brother or sister, is still in the darkness" (2:9). To the contrary, both must go together: "Whoever loves a brother or sister lives in the light, and in such a person there is no cause for stumbling" (2:10). This "love," like that of Jesus, is evident in real concern for the material needs of another,

> We know love by this, that he laid down his life for us—and we ought to lay down our lives for one another. How does God's love abide in anyone who has the world's goods and sees a brother or sister in need and yet refuses help? (3:16–17)

Finally, the letter concludes that there is only one source for loving other human beings and the love of God: "Beloved, let us love one another, because love is from God; everyone who loves is born of God and knows God" (4:7). Negatively, "Whoever does not love does not know God, for *God is love*" (4:8). This last statement, "God is love," is unique in the entire Bible. It expressed very simply that there is really one love in the world, God's great universal love for all. When we love others, we are part of it and at the same time closely united to the very essence of God. Justice flows from true human love which at the same time is divine love.

Summary

John's Gospel moves toward equality in justice regarding status and relationships. Women—the Samaritan, Martha, and Mary—take on leadership roles exercised by men in the other Gospels. Mary Magdalene is the first to see the risen Jesus and bring the news to others. Oneness despite the diversity in levels of belief is a central theme illustrated by the Samaritans, John the Baptist believers, conservative Jewish Christians, and "apostolic Christians" led by Peter. The hierarchies within the 12 in the first three Gospels yield to a oneness in discipleship guided by the Paraclete. The first letter of John tries to neutralize the impact of the fourth Gospel on gnostic-oriented believers by emphasizing practical love for others as being the same as "love of God."

9

Paul the Apostle:
Oneness Through Diversity

The letters of Paul[36] are the earliest Christian literature; his first letter to the Thessalonians dates from around A.D. 50. Christianity as we know it today is largely the result of the pioneering efforts of this extraordinary apostle. He became a convert within a few years after the death of Jesus, but there is no evidence in his letters that he ever knew Jesus in the flesh. His first experience of Jesus was through a direct vision of the risen Christ. Before this, he was a dedicated teacher of Judaism, zealous to the extreme when it came to faithful response to God in the Jewish Torah. His conversion was not from a bad life to a good one, but a change of focus to a total gift of himself to God the Father through Jesus, instead of through the Torah.

However, his letters were not meant to be summaries of his teachings. Essentially, he wrote ad hoc responses to questions and difficulties brought to his attention by messengers or letters. Paul considered his mission to be that of an apostle establishing new communities in new places and then moving on after he felt they could continue on their own. As far as we know, the most time he ever stayed in one place was at Ephesus for a period of three years.

Regarding Social Justice, we can only draw on the limited materials in some of his letters. He was a man driven by the conviction that "time was of the essence." He felt that Jesus might return as early as within his own lifetime. He wrote to the Thessalonians about those who would be alive at Jesus' return and even "meet the Lord in the air" when he returned (1 Thess 4:17).

Within this time limitation, his intention was not to convert the world or make great changes in society. Within the oppressive, authoritarian Roman Empire, there was little opportunity for ordinary citizens to effect social change and very few of Paul's converts were even citizens.

Paul's goal was to create a circle of small house-church communities around the Roman Empire, which could be influential models and examples of what the world itself should be. Each could spread out to establish new centers in regions around them. His approach was to first visit a Jewish synagogue or place of prayer. There were always some Gentiles who were close to the synagogue—attracted by Jewish belief in one God who was just and asked for justice in those who believed in him. These Gentiles in turn influenced others outside the synagogue and brought them to Paul.

Eventually, this last group became the most responsive because Paul was not asking them to first of all adopt all Jewish law. He taught that faith in Christ was sufficient to receive the Spirit of God through conversion and baptism. However, this approach was not shared by other Christian apostles. Some required Gentiles to be circumcised and keep the law before they could become Christians (Acts 15:1). Others taught Gentiles to embrace as many biblical directives as possible in order to add a certain "perfection" to their basic belief in Christ. Still other believers continued to observe all the Jewish food regulations even to the extent of not eating together with Gentile Christians. Paul later wrote letters to deal with these problems; this is especially true of his letter to the Galatians.

Oneness Through Diversity—Christian and Gentile Jews

Paul's basic view on this oneness despite diversity is expressed in the following text:

> For in Christ Jesus you are all children of God through faith. As many of you as were baptized into Christ have clothed yourselves with Christ. *There is no longer Jew or Greek,* there is no longer slave or free, there is no longer male and female; for all of you are one in Christ Jesus. (Gal 3:26–28)

228

Paul is writing to believers about the relationships that should exist *within* a Christian community. When he first came to Antioch in Syria, he had the experience of living in the first joint community of Gentile and Jewish believers in which these distinctions were not present, especially in table fellowship (Acts 11:19–26). Later, Paul explained his own work among the Gentiles to the church leaders, Peter, James, and John. They placed no admission restrictions on the Gentiles, except that they should "remember the poor" (Gal 2:10). This meant to share possessions as a sign of real fellowship. They agreed that Peter and the others would continue to work with the Jews, while Paul would devote himself especially to the Gentiles (2:7–9).

However, Paul was thoroughly shocked on the occasion of a visit of Peter and some Christian Jews "from James" (2:11–14):

> But when Cephas (Peter) came to Antioch, I opposed him to his face, because he stood self-condemned; for until certain people came from James, he used to eat with the Gentiles. But after they came, he drew back and kept himself separate for fear of the circumcision faction. And the other Jews joined him in this hypocrisy, so that even Barnabas was led astray by their hypocrisy.

Paul was so disturbed because table fellowship was central to the Christian community. The exclusion of Gentiles from meals with their Jewish Christian brothers gave the appearance that something was lacking in them, or that they were "second class citizens." Peter's conduct was likely a practical gesture to appease the rigid views of some Jerusalem Christians who accompanied them. He was afraid that their disapproval would hurt his relationships with other Christians at Jerusalem and hinder his work among the Jews. However, Paul saw this as hitting at the heart of the Christian community. He felt it amounted to putting pressure on Gentile Christians to conform to Jewish practices. He told Peter publicly, "If you, though a Jew, live like a Gentile and not like a Jew, how can you compel the Gentiles to live like Jews?" (2:14).

Paul's arguments to the Galatians in the cited text above (3:26–29) are the following: They are first of all joint children of God through faith. A proof of this was the experience of their baptism or plunging into union with Christ. As a result of this, they received the gift of the one Spirit, through which they cried out, "Abba, Father," in the same way as Jesus himself did (4:6). This made them part of Jesus' own family of God, "one in Christ Jesus" (3:28). All were also "Abraham's offspring" because of God's promise to him. It amounted to a complete new creation or beginning made possible by the Spirit of God. So he can close his letter by writing, "For neither circumcision nor uncircumcision is anything; but a new creation is everything!" (6:15). Consequently, no external diversity whether of laws or marks on the flesh can affect the interior oneness of the Spirit.

Gender Diversity—There Is No Longer Male or Female (Gal 3:28)

Apparently Negative Pauline Views

In teaching Paul's letters over the years, I have found that one of the great obstacles facing students is the "bad press" about Paul and women. This is especially true of women who remember or have been told about the signs that were placed in some church entrances forbidding women to enter unless they had hats or veils. The authority quoted was St. Paul. Or they vividly recall weddings when the priest or minister looked intently at the bride while reading Paul's instruction: "Wives, be subject to your husbands" (Col 3:18). It is worse yet if they read the Pauline letter to Timothy with the injunction that women should not be teachers and should be silent in church and work out their salvation through childbearing (1 Tim 2:12–15).

Of course, we could easily answer that Paul was living in a patriarchal world 2,000 years ago, and we could not possibly judge him from modern standards. Yet, even so-called modern standards have a long ways to go. For example, women's legal right to vote only began in the United States in the first part of the twentieth century, after a long bitter struggle. Our Constitution reads that all *men* have been created equal. A constitutional amendment defining that this means both men and women has not yet been passed. In the early 1960s, President Kennedy signed a bill requiring equal wages to women for equal work. At that time, women's wages were only 60 percent that of men. Yet, even now after almost 40 years, this percentage has only reached 75 percent. This is a special hardship because many more women than previously are single heads of household.

However, we must still look to see what basis Paul has to proclaim to the Galatians, "There is no longer male or female for all of you are one in Christ Jesus" (3:28). First, we must remove difficulties with Paul that have very definite answers. In regard to marriage and obedience, the above injunctions in Colossians and similarly in Ephesians 5:21–44 are found in collections of "household instructions" belonging to a later period after Paul's original letters. These are generally considered to be Romans, 1 and 2 Corinthians, 1 Thessalonians, Galatians, Philippians, Philemon, and 2 Timothy. The others were written by Paul's disciples, not Paul himself. This is especially true about the first letter of Timothy with the orders that women are not to be teachers and are to remain silent in church.

This still leaves 1 Corinthians with its famous passage on "women's veils." The following is the background: In the Corinthian community, Paul has learned by letters that women, like men, were standing up to pray and prophesy. For women, this was a new sense of freedom especially because women were silent in Jewish synagogues, although Greek women felt less restrained. Paul wrote in return, "Any woman who prays and prophesies with her head unveiled disgraces her head—it is one and the same thing as having her head shaved. For if a woman will not veil herself, then she should cut off her hair; but if it is disgraceful for a woman to have her hair cut off or to be shaved, she should wear a veil" (11:5–6).

We note that Paul does not silence the women but is concerned about how they dress and act. Because both men and women wore long robes, the veil was a distinguishing feature of women's garb. Paul was very concerned about women trying to imitate males especially in clothing because transvestitism was strictly forbidden in the Jewish law. He does revert to quoting scriptural texts about woman's inferior position to man as shown in the (second)[37] creation story in which man is created first and then the woman: "Indeed, man was not made from woman, but woman from man. Neither was man created for the sake of woman, but woman for the sake of man" (11:8–9; Gen 2:15–25).

Yet, he realizes that this is the "old creation." In the Christian community, a new creation is beginning. At the close of Galatians he wrote: "A new creation is everything" (6:15). In this new creation, Paul continues, there is perfect equality between men and women: "Nevertheless, *in the Lord* woman is not independent of man or man independent of woman. For just as woman came from man, so man comes from woman; but all things come from God" (1 Cor 11:11–12). Paul sees the old and new creation in tension and does not wish anyone to be unnecessarily offensive in pushing his or her new freedom on others. So, he ends with what resembles a patriarchal decree: "If anyone is disposed to be contentious...we have no custom, nor do the churches of God" (11:16).

A second troubling passage is that in 1 Corinthians 14:34–36:

> As in all the churches of the saints, women should be silent in the churches. For they are not permitted to speak...as the law also says. If there is anything they desire to know, let them ask their husbands at home. For it is shameful for a woman to speak in church. Or did the word of God originate with you? Or are you the only ones it has reached?

At first, this passage appears to contradict the passage above about women praying and prophesying (11:5). There, we notice that Paul did not silence them but told them to wear veils in order to avoid imitating men. However, in that passage, the praying and prophesying were moved by the Spirit and governed by the freedom of the new age. But in the above verses, it seems to be a matter of ordinary speech, and the rules are from the "old creation" with its subordination of women. There is some mitigation in the fact that this is part of a rule of order in which others are told to maintain silence also. For example, those with the gift of tongues are told to be quiet if there is no one to interpret for them (14:28), and those prophesying are told not to go on and on but to yield to another prompted by the same gift (14:30). The same appeal to custom is made to them regarding the veils for women: "as in all the churches of the saints," a likely reference to Jewish Christian churches in which the rules of silence for women, according to custom, were observed.

In defense of Paul, it has been pointed out that the above verses (34–36) are not in this location in some Greek manuscripts but instead appear after verse 40. This leads to the suspicion that they were a moveable fragment. Perhaps the collector of the Pauline letters[38] inserted the passage at this point to go along with the text in 1 Timothy ordering women to be silent in church (2:11). However, a suspicion is only a possibility, not a proof to be used even with the best of intentions to defend Paul. He must have been deeply affected by the patriarchal environment in which he grew up.

Positive Features in Paul's View of Women

Some of His Views in 1 Corinthians 7

Paul starts, "Now concerning the matters about which you wrote (me): 'It is well for a man not to touch a woman'"(7:1). If we knew all the actual questions the Corinthians addressed to Paul, this chapter would be much easier to understand. We can only try to reconstruct some of the concerns newly baptized converts might have had. They knew that baptism meant a covenant to begin a whole new life in the new creation. In view of this, they had to examine their entire life, their occupations, business, friendships, and even marriage to see whether changes needed to be made. Some asked Paul (in view of Greek depreciation of the human body as evil) whether it might be better "not to touch a woman," meaning to have no sexual relations at all or to limit these in marriage.

Here, we note how Paul responds. In each case, he mentions equally both the man and the woman. This was contrary to the usual primacy of the man's choice in such matters by custom and law. So, he answers, "Because of cases of immorality, each man should have his own wife, and each woman her own husband" (7:2). In regard to conjugal rights, the same equal response is given for each person (7:3). This is repeated to show that neither (especially as the man was considered to have that authority) had authority over their own bodies (7:4). To those who asked whether they should not abstain from use of sex, he answers, "Do not deprive *one another* except by agreement for a set time, to devote yourselves to prayer" (7:5).

Another important question concerned the situation of a couple who married and then only one of them became a Christian. Today, this is often not a serious problem. However, in the ancient world, religion concerned every facet of domestic and social life. Many prayers and religious rites were performed at home. Types of foods could be potentially explosive issues. For example, was it permitted to eat meats that had been offered in sacrifice in pagan temples, where most of the meat came from? Paul must have been asked many questions about this mixed-marriage situation. Would it be best if they separated? And if the couple did, could they marry again? Paul answers,

> To the rest I say—I and not the Lord—that if any believer has a wife who is an unbeliever, and she consents to live with him, he should not divorce her. And if any woman has a husband who is an unbeliever, and he consents to live with her, she should not divorce him. For the unbelieving husband is made holy through his wife and the unbelieving wife is made holy through her husband....But if the unbelieving partner separates, let it be so; in such a case the brother or sister is not bound. It is to peace that God has called you. (7:12–15)

Paul writes, "I and not the Lord," because part of his answer will not be in literal accord with Jesus' saying about divorce to which he has just referred in Verse 12. Paul knows that Jesus' statement must be understood in terms of the total baptismal covenant of the newly baptized. First, Paul answers that they should stay together and not divorce if the unbeliever consents to live together in peace. He carefully frames the answer with both husband and wife represented equally, although divorce was usually considered something the man should decide. Then, he states the motivation that each, whether man or woman, can sanctify his or her partner through good example. However, Paul then adds that if either one of the partners decides to separate, the other is no longer bound, because God has called them to peace.

In both cases, whether to stay together or separate, the woman's initiative is placed fully equal to that of the man. This whole statement of Paul is remarkable for its time for the presentation of the equal rights of women.

Paul and Women's Leadership in the Apostolate

From what we know of Paul's life in his letters and in the Acts of the Apostles, we see the remarkable role that women played in missionary work. For example, the Gospel first came to Europe when Paul came to Philippi and found a group of women praying on the Sabbath outside the city near a river. He sat down and spoke to them. As a result, one of them, Lydia, the head of a household and a prominent dealer in purple cloth, became a convert along with her household. Paul stayed there and made it a center of his apostolate (Acts 16:13–15).

This community followed Paul with letters and gifts no matter where he went. He acknowledged in writing to the Philippians that they were the only ones he permitted to do so: "You Philippians know that in the early days of the Gospel, when I left Macedonia, no church shared with me in the matter of giving and receiving, except you alone. For even when I was in Thessalonica, you sent me help for my needs more than once" (4:15–16). Paul wrote this letter from prison, where he received daily food and help from a personal representative, Epaphroditus, that the community sent him (2:25–30).

Another prominent woman leader was Priscilla, wife of Aquila. They were a Jewish couple whom Paul met in Corinth, where they had recently arrived from Rome. They were tent makers, like Paul, and worked together with him in that trade. Paul converted them to Christianity while they were in Corinth. The couple was responsible for the conversion and instruction of Apollos, a brilliant Jewish preacher from Alexandria, Egypt. Apollos had great influence among Corinthian Christians: "He was an eloquent man, well versed in the scriptures,...though he knew only the baptism of John." Priscilla and Aquila "took him aside and explained the Way of God to him more accurately" (Acts 18:24–26). The fact that Priscilla is named first in the story seems to indicate she was the most active of the couple in missionary work.

Priscilla and Aquila collaborated with Paul during his year-and-a-half stay at Corinth. Afterward, Paul decided to start work in Ephesus, capital of the Roman province of Asia (mostly modern Turkey) and one of the largest cities of the Roman Empire. Before doing so, Paul had to return to Syria and left the couple at Ephesus to prepare the way for his return. We have no details of their work in the city, but Paul had great success there and remained about three years. Priscilla and Aquila must have played an important part in his success because they had gathered a church that used to meet in their house. In writing to the Corinthians from Ephesus, Paul sends this message: "Aquila and Priscilla, together with the church in their house, greet you warmly in the Lord" (1 Cor 16:19). The end of the letter to the Romans has a long list of greetings in which the couple is singled out for their extraordinary devotion: "Greet Priscilla and Aquila who work with me in Christ Jesus, and who risked their necks for my life, to whom not only I give thanks, but also all the churches of the Gentiles. Greet also the church in their house" (16:3–4).

In the same chapter 16 of Romans, Paul greets a long list of women who have been prominent in the churches. Among them: "I commend to you our sister Phoebe, a deacon (or minister) at Cenchreae, so that you may welcome her in the Lord as is fitting for the saints, and help her in whatever she may require from you, for she has been a benefactor of many and of myself as well" (2); "greet Mary who has worked very hard among you" (6); "greet Androni-cus and Junia, my relatives who were prominent among the apos-tles, and they were in Christ before me" (7); "greet those workers in

236

the Lord, Tryphaena and Tryphosa" (12); "greet the beloved Persis who has worked hard in the Lord" (12); greet Rufus, chosen in the Lord; and greet his mother—a mother to me also" (13).

Overcoming Class Distinctions in the Corinthian Eucharist

Social Justice concerns a just sharing of resources (property, material goods, etc.) and relationships. The letter to the Galatians explained the necessary basic freedom for this sharing to take place. The new relationships are based on the joint and equal relation to one *Abba,* resulting in a family that can address one another in the familiar form of "brother and sister." Consequently, the old divisions based on culture, race, gender, and obligatory religious observances are broken down. In the ancient Mediterranean world, familial relationships would also involve material resources. Paul's letters are necessarily brief and do not give a complete picture of the practices of the Christian community. However, we can learn much from his response to information he received from Corinth about the celebration of the Lord's Supper in the church in that city.

In this earliest description of the Eucharist, written about the year A.D. 55, we find that Paul wrote to the Corinthians about a special meal that preceded or accompanied the Lord's Supper celebration. Paul had received shocking news from Corinth about how the Lord's Supper was being celebrated: "To begin with, when you come together as a church, I hear that there are divisions among you; and to some extent I believe it" (1 Cor 11:18). These divisions or cliques were people who shared a common meal as a prelude to the ritual celebration of the Lord's Supper. However, they shared in accord with their social class or economic status. Many Christians sought friends of similar status and shared sumptuous meals with them. As a result, there was a glaring difference between the meals of the poor and those of the rich. So, Paul writes,

> When the time comes to eat, each of you goes ahead with
> your own supper, and one goes hungry and another becomes
> drunk....do you show contempt for the church of God and

humiliate those who have nothing? What should I say to you? Should I commend you? In this matter I do not commend you! (1 Cor 11:21–22)

Paul declares that eating Christ's bread/body is an act of sharing that makes the communicants become one body: "Because there is one bread. We who are many are one body, for we all partake of the one bread" (10:17). In Paul's view, becoming one body implies a serious responsibility to brothers and sisters who are poor or needy. Before eating, they should do the following: "Examine yourselves and only then eat and drink of the bread and drink of the cup" (11:28). Such a warning is necessary because a special sign of membership in the body of Christ is love and concern for those who are hungry and in need. Paul sees members of the body of Christ as interdependent, for he wrote, "If one member suffers, all suffer together" (12:26).

Paul's Ecumenical Collection as a Sign of Covenant Oneness

The feeling of covenant brotherhood under one *Abba* was not only in the immediate neighborhood or city but also even extended to others far off. When Paul spoke with Peter and other "pillars" of the church, they agreed that Paul was to concentrate on an apostolate to the Gentiles, while Peter and the others would continue working with their fellow Jews: "When James and Cephas and John, who were acknowledged pillars, recognized the grace that had been given to me, they gave to Barnabas and me the right hand of fellowship, agreeing that we should go to the Gentiles and they to the circumcised. They asked only one thing, that we remember the poor, which was actually what I was most eager to do" (Gal 2:9–10).

These "poor" in question were Jewish-Christian brothers and sisters in Jerusalem and Judea who were poor in comparison with many of the Greeks. Peter was concerned that real covenant fellowship meant not only having the same spiritual faith but also generously sharing possessions to prove themselves to be really one family under the same Father. Paul agreed with this totally and adopted a very practical way to make it a reality. He chose the form of a special collection each Sunday in all of his churches. When this was completed, representatives of the churches would accompany Paul to Jerusalem with the offerings and present them as a special gesture of oneness with Jewish Christians:

> Now concerning the collection for the saints: you should fol-
> low the directions I gave to the churches of Galatia. On the
> first day of every week, each of you is to put aside and save
> whatever extra you earn, so that collections need not be
> taken when I come. And when I arrive, I will send any whom
> you approve with letters to take your gift to Jerusalem. If it
> seems advisable that I should go also, they will accompany
> me. (1 Cor 16:1–4)

Paul draws attention to the motivation behind such an extraordinary "ecumenical" collection. He wants it to be an expression of real equality. The Gentile Christians have received their gift of grace through the Jews. Now, the Gentiles should return the favor/grace by sharing material possessions. "It is a question of a fair balance between your present abundance and their need, so that their abundance may be for your need, in order that there may be a fair balance" (2 Cor 8:13–14). The Greek word behind the translation of *balance* means literally "equality," which is mentioned twice.

Paul follows with a scriptural reference to the most remarkable sharing miracle in Hebrew history: "As it is written, 'the one who had much did not have too much, and the one who had little did not have too little.'" It refers to what happened in God's miraculous gift of manna to the Hebrew people when they were desperately hungry during their journey through the Sinai desert to the promised land. When the breadlike substance was distributed, each person had an equal and sufficient amount to eat (Exod 16:16–18). The miracle of equal and just sharing was regarded as even greater than the gift of manna itself.

For Paul, this unusual collection was one of the crowning events in his missionary career. He hoped it would make a great impression on both Jews and Jewish Christians in Jerusalem. On his way to Jerusalem with the offerings, accompanied by representatives of the churches involved, he wrote to the Christians at Rome:

At present, however, I am going to Jerusalem in a ministry to the saints; for Macedonia and Achaia have been pleased to share their resources with the poor among the saints at Jerusalem. They were pleased to do this, and indeed they owe it to them. For if the Gentiles have come to share in their spiritual blessings, they ought also to be of service to them in material things. So, when I have completed this, and have delivered to them what has been collected, I will set out by way of you to Spain; and I know that when I come to you, I will come in the fullness of the blessing of Christ. (Rom 15:25–29)

Status Distinctions Derived from Prominent Teachers

Paul opens his first letter to the Corinthians to respond to news he has received about divisions in the community:

For it has been reported to me by Chloe's people that there are quarrels among you, my brothers and sisters. What I mean is that each of you says, "I belong to Paul," or "I belong to Apollos," or "I belong to Cephas," or "I belong to Christ." Has Christ been divided? Was Paul crucified for you? Or were you baptized in the name of Paul? (1:11–13)

Some Christians were influenced by the ways of Greek philosophical clubs and organizations. The reputation of famous teachers rubbed off on their students and gave them special prestige and recognition. Among Christians, some felt that the effect of baptism by a noted teacher added a special power to the rite, which led them to make a point of who their teacher was or who baptized them. For example, Apollos was a popular teacher, known for his eloquence (Acts 18:24). Paul was very disturbed about the tendency because it indicated worldly wisdom and a feeling of superiority over others that could destroy community oneness.

He responds to this in several ways to make his position as clear as possible. First, he writes that he made it a point (with some exceptions) not to perform baptisms himself lest this give occasion for any kind of boasting. "For Christ did not send me to baptize but to proclaim the Gospel, and not with eloquent wisdom, so that the cross of Christ might not be emptied of its power" (1 Cor 1:17). This "eloquent wisdom" is that of Greek wisdom teachers who relied on their powers of eloquence to win people over and is the very opposite of the wisdom of the cross, which works through human weakness: "We proclaim Christ crucified, a stumbling block to Jews and foolishness to Gentiles, but to those who are called, both Jews and Greeks, Christ the power of God and the wisdom of God" (1:23).

Such a contrast was evident in Paul's audience. They were not eminent philosophers or rich members of the nobility: "God chose what is foolish in the world to shame the wise; God chose what is weak in the world to shame the strong" (1:27). It was also true of Paul's approach. He was not gifted with eloquent speech or attractive appearance: "When I came to you, brothers and sisters, I did not come proclaiming the mystery of God to you in lofty words or wisdom. For I decided to know nothing among you except Jesus Christ, and him crucified" (2:1–2). This guaranteed that their faith "might rest not on human wisdom but on the power of God" (2:5).

Regarding other preachers in making comparisons, each has a role to play according to his or her particular gift. But behind each gift it is the same God at work: "What then is Apollos? What is Paul? Servants through whom you came to believe, as the Lord assigned to each. I planted, Apollos watered, but God gave the growth" (3:5–6). So, the community should regard the various ministers of the Gospel as "servants of Christ" and "stewards of God's mysteries" (4:1). To judge and compare them for personal prestige is to take the place of God, who will examine their work at the Judgment. "Therefore do not pronounce judgment before the time, before the Lord comes, who will bring to light the things now hidden in darkness and will disclose the purposes of the heart. Then, each one will receive commendation from God" (4:5).

Social Status, Special Gifts, and the Common Good

Paul's first letter to the Corinthians, chapters 12–14, furnishes valuable information about community meetings in house churches. It was the occasion for exercising a variety of gifts and talents on the part of believers. Paul writes, "What should be done then, my friends? When you come together, each one has a hymn, a lesson, a revelation, a tongue, or an interpretation. Let all things be done for building up" (14:26). Other gifts included healing the sick, miracle working, discernment of spirits, teaching, and administration of charity. Among the gifts, that of tongues, for example, was especially sought after as very personally satisfying and also making a special impression on others. This lent itself to a competition for prestige and status in the community. For some, it was more important than any kind of material possession.

Some community members wrote to Paul and asked his advice about establishing proper order to overcome the chaos that competition for being "on stage" sometimes brought about. The first answer Paul gave was an emphasis on the oneness of the shared source of everyone's gift—the Spirit. In these chapters, he repeats again and again, *one Spirit* or *the same Spirit, Lord,* or *God,* or *one body.* God's purpose in any gift is for "the common good" (12:7). Paul repeats five times the phrase "build up" by itself or "build up the church" or other forms of *build.* A gift of God is meant to help the community grow in some way. Or Paul may say that the gift is "for another."

By way of example, Paul states, "If in a tongue you utter speech that is not intelligible, how will anyone know what is said?" (14:9). Paul does not condemn the gift of tongues, but suggests that the person so gifted should pray for an interpreter so others may benefit. Finally, he writes that if no interpreter is found, the person should just be quiet (14:28)! As regards gifts, people may desire to have them but should prefer those that are most beneficial to others, which is really what love means:

> Pursue love and strive for the spiritual gifts, and especially that you may prophesy. For those who speak in a tongue do not speak to other people but to God; for nobody understands them, because they are speaking mysteries in the Spirit. On the other hand, those who prophesy speak to other people for their upbuilding and encouragement and consolation. Those who

speak in a tongue build up themselves, but those who prophesy build up the church. (14:1–4)

Paul encourages prophecy because it is God's word speaking through a human mouthpiece and in contrast does not lend itself to praise and esteem because of human skills. In addition, it directly concerns the building up and encouraging of other people. As in the English word *edify,* the Greek root for *build* can have a personal meaning as well as a material one.

The apostle is concerned to show that the best way to help a community grow is not through everyone having the same gift but through a wide diversity of gifts that is mutually appreciated. True oneness comes through recognition and respect for diversity. Thus, it is the product of love. To the contrary, so-called unity is a shadow or parody of oneness that does not recognize diversity but attempts to impose itself through power.

As an example of oneness through diversity, Paul presents the image or model of the human body:

> For just as the body is one and has many members, and all the members of the body, though many, are one body, so it is with Christ. For in the one Spirit we were all baptized into one body—Jews or Greeks, slaves or free—and we were all made to drink of one Spirit. Indeed, the body does not consist of one member but of many. If the foot would say, "Because I am not a hand, I do not belong to the body," that would not make it any less a part of the body. (12:12–15)

Paul then goes on to apply this rule to the ears, eyes, and other bodily members. He declares that according to God's design no body member can say to another, "I have no need of you." And, in fact, so all will respect others for having something they themselves do not possess. The rule applies especially to those parts of the body that seem "less honorable" (in the sense of being displayed to others in public). These organs are especially clothed and are really the most important. In regard to spiritual gifts, Paul is thinking of those gifts that have less outward display but are really most important. God has designed this wonderful diversity, so the members will really care for one another. "If one member suffers, all suffer with it; if one member is honored, all rejoice together with it. So Paul will conclude, "You are the body of Christ, and individually members of it" (12:27).

Paul then describes "a more excellent way"—that of appreciating others' gifts and encouraging them in kindness and patience, rather than through "put downs" through competition, jealousy, comparisons, and control over others:

> Love is patient; love is kind; love is not envious or boastful or arrogant or rude. It does not insist on its own way; it is not irritable or resentful; it does not rejoice in wrongdoing, but rejoices in the truth. It bears all things, believes all things, hopes all things, endures all things. (13:4–7)

What Paul has put forth as a community model is really a blueprint for all of life and society. Social Justice cannot exist on an individual basis but as part of a joint effort for the *common good*. This common good recognizes, respects, and promotes the diversity that each person contributes toward it as the best way to achieve true oneness. Love is the energy that gently achieves oneness through diversity. It takes patience and time to achieve because it is people-centered. Control and power is the force that promotes uniformity and so-called unity. It attempts to work quickly for immediate results because it is not concerned primarily with people but with useful possession. So-called unity is a parody of true oneness and is an image used to deceive people through the outward appearance of apparent "good."

Eliminating the Roots of Injustice—the Training of Converts

Paul realized that conversion to a life of justice was not something that took place immediately but required a period of training and personal change. His letter to the Romans refers to such a preparation time for converts before their actual baptism: "You, having once been slaves of sin, have become obedient from the heart to the form of teaching to which you were entrusted, and...you, having been set free from sin, have become slaves of justice" (6:17–18). This "form of teaching" in Greek is *typon didachēs.* The radical change in lifestyle is stressed by the phrase "obedient from the heart."

Social Justice in a community could not take place without overcoming the inclinations to selfish conduct within each individual. Paul describes the way to victory in this struggle to change from "slaves of sin" to "slaves of justice" in terms of the conflict between "Spirit" and "flesh:"

> Live by the Spirit, I say, and do not gratify the desires of the flesh. For what the flesh desires is opposed to the Spirit, and what the Spirit desires is opposed to the flesh; for these are opposed to each other, to prevent you from doing what you want. (Gal 5:16–17)

Paul summarizes this theme with the opening words, "Live by the Spirit, I say, and do not gratify the desires of the flesh." To "live by the Spirit" is an inner-directed life of freedom in union with Christ for "Christ has set us free" (5:1). By the "flesh," Paul means a life limited by the weaknesses of human nature. In the Bible, the word *flesh* or *flesh and blood* means "human" in *contrast with* God. The translation "desires" of the flesh could be misleading. A better translation would be much stronger, e.g., "cravings," to mean "that a person is driven by outside forces that practically compel action." For example, a person might *desire* or prefer to enjoy food or wine, but gluttony or drunkenness often comes from *addictions.* This word means something or someone that is practically *dictating* what we should do, making us slaves.

"Spirit...is opposed to the flesh." The Spirit is a free gift within, while the "flesh" giving in to cravings and addictions is a force from without, promoting slavery that impedes the choice of good actions. Paul gives an itemized list of such cravings: "Now the works of the flesh are obvious: fornication, impurity, licentiousness, idolatry, sorcery, enmities, strife, jealousy, anger, quarrels, dissensions, factions, envy, drunkenness, carousing, and things like these. I am warning you as I warned you before: those who do such things will not inherit the kingdom of God" (5:19–21).

Once the hard struggle to overcome these addictions is won, the heart is open to a whole new inner life directed by the Spirit:

By contrast, the fruit of the Spirit is love, joy, peace, patience, kindness, generosity, faithfulness, gentleness, and self-control. There is no law against such things. And those who belong to Christ Jesus have crucified the flesh with its passions and desires. If we live by the Spirit, let us also be guided by the Spirit. (5:22–25)

However, the only way to let that Spirit flow is through removal of the cravings of the flesh. Paul expresses it very forcibly: "Those who belong to Christ Jesus have crucified the flesh with its passions and desires" (5:24). To merely say that one has the Spirit is not enough. The Spirit is not a static gift. The only evidence of its presence is when people allow themselves to be guided by it: "If we live by the Spirit, let us also be guided by the Spirit" (5:25). Paul then applies this to community divisions: "Let us not become conceited, competing against one another, envying one another" (5:26).

PART III

10

Social Justice in Christian Writings of the First Three Centuries

The *Didachē,* or "Teaching of the Twelve Apostles"

Outside of the New Testament, it is the earliest Christian document to have the Lord's Prayer along with instructions for liturgy and practice for baptismal candidates. These instructions had a great influence on later church liturgies and practices. The date of its origin is uncertain. The quotations of the New Testament point to a date at the earliest in the first part of the second century.

The instruction opens with a presentation of two ways that the convert must choose between:

> There are two ways, one of life and one of death; and great is the difference between the two ways. This is the way of life: First you shall love God who made you, secondly, your neighbor as yourself; and whatever you would not like done to you, do not to another. (1:1–2)[39]

We have seen that this statement about loving one's neighbor was in the Sermon on the Mount as a concluding summary of the Law and Prophets (Matt 7:12) . In the *Didachē,* it lies at the beginning and then is expanded upon with many similarities to the Sermon on the Mount. Along with the Sermon on the Mount, there is also a Christian instruction on the Ten Commandments.

Following the instruction, baptism, and fasting, the convert is ready to receive the great gift of the prayer of Jesus. The words of the Lord's Prayer are given, because it is presumed the convert does not know them as a formula. They are a personally entrusted gift and privilege so the convert can now pray in union with Christ in the very words that he gave to them.

The *Didachē* then introduces the Lord's Prayer with these words, "Do not pray as the hypocrites, but as the Lord directed in his Gospel" (8:2). Then, it quotes the text of the Lord's Prayer as it is in Matthew, beginning with the words "Pray then in this way." The only differences are the following: The fifth petition reads, "*Forgive us our debt* (in the singular) *as we forgive* (instead of "have forgiven") our debtors." The singular *debt* may be putting our various sins in totality. The *forgive* instead of *have forgiven* makes forgiving action accompany forgiveness. However, the instruction strongly enjoins later that confession of faults and reconciliation occur before taking part in the eucharistic sacrifice: "Offer the Eucharist, having first confessed your offenses, so that your sacrifice may be pure. But let no one who has a quarrel with his neighbor join you until he is reconciled, lest your sacrifice be defiled" (14:1–2).

The text above has no direct reference to forgiving the material debts of other people, but the instruction elsewhere has a strong emphasis on sharing:

> Give to everyone who asks, and ask nothing in return; for the Father wishes that a share of his own gifts be given to all. Blessed is the one who gives according to the commandment, for that person is without blame. Woe to the one who takes, but if the one who takes is in need, there is no fault. (1:5)

The model for imitation is God the Father. Believers will receive the gift of sonship, so they must be givers like him. The Father will be named seven times in this brief document. While debt forgiveness is not mentioned above, the writer goes even further by saying that anyone in need may even take from those with abundance, which shows the priority of the needs of others over the rights of private property.

The *Letter of Barnabas*

This Barnabas is not the same as Paul's companion apostle. The letter has no New Testament references and belongs to an early period before the Gospel writings were available to the author, perhaps around the beginning of the second century A.D. It is likely that the writer was a Jewish convert from around Alexandria, Egypt, where the allegorical interpretation of scriptures was popular. Most of the letter is an exegesis of the Old Testament, finding hidden meanings within the text in reference to Christ. Even the mention of Abraham's 318 men (Gen 14:14) prompts the author to find the name of Jesus in numerical arrangements and values of Hebrew letters (Barnabas 9:15).

At the close of the letter, the author describes the characteristics of men of darkness and emphasizes their lack of justice:

> They do not cleave to what is good or to just judgment, or pay attention to the cause of the widow and orphan....They are without pity for the poor and do nothing for the person oppressed by toil....They repel the needy and oppress the afflicted, are advocates of the rich, unjust judges of the poor, altogether sinful through and through. (20:2)

The *Shepherd of Hermas*

This is a long book of apocalyptic visions enjoining repentance. One of the mediators of revelation is an angel disguised as a shepherd who commands the author to write down the visions. The book was considered inspired in some church circles, especially in the Greek church, and widely read in the early centuries. Scholars disagree about the time of its authorship. Both Clement of Alexandria and the Muratorian fragment cite it. These citations indicate a time no later than the second half of the second century. The author states that he was originally sold as a slave in Rome. Later, he married and had children. The spirituality in the book is down to earth, appealing, especially, for consideration of the poor.

In his vision of a tower, the author asks the lady representing the church, "Who are the white round stones that do not fit into the building?" She answers him,

> Just as the round stone cannot be made square, unless it be cut and lose something, so also the rich of this world cannot be made useful for the Lord, unless their riches have been cut out of them. (*Visions* 6:6)

In his first parable, the shepherd contrasts the possessions of this Earth to riches before God:

> Instead of fields, then, buy souls that are in trouble, according to your ability. Look after widows and orphans and do not neglect them. Spend your riches and all your establishments you have received from God on this kind of fields and houses. It was for this that the Master bestowed wealth on you, to perform this ministry for Him. (*First Parable,* 8)

In another Shepherd's parable revelation, he explains the meaning of a true and genuine fast in a way that seems inspired from Isaiah 58:6–10:

> On the day of your fast do not taste anything except bread and water. Compute the total expense for the food you would have eaten on the day on which you intended to keep a fast and give it to a widow, an orphan, or someone in need. (*Parables* 3:7)

The *Letter of Diognetus*

This is a letter by an unknown author at an uncertain early date. It is written in polished, eloquent Greek by a fervent Christian. In it, the writer describes how true imitation of God is the basis of religion:

> Any person can be an imitator of God, if they take upon their shoulders the burden of their neighbors, if they choose to use their advantages to help another who is underprivileged, if they take what they have received from God and give to those who are in need—for such a person becomes God to those who are helped. (10)

St. Justin, Martyr

St. Justin was the great Christian apologist of the second century. He was born in Samaria, but of Greco-Roman rather than Jewish ancestry. As a young man, his parents gave him the best possible education in philosophy and the arts. He became a convert around A.D. 130 when he was about 25 years old. Sometime afterward, he went to Rome where he opened a school of philosophy, which had great influence. He also authored many publications. The most important of those that have remained are his two apologies and his *Dialogue with Trypho*. He was executed in Rome as a martyr around A.D. 165.

Especially valuable is his description of the Eucharist as connected with justice and charity. In his *First Apology* he writes, "We who loved above all else the ways of acquiring riches and possessions now hand over to a community fund what we possess, and share it with every needy person" (chapter 14). Also, he has the following:

> The wealthy, as they wish, contribute what they desire, and the collection is placed in the custody of the president. (With it) he helps the orphans and the widows, those who are needy because of sickness or any other reason, and the captives and strangers in our midst; in short he takes care of all those in need. Sunday, indeed, is the day on which we all hold our common assembly because it is the first day on which God, transforming the darkness and matter, created the world and our Savior Jesus Christ arose from the dead on the same day. (*First Apology*, chapter 67)

St. Clement of Alexandria

St. Clement (about A.D. 150 to 215) was the most famous teacher of the Alexandrian school of catechetics and scripture interpretation. He became its director around A.D. 200. Clement wrote the first complete book on Christian instruction and ethics, called *The Instructor*, or *Paidogogus*. His view on possessions as gifts to be shared by all permeates his teaching:

It is God himself who has brought our race to possession in common, by sharing himself, first of all, and by sending his Word to all people alike, and by making all things for all. Therefore, everything is common, and the rich should not grasp a greater share. The expression, then, "I own something, and have more than enough; why should I then not enjoy it?" is not worthy of us nor does it indicate community feeling. The other expression does, however: "I have something, why should I not share it with those in need?" Such a one is perfect and fulfills the command: "You shall love your neighbor as yourself." (*The Instructor*, Book II, 12:120)[40]

In all his teaching, Clement is never satisfied with externals but always goes to the inner root or disposition that must be dealt with. This comes out in another book called *The Rich Man's Salvation*, which was written to deal with the problems that wealthy Christians faced as they read the story of the rich young man in Mark 10:17–31. The following is an excerpt:

We must not fling away the riches that are of profit to our neighbors as well as to ourselves. For they are called...wealth because they have been prepared by God for the welfare of people...they are put at our disposal as a sort of material and as instruments to be well used by those who know. You can use it rightly; it ministers to righteousness. But if one uses it wrongly, it is found to be a minister of wrong...we must put the responsibility on that which has the power of using things either well or badly, as the result of choice...and this is the mind, which has in itself both free judgment and full liberty to deal with what is given to it. So let a person do away not with possessions but with the passions of his soul which do not consent to the better use of what someone possesses.[41]

Origen

Origen was born in Alexandria and lived from around A.D. 185 to 255. His father, Leonides, died as a martyr when Origen was only 17. From then on, he gave his whole life to teaching, especially converts who had to attend a three-year catechumenate to prepare for baptism. Most of his voluminous writings grew from the commentaries on scripture that he used in his teaching. In his own personal life, he was a devoted Christian, rigorous in ascetic practices, which sometimes went to extremes. An important part of training for baptism was the explanation of the Lord's Prayer. In Origen, we find one of the earliest of such teachings. Of special interest is his treatment of "Forgive us our debts as we forgive our debtors." Origen goes into every kind of debt whether to or from others. He also has the following application to financial debts:

> Whenever, therefore, any of our numerous debtors (of all kinds, from Origen's previous words) show neglect about paying back what is due to us, we shall act with fellow-feeling and not bear malice toward them, remembering our own debts, how often we have failed to pay them, not only to people but to God himself. For when we remember those to whom we were in debt yet did not pay...we shall be gentler towards those who have incurred a debt toward us and have not paid what is due. (*Treatise on Prayer* 28:6)[42]

Tertullian

Tertullian was born around A.D. 160 in Carthage, North Africa. He was the son of a Roman centurion, trained as a youth to be a lawyer. After his conversion, around 195 he became a fierce, colorful, and eloquent defender of the church in his writings and teachings. His military training and perfectionism helped form an attitude of complete separation from secular culture. Ultimately, this led him to severe attacks against the "moral laxity" of the Catholic Church. He later embraced the strict views of the Montanist heresy. He died sometime after 206. The following is an excerpt from his *Apology* attacking the unjust treatment of Christians in Roman courts.

> We are a body knit together as such by a common religious profession, by unity of discipline and by the bond of a common group. We meet together as an assembly and congregation offering up prayer to God as with united force so we may wrestle with him in our supplications....It is mainly the deeds

of a love so noble that lead many to put a brand on us. "See," they say, "how they love one another," for they themselves are animated by mutual hatred....one in mind and soul, we do not hesitate to share our earthly goods with one another. All things are common among us but not our wives. (*Apology,* chapter 39 ff.)[43]

St. Irenaeus, Bishop of Lyons

Irenaeus (c. A.D. 125–202) was the first great ecclesiastic theologian of the west, defending the church against gnosticism and other heresies. His view was that all the kingdoms of the Earth belonged to God, who has appointed rulers to establish justice over an evil-inclined world. He develops St. Paul's directive in the letter to the Romans: "Let everyone be subject to the higher authorities; for there is no authority except from God, and those authorities that exist have been instituted by God. Therefore whoever resists authority resists what God has appointed and those who resist will incur judgment" (13:1–2). The following are excerpts from Irenaeus on this subject:

Human beings, by departing from God, reached such a fury as to even look upon a brother as an enemy, and engaged without fear in every kind of restless conduct, and murder and avarice.

God imposed upon them the fear of human beings since they did not acknowledge the fear of God and kept them under restraint by their laws. The purpose was so they might attain to some degree of justice and exercise mutual forbearance through dread of the sword suspended full in their view....For this reason, magistrates themselves, having laws as a clothing of righteousness, whenever they act in a just and legitimate manner, shall not be called in question for their conduct. (*Against the Heresies,* chapter 24)[44]

St. Cyprian of Carthage

St. Cyprian (c. A.D. 205–251) was born in Carthage, North Africa, of a wealthy non-Christian family. After his conversion, he became disillusioned by the corruption and immorality in public life and government. He decided to sell all his property and give the proceeds to the poor. His concern for the poor was characteristic of his whole life and writings. He gives more attention to justice to the poor than any other writer of the early centuries. On the occasion of a pestilence in Carthage from 252 to 254, he wrote a long treatise, *Works and Almsgiving*, to encourage help for the needy, sick, and dying. Each of the 26 chapters presents examples and motivation for justice and charity taken mainly from the scriptures. The following is one example:

> Be to your children such a father as was Tobias: "Do justice all the days of your life....Give alms out of your substance, and turn not your face from any poor person, for it shall come to pass that the face of the Lord shall not be turned from you. As you have, my son, so give: if you have an abundant supply, give alms the more from that. If you have a little, give a share from that little. Have no fear when you bestow an alms; you are storing up for yourself a good reward for the day of necessity, for alms delivers from death and does not suffer one to go into darkness. Alms proves a great confidence for all who do it before the most high God. (chapter 20; scripture quote is from Tobit 4:5–12)

11

The United Nations Millennium Declaration and the New Testament

In our introduction, there was a brief description of this eight-page declaration signed by all the participants in the world. The opening statement of this declaration is reprinted here for easy reference:

> We believe that the central challenge we face today is to ensure that globalization becomes a positive force for all the world's peoples. For while globalization offers great opportunities, at present its benefits are very unevenly distributed.

This statement is rather mild and was made after many compromises in order to please the 150 world leaders with their 8,000 delegates. Yet, it does bring out the interconnectiveness of our world and the lack of justice in the distribution of its limited resources. Behind the above statement is the basic world view and vision that must precede any hope for meaningful change: We are all fellow travelers on our planet spaceship Earth, which belongs to all of us equally. There are only a limited number of seats and space on the ship. If these are selfishly hoarded by any person, group, or nation, this is an evil injustice because it hurts others. In other words, the future of Earth depends on realization that there are limited resources and that the overabundance of some is an injustice to others. No longer can we live with the imaginary myth that there are unlimited resources and that it is sufficient to provide generous gifts and handouts to those in need.

The Preparations for the Millennium Declaration

The Declaration was not a hasty summary of ivory-tower discussions. It was drawn up after years of study. Part of the study was an unprecedented poll of 57,000 adults in 60 countries spread over six continents to ascertain the actual needs and concerns of more than six billion people on this Earth. An underlying conviction was that *"no shift in the way we think or act can be more critical than this: we must put people at the center of everything we do."*

Who are these people, and what are their concerns? The following is an excerpt from a summary drawn up by the Secretary General of the United Nations:

> Let us imagine for a moment, that the world really is a "global village." Say this village has 1,000 individuals, with all the characteristics of today's human race distributed in exactly the same proportions. What would it look like? What would we see as its main challenges?
>
> The average income per person is $6,000 a year...but just 200 people dispose of 86% of all the wealth, where nearly half the villagers are eking out an existence on less than $2 a day. Men outnumber women by a small margin, but women make up a majority of those who live in poverty....Some 200 villagers—two-thirds of them women—are illiterate. Of the 390 inhabitants under 20 years of age, three-fourths live in the poorer districts and many are looking desperately for jobs that do not exist. Fewer than 60 people own a computer, and only 24 have access to the Internet. More than one-half have never made or received a phone call.
>
> Life expectancy in the affluent areas is nearly 78 years, in the poorer areas 64 years and in the very poorest neighborhoods a mere 52 years. Each marks an improvement over previous generations but why do the poorest lag so far behind? Because in their neighborhoods, there is a far higher incidence of infectious diseases and malnutrition, combined

with an acute lack of access to safe water, sanitation, health care, adequate housing, education and work.

There is no predictable way to keep the peace in this village. Some districts are relatively safe while others are wracked by organized violence. The village has suffered a growing number of weather-related natural disasters in recent years, including unexpected sudden and severe storms, as well as sudden swings from floods to droughts, while the average temperature is perceptibly warmer....

Who among us would not wonder how long a village in this state can survive without taking steps to insure that all its inhabitants can live free from hunger and safe from violence, drinking clean water, breathing clean air, and knowing that their children have real chances in life?

The Millennium Declaration Response to the Challenge

While the document itself is only 8 pages long, it builds on an 80-page detailed report presented to the delegates by the Secretary General of the United Nations. This report incorporates and summarizes a thorough investigative study made over several years. The Declaration as well as the detailed report is easily available from the United Nations Web site. The following is an outline:

    I. Values and Principles.
    II. Peace, security and disarmament.
    III. Development and poverty eradication.
    IV. Protecting our common environment.
    V. Human rights, democracy and good governance.
    VI. Protecting the vulnerable.
    VII. Meeting the special needs of Africa.
    VIII. Strengthening the United Nations.

The first section (I) on values and principles is the core of the document. Parts II–VIII are the key objectives. Part I begins with the words "We consider certain fundamental values to be essential to international relations in the twenty-first century." These values include (shortened version):

Freedom: Men and women have the right to live and raise their children in dignity, free from hunger and from the fear of violence, oppression or injustice. Democratic and participatory governance based on the will of the people best assures these rights.

Equality: No individual and no nation must be denied the opportunity to benefit from development. The equal rights and opportunities of women and men must be assured.

Solidarity: Global challenges must be met in a way that distributes the costs and burdens fairly in accordance with basic principles of equity and social justice.

Tolerance: Human beings must respect one another, in all their diversity of belief, culture, and language. Differences within and between societies should be neither feared nor repressed, but cherished as a precious asset of humanity. A culture of peace and dialogue among all civilizations should be actively promoted.

Respect for nature: Prudence must be shown in the management of all living species and natural resources, in accordance with the precepts of sustainable development. Only in this way can the immeasurable riches provided to us by nature be preserved and passed on to our descendants. The current unsustainable patterns of production and consumption must be changed in the interest of our future welfare and that of our descendants.

Shared responsibility: Responsibility for managing worldwide economic and social development, as well as threats to international peace and security, must be shared among the nations of the world and should be exercised multilaterally. As the most universal and most representative organization in the world, the United Nations must play the central role.

The New Testament Contribution to the New Millennium

In addition to the values shared with the Millennium Declaration, we will outline the following areas of New Testament contribution:

1) A more realistic view of the evil nature and roots of injustice. 2) The dynamic energy needed to actuate justice. 3) The compassion that moves each person to do his or her part. 4) Community cooperation instead of individualism. 5) Joyful appreciation of the goodness and beauty of life. 6) A blueprint for a Missionary Church.

A More Realistic Vision of the Evil Nature of Present Injustice

This vision offers much agreement with the United Nations' opening summit declaration. However, the declaration had to be softened to obtain a consensus, even when some participating nations actually contribute to injustice. The Gospels open with God's call through the prophets for repentance with specific demands for change. We have seen that the ancient prophetic view of justice was based on the premises of equality in sharing limited land resources and relationships. Anything less is evil. There are no gray areas of compromise. The New Testament ethic is not really "new," but a return to a return to the ancient radical prophetic justice. However, a merely intellectual assent to this justice is fruitless. The New Testament calls for making justice a complete priority in one's lifestyle: "Seek *first* the kingdom of God and its justice" (Matt 6:33).

The Roots of Injustice

The Sermon on the Mount describes injustice very forcibly in its pure and simple greed. Jesus said, "No one can serve two masters; for a slave will either hate the one and love the other, or be devoted to the one and despise the other. You cannot serve God and wealth" (Matt 6:24). *Wealth* is a literal translation of *Mammon,* a personification in godlike terms of the evil of attachment to possessions. The modern equivalent of "serving a master" is addiction. People, things, situations can infallibly "dictate" or demand that we act in certain ways. Jesus asks for a definite choice. A total service to the Creator of an Earth made to be shared by all cannot coexist with a total service of selfish needs.

Dynamic Energy Resources

The Source of Energy

A building contractor can work efficiently and confidently if there is an architectural plan for the structure to be built. All that is needed is to *just do it*. Yet, the cooperation of many workers is needed to make the plan a reality. If there is a full-time commitment of skilled people along with the availability of all necessary materials, the project will rapidly and satisfactorily be completed.

In the analogy of creating a just, compassionate world, there must be confidence in an underlying energy beneath the surface of reality that can move the Earth in that direction. Paul wrote to the Romans, "We know that God makes all things work together for good" (8:26). Originally, Paul wrote these words about believers' call to faith. However, if we believe that God is calling for a just world, the text should also apply to a divine energy at work in the world to make possible that justice. This does not work automatically but in and through people who trust in prayerful action: "All things can be done for the one who believes" (Mark 9:23). This brings out the essential contribution of religion and faith in the process of changing the world.

The Total Commitment Asked by Gospels

God is a God of Justice, working through people. The complete divine energy in the world is only activated when people make a full commitment to a just world. The Gospels presuppose such totality. The call of Jesus and the Baptist for repentance requires a total commitment. The initial baptism was a "plunging into" not only water but also an entirely new lifestyle with new priorities in work, relationships, time, and activity. The Jewish traditional prayer, the *Shemah Israel* was a reminder to serve God with the *whole* heart, the *whole* soul, and one's *whole* strength (Deut 6:4–9).

Matthew often quotes Jesus' statements and parables about total, *joyful* commitment.

The kingdom of heaven is like a treasure hidden in a field which someone found and hid; then *in his joy* he goes out and sells *all* that he has and buys that field. Again the kingdom of heaven is like a merchant in search of fine pearls; on finding one pearl of great value, he went and sold all that he had and bought it. (13:44–45)

This inner life direction is a mysterious force that transforms all of life, relationships and activities, like yeast changing the whole nature of a batch of wheat dough: "The kingdom of heaven is like yeast that a woman took and mixed with three measures of flour until all of it was leavened" (13:33).

For this reason, the Sermon on the Mount teaches that it is not enough to simply wish for justice, it must be a burning desire like hunger. So, Jesus declares in the fourth Beatitude, "Blessed are those who *hunger and thirst* for justice, for they will be filled" (5:6). Such a desire risks suffering, sometimes death, but always entails a difficult struggle: "Blessed are those who are persecuted for justice's sake, for theirs is the kingdom of heaven" (5:10). Even in the world, inner drive is what distinguishes some people from others. I once asked a famous basketball coach why it was that some teams with outstanding athletes often lose to much poorer quality opponents. He answered that, besides working together, they had learned to play with *great intensity.*

A Very Practical Dimension

We have seen how Luke adds a very practical dimension to this commitment. At the baptismal scene, the question asked by the crowds is meant to represent that of the audience: "What then should we do?" (3:10). The Baptist gives a very simple direct answer—equal sharing with others: "Whoever has two coats must share with anyone who has none; and whoever has food must do likewise" (3:11). Jesus' journey to Jerusalem is a model for the believer's journey through life. As a final scene in that journey, Luke presents Zacchaeus as a model for a real turning of one's life to God. Zacchaeus, a notorious chief tax collector, was short in stature in more ways than one. When Jesus invited himself to come to his house, Zacchaeus rose to full stature and pledged to restore all the money he had taken from others and to share an equal half of all he had with the poor (19:1–10).

The Deep Compassion That Really Moves People to Act

A hard-nosed challenge of justice appealing to a sense of duty can have short-time effects and will often shake up people temporarily to make a change. However, compassionate justice has long-term, total effectiveness. In the Hebrew scriptures, the compassion and justice of God always go together. Matthew makes great efforts to unite justice and compassion. The fourth Beatitude bestows a blessing on those who hunger and thirst for *justice*. However, the fifth immediately balances the fourth with the words "Blessed are the merciful, for they will receive mercy" (5:6–7).

Matthew knows that this mercy is within people, but needs a practical way to be tapped into. So, only this Gospel contains Jesus' Golden Rule of identification with others three times: First, in the Sermon on the Mount, in the concluding teaching, "In everything do to others as you would have them do to you; for this is the law and the prophets" (7:12). Then, we have it again with the advice to the rich young man (19:19). It finally appears a third time as an answer to a question about the greatest commandment in the law (22:38–40).

However, Matthew is concerned about presenting Jesus as a model of sensitivity toward others rather than as an armchair philosopher. In his Gospel, the Baptist is shocked when Jesus comes to the Jordan River seeking baptism and tries to prevent him from doing so. Jesus replies in his first Gospel words that it was proper for him to do so in order to fulfill all justice (3:15). Then, Jesus stepped into the Jordan River, identifying himself with so many people who had come from afar to break from the past and begin a new life.

The Sermon on the Mount is introduced by a description of Jesus' ministry to the sick and afflicted: "They brought to him all "the sick, those who were afflicted with various diseases and pains, demoniacs, epileptics, and paralytics, and he cured them" (4:24). Matthew likes to single out Jesus' quality of mercy and identification with others in his healing ministry. After Jesus cures Simon's mother-in-law, crowds of people came to the house after sunset: "They brought to him many who were possessed with demons; and he cast out the spirits with a word. This was to fulfill what had been spoken through Isaiah the prophet, 'He took our infirmities and bore our diseases'" (8:17; Isa 53:4).

Yet, Matthew does not us want to think that this compassion is only a generic one—such as like feeling sorry for all the starving people in the world. On the contrary, it is an active reaching out to each person in the daily, ordinary circumstances of life. The last judgment scene centers on sensitivity to people in everyday needs: giving food to the hungry, drink to the thirsty, lodging for the stranger and homeless, clothing for the naked, visits to those sick and in prison (25:35–36). In fact, Jesus feels so closely identified with these people's needs, that ministry to them is personal service to himself: "Amen, I say to you, just as you did it to one of the least of these my brothers, you did it to me" (25:40).

The Sermon on the Mount does not restrict this divine compassion to human beings but sees it mirrored in all of nature. God *makes his sun* rise equally on the evil and the good and also *sends rain* on the just and unjust (5:45). The divine care makes sure that the birds are fed (6:26). The Earth is colored and covered with garments of grass and flowers (6:28–30). A reference to Solomon (6:29) is a reminder of the wisdom tradition of the divine mysteries hidden in nature:

> He (Solomon) composed three thousand proverbs, and his songs numbered a thousand and five. He would speak of trees, from the cedar that is in Lebanon to the hyssop that grows in the wall; he would speak of animals, and birds and reptiles and fish. People came from all the nations to hear the wisdom of Solomon. (1 Kings 4:32–34)

Community Cooperation Instead of Individualism

The Corporate Nature of Evil Demands a Corporate Response

Community cooperation is not an option but an imperative because the forces of injustice have a worldwide corporate nature.

While globalization has many positive benefits, the opening United Nations declaration pointed out that this globalization has left a large part of our world behind. The text that follows makes this much more definite: "We will spare no effort to free our fellow men, women and children from the abject and dehumanizing conditions of extreme poverty, to which more than a billion of them are currently subjected."

The cause of such poverty is vividly expressed in the executive summary of the role of the United Nations with these words, "The gross disparities of wealth in today's world." Also, "the combination of extreme poverty with extreme inequality between countries, and often also within them, is an affront to our common humanity." The specific corporate nature of this injustice is expressed as follows: "Groups and individuals more and more often interact directly across frontiers. This has its dangers. Crime, narcotics, terrorism, pollution, disease, weapons, refugees and migrants: all move back and forth faster and in greater numbers than in the past."

The New Testament strongly emphasizes the corporate nature of evil. This is especially evident in what we have previously seen in Luke's description of a cosmic battle against the forces of evil. It is summed up by Jesus' statement at his arrest, "This is your hour and the power of darkness" (22:53). Because these powers go beyond any one person, they have a virtual superhuman force. Luke begins and ends Jesus' own struggle and prayer in the agony in the garden with the words "Pray that you may not come into the time of trial" (22:40, 56).

Community Cooperation vs. Individualism

The Lord's Prayer begins with the words "Our Father." In all the petitions, there is no *I* or *me*. For example, the petition for food does not have the words "Give *me* today *my* daily bread." Instead, the plural in the form of *we, us,* or *our* is found eight times. In this way, the prayer contrasts with the egocentric individualism that keeps increasing in our modern world. The tendency is to want everything as *my own,* as in *my* house, *my* car, and so on. This tendency accompanies the desire to be completely independent—to be able to take care of oneself without the help of others whether in sickness, old age, or special needs. It has created an ever increasing need for money to provide insurance for a life built around perishable things, rather than an interdependence built on people and relationships. It took many people to bring us into this world, yet we want to live as if we need no one to help us out of this world.

In the past, people trusted in their immediate families for this interdependence whether in sickness or old age. Now interdependence has become more difficult, with an increasing number of families whose members are scattered, sometimes thousands of miles away. The need of voluntary support communities has increased, not just for prayer but also for total support of one another.

Christianity began with small house churches, which were really extended families, including workers, their families, and others. These households were the basic economic and social units of society at large, until the industrial age began around 200 years ago. No church buildings to accommodate large numbers were built until the fourth century, when Christianity became the state religion. While the United Nations works on a global basis, everything depends on what happens at the grass-roots level. Large church buildings have a purpose in assembling all the faithful at special formal occasions. The informal atmosphere of dedicated small groups in which people know one another, pray together, exercise their gifts, and work for the common good is necessary to prevent excessive formalism in larger meetings of the faithful.

Joyful Appreciation of the Goodness and Beauty of Life

This joyful appreciation is the contribution of the wisdom component of the Old and New Testaments. The Sermon on the Mount teaches us to live each day as it comes, appreciating the beauty of nature and creation. People are led to avoid constant overconcern for the future and treasure the simple joys and pleasure of friendship, family, nature, animals, literature, music, and the arts. Without voluntary joyful simplicity in life, the tendency to multiply possessions will always be an impediment to sharing with those in need. Above all, others want to share our joy of life itself, not the misery that comes from artificial outward "necessities."

A Blueprint Sketch for a Missionary Church

There are various meanings for *church*. One very valuable one is associated with the original late-Greek root for *church,* which is traced back through Middle and Old English to *kyriakon,* meaning "the Lord's house or home." The two roots of the word are *kyrios,* for *Lord,* and *oikos,* for *house.* This latter word is found more than 100 times in the Gospels, often signifying the gathering place for Jesus' disciples or those whom he calls. This "gathering" function is essential to Jesus' *mission,* from the Latin root for *sending*—referring to what God has sent him to Earth to do. John's Gospel calls this "gathering" to be the prime reason for Jesus' death, that Jesus was to die, "not for the nation only, but to *gather* into one the dispersed children of God" (11:53). In discussing this text in chapter 8, we have seen that such gathering refers to the whole human race, as God's children, scattered over all the world after the story of the Tower of Babel and the confusion of tongues.

However, among the "scattered children" there are some for whom God is especially concerned in this "gathering together." We find them in the prophet Ezekiel's description of God as a "Good Shepherd." God declares:

> I myself will be the shepherd of my sheep, and I will make them lie down, says the Lord GOD. I will seek the lost, and I will bring back the strayed, and I will bind up the injured, and I will strengthen the weak, but the fat and the strong I will destroy. I will feed them with justice. (34:15–17)

Jesus took upon himself the mission of imitating God as a Good Shepherd. His first concern was "to gather" and serve those lost and abandoned, the outcasts of society, the sick, the unclean and unwanted. A "missionary church," as the body of Christ, takes upon itself the continuation and actuation of Jesus' "gathering" work in today's world. Such a church will not have a stereotyped form, nor will it try to do all things at once. What would be the example of what one might look like today?

One Practical Example

Recently, I visited Old Saint Mary's Cathedral, built in 1854 as California's first cathedral. In the pew I picked up the parish bulletin of the previous Sunday. The heading across the top caught my attention: "A Welcoming Missionary Community of Faith Led by the Paulists for over 100 years." Underneath was a self description of a "gathering community":

We Welcome...	*We Celebrate...*
People of All Faiths & All Races	Diversity
Divorced or Separated Persons	A Spirit of Hospitality
Families with Children	The Unity That God Wills
Gays & Lesbians	Enlightening Those Who Seek God
Homeless Persons	Forming Small Faith Communities
Loving Relationships	Reaching Out to Alienated Catholics
Married Couples	Reverencing the Dignity of Each Person
Single Persons	Caring for the Needs of the Less Fortunate
Those in Recovery	Empowering Christians to Realize Their Call
Travelers from Far and Near	Honoring Understanding among All Faiths
Widowers & Widows	Nurturing Our Gifts and Sharing Them
Visitors	Supporting the Arts Through Concerts
	Pursuing New Ways to Serve
	Being a Good Neighbor

*We Seek...*To Live the Gospel of Jesus Christ
To Gather the Community and Tell the Story
To Break the Bread and Share the Cup

We Treasure Our Past
We Hope in the Future

The question came to my mind, "Do they really accomplish this?" And the answer came, "Of course not. It's humanly impossible, yet it's so important that they openly announced their objectives so that, with divine help, they can progress toward them each day."

Notes

1. An excellent survey is that of J. David Pleins, in the *Social Vision of the Hebrew Bible* (Nashville: Westminster/John Knox, 2000).

2. An explanation of this method will be found in the introduction to part I.

3. The special nature of biblical justice is brought out by John R. Donohue, in "Biblical Perspectives on Justice," in John C. Haughey, *The Faith That Does Justice* (New York: Paulist Press, 1977).

4. A detailed explanation and history of the biblical meaning of covenant is found in Lawrence Boadt, *Reading the Old Testament* (Mahwah, N.J.: Paulist Press, 1984), pp. 173–179.

5. The centrality of Deuteronomy as the preeminent book of the Torah is explained by S. D. McBride in "Polity of the Covenant People: The Book of Deuteronomy," *Interpretation* 3 (1987), pp. 229–244.

6. For the unique place of Deuteronomy 15 in that book and in the Bible, see Jeffries M. Hamilton, *Social Justice and Deuteronomy: The Case of Deuteronomy 15* (Atlanta: Society of Biblical Literature, 1992).

7. This process is traced by William J. Doorly, *Obsession with Justice, the Story of the Deuteronomists* (Mahwah, N.J.: Paulist Press, 1994).

8. For Amos and pre-exile prophecy, I have drawn from Bruce Vawter, *The Conscience of Israel: Pre-exilic Prophets and Prophecy* (New York: Sheed and Ward, 1961).

9. Mark opens his Gospel with a scripture quotation putting together Isaiah 40:3 with Malachi 3:1, "Behold I am sending my messenger ahead of you, who will prepare your day" (1:2). He also writes that John the Baptist was clothed with camel's hair, with a leather belt around his waist (1:6). This recalls the garment of Elijah the prophet in 2 Kings 1:8.

10. According to Malachi, Elijah was to return to Earth before the last days (4:4).

11. The section on Lady Wisdom and Proverbs owes much to Claudia V. Camp and Carole R. Fontaine, authors of the annotations on the Book of Proverbs in *The HarperCollins Study Bible* (New York, San Francisco: HarperCollins, 1993).

12. This chapter is especially indebted to Catherine M. Murphy, *The Disposition of Wealth in the Literature and Practice of the Qumran Community and Its Relevance for the Study of the New Testament* (Notre Dame, Ind.: Dept. of Theology, 1999). Also very helpful was, Michael Wise, Martin Abegg Jr., and Edward Cook, *The Dead Sea Scrolls: A New Translation* (San Francisco: HarperCollins, 1996).

13. The translations from Philo and Josephus are from Catherine Murphy, *op.cit.*

14. Donald Senior has brought out the background of Roman abusive power in his article "With 'Swords and Clubs'—the Setting of Mark's Community and His Critique of Abusive Power," *Biblical Theology Bulletin* 17 (1987), pp. 10–20.

15. See Douglas E. Oakman, *Jesus and the Economic Questions of His Day* (Lewiston/Queenstown: Edward Mellen Press, 1966), p. 73.

16. In reference to the two multiplications of loaves: In the first story, the number of people is 5,000, and the number of leftover loaves is 12. It reminds us of the five books of the Law and the 12 tribes of Israel. The "blessing" of the loaves reflects Jewish usage. However, in the second multiplication, the number of people is 4,000, a multiple of the universal number 4 as in Matthew 24:31, "The four winds from one end of heaven to the other." The 7 loaves left over is a number of fullness, like the traditional 70 nations of the world. Here, when Jesus takes the loaves, he "gives thanks," which is the Greek equivalent for blessing.

17. Regarding the two creation accounts: The first begins in Genesis 1:1 and goes to 2:3–4 forming a literary unit from a distinct source. In this story, God creates man and woman equally to the divine image: "In the image of God he created them; male and female he created them" (1:27). However, a second story begins in 2:4–5 from another source. Here, God creates first the man and then, from him, the woman, which shows a strong hint of subordination. After the couple disobey God's commandment, God tells the woman, "He (the man) shall rule over you" (2:16).

18. This special exegesis has been pointed out by Elizabeth Fiorenza, *In Memory of Her* (New York: Crossroads, 1983).

19. The term *literary frame* or *inclusio* means "a story with a preceding and ending frame that helps explain it." The frame often has similar

elements at each end. In regard to the fig tree, Mark wants to emphasize the power of Jesus' word to bring about a new temple for all nations. So, the effect of his word on the fig tree points to this.

20. For Matthew and Social Justice, I am very much indebted to the research of Michael J. Crosby in *House of Disciples: Church, Economics, and Justice in Matthew* (Maryknoll: Orbis, 1988).

21. On the patriarchal household and Matthew's plan to subvert it, I have drawn considerably from the work of Warren Carter and John Paul Heil in *Matthew's Parables* (Washington, D.C.: Catholic Biblical Association Monograph Series 30, CBA, 1998).

22. Aristotle treats of the household in his *Politics* I, ii.1–2.

23. Philo's texts are in his *Decalogue* 165–167 and *Posterity and the Exile of Cain* 181.

24. See Warren Carter, *Matthew and the Empire: Initial Explorations* (Harrisburg: Trinity Press, 2001) for the "Fatherhood" of the Roman emperor and Matthew's hidden agenda against it.

25. For a study of justice in Matthew based on this basic literary enclosure, see Adolfo Fonseca and M. Castano, *DIKAIOSYNE en Mateo: Una Interpretacion Teologica a partir de 3,15 y 21,32,* Tesi Gregoriana, Serie Teologica 29. Rome: Editrice Pontifica Universita Gregoriana, 1997.

26. Carter, Warren, pp. 135–146.

27. The seven texts in Matthew for *justice, dikaiosynē,* are 3:15 and 21:32, plus five in the Sermon on the Mount: 5:6, 10, 20; 6:1, 33. (Although 6:1 is sometimes translated as *piety.*)

28. The similarities between Matthew and Deuteronomy are pointed out in the following article: Joseph A. Grassi, "Matthew as a Second Testament Deuteronomy," *Biblical Theology Bulletin* 19 (1989, 23–30).

29. Regarding the political and social situation behind Luke, I have been helped by Richard J. Cassidy, *Jesus, Politics, and Society: A Study of Luke's Gospel* (Maryknoll: Orbis, 1988).

30. This Lukan theme of combat against the forces of evil is presented by Jerome Neyrey, *The Passion According to Luke* (Mahwah, N.J.: Paulist Press, 1985).

31. The special role of women, not only in Luke but also in the other Gospels, is described by Joseph A. Grassi in *The Hidden Heroes of the Gospels* (Collegeville: Liturgical Press, 1989).

32. The fourth Gospel author was familiar with the other three at least in the sense of knowing the tradition behind them, although there are

few exact verbal similarities. Of the other three, John is closest to Luke with whom he shares a number of things not found in Mark or Matthew.

33. Among the similarities to the Song of Songs are the following: the *nard* (1:12; 4:13), *anointing* (1:3), *banquet,* (5:1–2), the *hair* (7:5). In addition, see the article of M. Cambe, "L'Influence du Cantique des Cantiques sur le Nouveau Testament," *Revue Thomiste* 62 (1962), pp. 5–26.

34. In this area, I have drawn much from Raymond E. Brown, *The Community of the Beloved Disciple* (Mahwah, N.J.: Paulist Press, 1979).

35. On this background, see Joseph A. Grassi, *The Secret Identity of the Beloved Disciple* (Mahwah, N.J.: Paulist Press, 1992).

36. For the background of the letters of Paul, I have followed Jerome Murphy-O'Connor, *Paul: A Critical Life* (Oxford: Clarendon Press; New York: Oxford University Press, 1996). For the social and urban background, Wayne A. Meeks, *The First Urban Christians: The Social World of the Apostle Paul* (New Haven: Yale University Press, 1983).

37. Paul starts with the second creation story in 1 Corinthians 11:7, when he writes, "he (man) is the image and reflection of God; but the woman is the reflection of man. Indeed, man was not made from woman but woman from man." However, he tries to balance it at the end by describing a new dispensation, rooted in the first creation story: "Nevertheless, in the Lord woman is not independent of man or man independent of woman...but all things come from God" (11:11–12).

38. Paul's letters were originally written to various local churches, which sometimes interchanged them. At an unknown date, a later disciple of Paul visited these churches to make a collection of them, sometimes putting together fragments from different scrolls to form a unified letter. Some scrolls may have been written by later disciples of Paul rather than by Paul himself.

39. Translations of the *Didachē, Letter of Barnabas, Shepherd of Hermas,* and *Letter of Diognetus* are from Francis X. Glymm, Joseph M. Marique, and Gerald G. Walsh, *The Apostolic Fathers* (New York: Christian Heritage, 1947).

40. The translation is from Simon P. Wood, *Clement of Alexandria: Christ the Educator* (New York: Fathers of the Church, 1954).

41. The translation is from Henry Chadwick, *Alexandrian Christianity* (Philadelphia: Westminster, 1954).

42. Ibid.

43. The translation is from George W. Forell, *Christian Social Teachings* (Garden City, N.Y.: Doubleday, 1966).

44. Ibid.

Bibliography

This is not meant to be a complete bibliography of sources but a selection of those most frequently used in writing this book.

The translation used throughout is that of the *New Revised Standard Version,* except where a literal translation best serves the purpose.

Allison, Dale C. *The Sermon on the Mount.* New York: Crossroads, 1999.

Boadt, Lawrence. *Reading the Old Testament: An Introduction.* Mahwah, N.J.: Paulist Press, 1984.

Brown, Raymond E. *The Community of the Beloved Disciple.* Mahwah, N.J.: Paulist Press, 1979.

Cambe, M. "L'Influence du Cantique des Cantiques sur le Nouveau Testament," *Revue Thomiste* 62 (1962) 5–26.

Camp, Claudia V., and Carole R. Fontaine. Their annotations on the Book of Proverbs on Lady Wisdom in *The HarperCollins Study Bible.* New York, San Francisco: HarperCollins, 1993.

Carter, Warren, and John Paul Heil. *Matthew's Parables.* Washington, D.C.: Catholic Biblical Association Monograph Series 30. CBA, 1998.

———. *Matthew and the Empire: Initial Explorations.* Harrisburg: Trinity Press, 2001.

Cassidy, Richard J. *Jesus, Politics, and Society: A Study of Luke's Gospel.* Maryknoll: Orbis, 1978.

Chadwick, Henry. *Alexandrian Christianity.* Philadelphia: Westminster, 1954.

Crosby, Michael J. *House of Disciples: Church, Economics, and Justice in Matthew.* Maryknoll: Orbis, 1988.

Deferrari, Roy J., trans. *Saint Cyprian: Treatises.* New York: Fathers of the Church, 1958.

Donohue, John R. "Biblical Perspectives on Justice," in Haughey, John C. *The Faith That Does Justice.* Mahwah, N.J.: Paulist Press, 1977.

Doorly, William J. *Obsession with Justice: The Story of the Deuteronomists.* Mahwah, N.J.: Paulist Press, 1994.

Falls, Thomas B., trans. *Saint Justin, Martyr.* New York: Christian Heritage, 1948.

Fiorenza, Elizabeth. *In Memory of Her.* New York: Crossroads, 1983.

Forell, George W. *Christian Social Teachings.* Garden City, N.Y.: Doubleday, 1966.

Glymm, Francis X., Joseph M.-F. Marique, and Gerald G. Walsh, trans. *The Apostolic Fathers.* New York: Christian Heritage, 1947.

Grassi, Joseph A. *The Hidden Heroes of the Gospel.* Collegeville: Liturgical Press, 1989.

———. *The Secret Identity of the Beloved Disciple.* Mahwah, N.J.: Paulist Press, 1992.

Hamilton, Jeffries M. *Social Justice and Deuteronomy: The Case of Deuteronomy 15.* Atlanta: Society of Biblical Literature, 1992.

Malina, Bruce. *The New Testament World: Insights from Cultural Anthropology.* Atlanta: John Knox, 1981.

Meeks, Wayne A. *The First Urban Christians: The Social World of the Apostle Paul.* New Haven: Yale University Press, 1983.

Murphy, Catherine M. *The Disposition of Wealth in the Literature and Practice of the Qumran Community and Its Relevance for the Study of the New Testament.* Notre Dame, Ind.: Dept. of Theology, 1999.

Murphy-O'Connor, Jerome. *Paul: A Critical Life.* Oxford: Clarendon Press; New York: Oxford University Press, 1996.

Nardone, Enrique. *Los Que Buscan la Justicia: Un Estudio de la Justicia en el Mundo Biblico.* Aldecoa, S. L. Burgos, Spain: Editorial Verbo Divino, 1997.

Neyrey, Jerome. *The Passion According to Luke.* Mahwah, N.J.: Paulist Press, 1985.

Oakman, Douglas E. *Jesus and the Economic Questions of His Day.* Lewiston/Queenstown: Edwin Mellen Press, 1986.

Pleins, J. David. *The Social Vision of the Hebrew Bible.* Nashville: Westminster/John Knox, 2000.

Senior, Donald. "With 'Swords and Clubs'—the Setting of Mark's Community and His Critique of Abusive Power," *Biblical Theology Bulletin* 17 (1987) 10–20.

Bibliography

Vawter, Bruce. *The Conscience of Israel: Pre-exilic Prophets and Prophecy.* New York: Sheed and Ward, 1961.

Wise, Michael, Martin Abegg Jr., and Edward Cook. *The Dead Sea Scrolls: A New Translation.* San Francisco: HarperCollins, 1996.

Wood, Simon P., trans. *Clement of Alexandria: Christ the Educator.* New York: Fathers of the Church, 1954.

Index